CW01551748

CONTEMPORARY FRENCH AND SCANDINAVIAN CRIME FICTION

INTERNATIONAL CRIME FICTIONS

The International Crime Fictions Series aims to build on the success of its precursor, European Crime Fictions, to profile transnational and intercultural approaches to crime fiction from around the world. The extended mission of the Series is conceived to analyse and document the fruitful exchanges between creative and critical work on crime fiction in an international context today.

The scope of the Series includes literary and cultural studies, translation studies, popular culture studies, film, photography and comics, fandom studies, genre studies, and national and transnational histories of crime, writing and practice.

INTERNATIONAL CRIME FICTIONS

CONTEMPORARY FRENCH AND SCANDINAVIAN CRIME FICTION

Citizenship, Gender and Ethnicity

Anne Grydehøj

UNIVERSITY OF WALES PRESS

www.uwp.co.uk

British Library Cataloguing-in-Publication Data
A catalogue record for this book is available from the British Library.

ISBN 978-1-78683-718-9
eISBN 978-1-78683-719-6

Typeset by Marie Doherty
Printed by CPI Antony Rowe, Melksham, United Kingdom

Contents

Acknowledgements

This book would not have come into being without the support and help from a number of people, to whom I owe my gratitude.

First of all, I am enormously indebted to my PhD supervisor Lucy O'Meara for her expert guidance and inspiration during the project's research and writing phases, and to my secondary supervisor Tom Baldwin for his always constructive criticism and involvement. Katya Haustein and Claire Gorrara as my PhD examiners deserve warm thanks for reading through the manuscript, providing constructive feedback and encouraging me to publish a revised version.

I would also like to express my gratitude to the University of Kent for granting me a Graduate Teaching Assistantship which made my research financially viable, and to Ana de Medeiros, who in the first instance encouraged me to embark on the project.

Throughout the project, colleagues and friends at the University of Kent and University College London have provided a supportive atmosphere for seeing the book to fruition, for which I am thankful. I owe a special debt of thanks to Mathilde Poizat-Amar for efficient work sessions in her office, and to Heide Kunzelmann for chats, coffees and collegiality, and for her help with the Nordic Research Network conference that I co-organised at the IMLR in 2016. I was also exceedingly fortunate in having the support and friendship of Giovanna Piga and Victoria Bennett; in our writing group, I found an intense and productive work environment combined with breaks of laughter that got me through the final chapters.

I also owe considerable thanks to friends and family who opened their homes to me during research trips: Mirjam Kofod-Pihl for accommodation during the Krimimessen crime festival in Horsens, Carolina Boe and François Lê Xuân for use of their apartment in Paris on multiple occasions, William Frost for bed and breakfast in Edinburgh, and my mother Ena Nygaard Jørgensen and her husband, Svend Nygaard, for providing a full-board writing retreat at their house in Silkeborg. I am also grateful to my father, Peter Grydehøj, and his wife, Jolanta Grydehøj, as well as to my two sisters, Mette

Grydehøj Post and Stinne Grydehøj, for their continuous sincere and curious interest in what I do.

Finally, a very special thanks to my children, Sigurd Grydehøj and Marta Grydehøj Duffy, for their unique way of keeping me afloat throughout the process, and to Larry Duffy for his always knowledgeable inputs, continuous encouragement and love.

I could not have done it without you.

Introduction

Of all contemporary European crime fiction traditions, the French and the Scandinavian variants arguably stand out. These two manifestations of the genre have been crucial to the shaping of its present conception, albeit for different reasons. In the case of France, the long-standing influence of the *roman noir* (especially in the incarnation of Gallimard's Série noire) is recognised internationally, and, as Andrea Goulet and Susanna Lee write in their introduction to a crime fiction issue of *Yale French Studies* published in 2005, 'France has set the aesthetic tone and template for modern representations of crime ... [and is] perhaps the country where crime fiction ... has met with the most commercial and critical success.'[1] The special status of French crime fiction has in recent years found a competitor in the international publishing phenomenon of 'Nordic Noir', which since the 1990s – and increasingly in the new millennium following the international success of Stieg Larsson's *Millennium* trilogy – has established itself as a distinctly geographically and culturally defined variant of the genre.

The origins of this book may be situated in this broad intercultural context, alongside a consideration of the reception of *le polar scandinave* (the Scandinavian crime novel) in France. Many of the front covers of Scandinavian crime fictions translated into French feature an exoticised vision of the north: the covers show snow-covered, barren landscapes, frequently framing the silhouette of a lonesome male character. Upon closer examination, the dust-jacket texts, alongside further allusions to the Nordic climate, frequently comment on the novels' engagement with 'le côté obscur' – the dark side – of the Scandinavian welfare states. This publishing phenomenon and the historically unprecedented explosion of translated Scandinavian literature in France are closely connected with the uniform marketing template and the French media's preoccupation with *polars polaires*.

The present work initially set out to investigate the ways in which the French reception of Scandinavian crime fiction was culturally specific, and whether, in fact, it had as much to with ideological and cultural debates within France as with the nature and content of the translated fiction. The central research question was, then, whether this variant of the crime novel could, once transposed to France, provide something, by way of social critique, that the domestic *polar* could not. The assumption was that this was the case particularly in relation to issues inherently problematic within the secular and ostensibly egalitarian framework of the modern French polity, such as religion, gender, ethnicity and other arenas where questions of identity are foregrounded.

It soon became apparent, however, that there was a much more complex, and critically more urgent, picture. The socially critical dimension of the *polar scandinave* concerned with the relationship between the citizen and the welfare state – which was continuously emphasised by French media and academic criticism – does, in fact, have a parallel in French crime fiction, but in the form of a much more fundamental critical engagement with the relationship between citizen and polity. Rather than the post-war welfare state per se – which is nevertheless an important feature of crime fiction's engagement with French society during 'Les Trente Glorieuses', the prosperous three decades following the end of the Second World War, and their aftermath – it is primarily the republican state and the egalitarian philosophical ideals underpinning it that are interrogated in the French variant of the genre. Moreover, as in the case of its Scandinavian counterpart, the state with which the French *polar* engages is one that is decidedly in crisis.

This book, then, explores how contemporary French and Scandinavian crime fictions have responded to a generalised sense of social and political crisis in the late twentieth and early twenty-first centuries. It covers a five-decade period from 1965 to the present day, during which both Scandinavian and French societies underwent significant transformations. The crime fictions of the respective contexts responded to these shifting social realities, which in turn played a part in transforming the codes and conventions of the crime novel. At the centre of the analysis are the two distinctive social models that these crime traditions have as their benchmarks: the French model of republican universalism and the Scandinavian welfare state, routinely referred to as the 'Nordic model'.

French crime fiction: the Republic in conflict

The modern French Republic is secular, and the relationship between state and citizen is based on a national civic identity informed by the concept of universalism and anchored in the idea of a sharp distinction between the public and the private spheres.[2] The two main strands of ongoing debate in French political life regarding questions of identity may be summarised briefly. On the one hand, there are arguments for the effectiveness of political and social integration within the idea of republican universalism. On the other hand, this social model is challenged by immigration, globalisation, the reality of a multicultural society and increased demands from various marginalised groups in society, all contesting the national discourse that in Naomi Schor's terms has 'for centuries claimed that France is the capital of universalism'.[3] Within official political debate, there is a strong reluctance to accept critical discussion about identity issues and minority rights because such claims are perceived as threats to the stability, integrity and coherence of the Republic: 'the pressure to assimilate in France is such that identity politics cannot thrive here; there is a logical and insuperable incompatibility between promoting assimilation and encouraging micro-communities based on gender, race, and sexual orientation'.[4]

Because crime fiction so frequently features representatives of the state in the form of the police and investigating magistrates, it offers an ideal platform for critical engagement with the state and the premises underpinning it. Since these premises are precisely those of a republican social order, they are open to critique and indeed subversion. Seen from the perspective of genre history, the classic French detective novel – in the form of the *roman à énigme* (mystery novel) – has traditionally dealt with re-establishing the social order. However, in the words of Claire Gorrara, there has been a shift to crime fiction having a 'subversive potential, an ability to confront and challenge the status quo'.[5] This shift occurring in the post-war era is reinforced with the introduction of the more politicised crime novel in the 1970s, considered to be one of the catalysts for a cultural legitimation of the genre.[6]

A dominant focus in criticism of French crime fiction has been the genre's marginalised status in the public and academic imagination. During the period this book covers, the genre has benefitted from a significant repositioning from being a 'minor genre' to becoming acknowledged as part of the 'cultural heritage'.[7] This shift in the cultural landscape has been attributed in part to the emergence of the *néo-polar* in the 1970s, which, for Christophe Evans, contributed 'not to bringing the crime novel out of its cultural ghetto ... but to placing it on higher ground permitting it to shine with greater force and further reach'.[8]

Despite this well-documented move beginning in the 1970s and consolidating itself in the 1990s towards a cultural legitimation of crime fiction – and of popular culture more widely – the distinction between high and low culture is still, according to Diana Holmes and David Platten, 'particularly powerful in France'.[9] It is indeed difficult to find French criticism addressing crime fiction that does not in some way or another comment on the marginalised position of the *polar* within the hierarchical organisation of French culture. Crime fiction, classified under the amorphous conglomeration of 'paralittérature' is, according to Marc Angenot, writing in 1974, 'outside the bounds of literary closure, like a product that is taboo, forbidden, subject to a blind spot, perhaps downgraded, held in esteem, but also rich in themes and obsessions that, in high culture, are suppressed'.[10] For Yves Reuter in 1992, the very fact of working academically in France on 'paralittératures' automatically has a dimension of anti-hegemony: 'The force of prejudice – including within the theoretical field – remains such that working on paraliteratures almost irremediably implies contesting and deconstructing ethnocentrism.'[11] A similar argument is proposed in 1997 by Patrick Raynal, then editor of Gallimard's Série noire: 'The twentieth century, as far as the novel is concerned, has for a long time been subject to a form of academic imperialism.'[12] For Raynal, the low status of 'la Noire' is caused by the genre's choice of characters: 'There was, thus, in opposition to noble literature, a literature that was – in the full sense of the term – ignoble, because it spoke of people who weren't supposed to be spoken about: criminals, whores, pimps, murderers, the poor, the unemployed, etc.'[13] Frequently, this cultural binarism is expressed in terms of an opposition between 'la littérature blanche' and 'la littérature noire'.[14] It is also reflected in the preoccupations of academic criticism, notably in contrast with English-speaking contexts. Holmes and Platten observe that 'in France more than in Anglophone cultures, where the impact of Cultural Studies has been much greater, the hegemonic attitude to "mass" literature in general and story in particular has been one of disdain for the "easy" pleasures provided by popular fictions'.[15] Conversely, it might also be argued that the impact of cultural studies in France has been less pronounced precisely because of 'disdain' for popular culture. Part of the explanation can perhaps be found in the conservatism of the French academic establishment, open to accusations of cultural elitism and of being unwilling to include 'new' study areas such as postcolonial studies or queer theory.[16] These are academic fields explicitly concerned with identity issues and, as such, they can be seen as challenging republican universalist assumptions in fundamental ways.

Scandinavian crime fiction: the People's Home on the market

Whereas post-war Scandinavia enjoyed a constant and peaceful political evolution, economic prosperity and high living standards with social-democratic governments safeguarding and nurturing the individual, the Nordic welfare state has, since the 1980s, embraced globalisation and increasingly been tied by the imperatives of neoliberalism. The ability of the Scandinavian countries to maintain welfare states with their previous levels of services is impeded by external forces. As sociologist Pekka Kosonen puts it, in the context of a study of globalisation and its impact on the Nordic welfare states, 'deregulated capital markets, internationalization of enterprises and Europeanisation set tighter limitations upon economic and social policies'.[17] In welfare state research, history, politics and social sciences generally, there has been a significant focus on the 'substantial reorientation' that 'the Nordic welfare states have undergone' in this period.[18] The erosion of the welfare state is also connected with changes in the preconditions for policy-making: the social-democratic parties in all three Scandinavian countries have shifted towards the centre during the 1990s, and anti-immigrant, populist parties have promoted an increasingly polarised discussion on immigration and integration. It has, however, also been argued that this crisis is part of a process that in fact was initiated much earlier, as Francis Sejersted argues in his influential history of twentieth-century Norway and Sweden: '[t]he Social Democratic order reached its zenith in the 1960s; thereafter it declined'.[19]

In more recent Scandinavian crime fiction research, there is a general consensus that '[t]he construction of the welfare state and its transformation ... are a crucial part of the background picture to an understanding of Scandinavian crime fiction'.[20] Indeed, a central and explicit thematic focus of the socially critical crime novel has been a critique of the welfare state and its development, an expression of anxiety over its transformation, or feelings of nostalgia or melancholy caused by the feeling of a 'paradise lost'.[21] Swedish crime writer Leif G. W. Persson, for example, employs the collective title *Välfärstatens fall*, the fall of the welfare state, for his trilogy (*The Story of a Crime*, 2002, 2003, 2007), whereas Henning Mankell subtitles his crime series featuring investigator Kurt Wallander as *Romaner om den svenska oron* (novels about the Swedish anxiety).[22] It is noticeable that the socially engaged crime novel in its Swedish form emerges in the mid-1960s at the moment when the welfare state reaches its 'zenith', that it develops significantly across Scandinavia during the 1980s and 1990s, and that it explodes in the 2000s as an international publishing phenomenon at the point when the crisis of the welfare state becomes irrevocable.

Scandinavia is here defined according to the common use of the term within the region as comprising the three countries of Denmark, Norway and Sweden.[23] Besides the geographic and linguistic closeness of the Scandinavian countries, they also share a number of common traits in terms of social organisation, institutions and their socio-historical and cultural development. However, perceiving these countries as one unity is clearly problematic. While the present study does not have the scope to prioritise a thoroughgoing inter-Scandinavian comparison, it is to be kept in mind that the notion of a unified Scandinavia fosters a reductive perspective of a region with complex, multifaceted and often divergent internal histories and cultures.[24] The same can be said of the idea of an integrated 'Scandinavian crime novel' – or a French one for that matter.

Indeed, notions such as the 'Scandinavian crime novel' and the 'Nordic Noir' phenomenon with which it is associated are based on geographical conflations (the latter term incorporating the wider Nordic region including Finland, Iceland, Greenland, Åland and the Faroe Islands). At a time of globalisation when cultural products become more and more fluid and transnational, does it make sense to make genre definitions based on nationally defined categories? The label Nordic Noir is itself a product of international success, exploited efficaciously as a recognisable brand in the marketing of crime novels produced in the Nordic countries. In many ways, it is clearly problematic to categorise distinct authorial voices within a rather inflexible and predetermined classification. In this regard, it is significant that the concept of Nordic Noir can best be understood as having been constructed *outside* the region; as Stougaard-Nielsen suggests: 'Scandinavian crime fiction is perhaps "only" Scandinavian when viewed or read from abroad'.[25]

Criticism dealing with the publishing phenomenon of Nordic Noir accordingly often modifies the regional epithet and points to both commonalities and particularities within the Nordic region's five countries, for instance by dealing with them in separate chapters.[26] Bergman, while agreeing that it makes sense to talk about 'Nordic crime fiction as a common, regional phenomenon', also argues that the different 'national crime fiction traditions display their own specificities and preferences – often based on national historical conditions rather than mainstream literary history'.[27] This tendency to specificity, Bergman contends, is frequently ignored in international reception.[28]

Notwithstanding the above caveats, occasional deployment of a broad-brush approach to Scandinavian crime fiction where appropriate does, however, facilitate an analysis of the relationship between the welfare state and the engaged crime novel. In international welfare studies, the Scandinavian countries are amalgamated in the same category with the argument that 'they share some basic characteristics representing similar internal welfare state logics'.[29] As the shortcomings of the welfare state and its institutions have been a common thematic concern in Scandinavian crime fiction, it is productive to consider these countries' crime fictions under the same umbrella. As testimony to this, the contemporary Scandinavian crime novel is in Denmark often referred to as 'velfærdskrimien' (welfare crime fiction).[30]

Another reason to consider Scandinavia as a whole for tactical purposes is the fact that the region has been considered a utopian enclave in post-industrial society inasmuch as these countries represent 'an island of national distinctiveness and social-democratic success in an increasingly neo-liberal economic ocean'.[31] While the most prominent early exemplars of critically engaged Scandinavian crime fiction are distinctively circumscribed by a specific national context (Sweden in the 1960s and 1970s), they share with later 'pan-Scandinavian' variants an imperative to challenge the outside world's often idealised and exoticised perception of their cultural context. Therefore, while there are localised particularities and concerns in the Danish, Norwegian and Swedish variants of the genre, which will be highlighted in the case studies of this book, there is also a thematic common ground, placing an emphasis on a pan-Scandinavian interrogation of the welfare state at large.

Methodology

The present study builds on existing research in crime fiction studies that has investigated the genre's narratives as socio-historical chronicles of their time and setting. In the Scandinavian context, the book acknowledges in particular the contributions to the field by Andrew Nestingen, whose methodology for looking at the transformation of the Nordic region since the 1980s through the lens of popular culture has provided a basis for understanding popular culture as 'a site where answers to the crisis of legitimacy [of the welfare state] in the Nordic countries are produced, circulated and contested'.[32] A fundamental proposition in Nestingen's analysis – and also of this book – is that genre literature negotiates the crisis brought about by the 'contradiction between neoliberalism and welfare-state corporatism'.[33] Attempts to grapple with this crisis are particularly privileged in crime fiction, doubtless at least in part because of the genre's inherent preoccupation with hierarchical societal structures and divides, frequently the cause of criminal acts, and because of its common character gallery of state representatives (the police and the judiciary).

In relation to French crime fiction, the study draws (predominantly) on Anglophone research, which since the early 2000s has seen an increased interest in the field. Claire Gorrara's *The Roman Noir in Post-War French Culture* (2003), an early contribution, seeks to explore how *noir* narratives 'intersect with wider social and historical forces'.[34] While Gorrara and Nestingen place their examination of the genre within a broader socio-historical analysis, both also value textual analysis. This goes against a critical trend in crime fiction studies, characterised, according to Gill Plain, by 'either an uncritical celebration of the history of detection or an analysis of readership patterns more concerned with *why* people read genre fiction than with the fiction itself'.[35] The current study prioritises textual analysis rather than a taxonomic survey of the chosen texts, and regards them, following Plain, as being 'as available for close reading and as open to literary theoretical interrogation as their more "respectable" counterparts'.[36]

The twenty-first century has also seen a growing critical interest in the relationship between crime fiction and identity, focused on the genre's successful exploration and discussion of identity issues relating to nationality, class, race, gender, sexuality, disability and other such categories.[37] Indeed, central to the texts investigated in the present study is their protagonists' search for identity or self-understanding. This search is entangled with and frequently reflected in the search for a solution to the crime committed. The book aligns itself with this identity-political strand of crime-fiction research, in which a common trope is the detective figure (or main protagonist) with a non-normative identity who serves the purpose of challenging hegemonic structures through a genre that traditionally has marginalised the former while embodying the latter, as John Scaggs outlines: 'all of these characters [female, lesbian, black, etc.] serve to expose the dominant ideology of white heterosexual masculinity through a textual hijacking of one of its principal vehicles: crime fiction'.[38]

The present study, then, recognises crime fictions as multidimensional research objects, appearing not only as literary texts or socio-historical chronicles, but also as sites for the negotiation of various identities. It enquires how the content and structures of crime fiction narratives reflect and support these dimensions in the two different culturally defined contexts. Going a step further, it investigates the ways in which crime fictions in these two settings challenge the status quo of political domination and throw light on the ideological underpinnings of the external public discourse that surrounds them. Aiming to position crime fictions in this broad discursive framework, the readings correspondingly embrace an intertextual and interdisciplinary methodological matrix drawing on the knowledge and applying texts from a wide range of disciplines (sociology, international relations studies, postcolonial studies, gender studies, queer theory, philosophy, history, law, welfare state studies, political philosophy, comparative literature).

Whereas the period covered here has been marked by conceptual keywords such as 'globalisation', 'transnationalism', 'hybridity', 'multiculturalism' – and the texts themselves are indeed characterised by a high degree of cultural mixing – crime fiction studies often take a nation-centred approach to the texts, and only a few studies directly compare crime fictions from different cultural settings.[39] However, the focus on national traditions within crime fiction studies might also, it can be argued, mirror the fact that questions about national identity have become an increasingly debated issue in the current political climate and social circumstances. The main objective of the study's comparative approach therefore is not to identify 'French crime fiction' or 'Scandinavian crime fiction' as typologies under which distinctive features and recognisable patterns can be found in order to reinforce the notion of the nation. Rather, the literary case studies are perceived as examples – without the claim of their being wholly representative – that contribute to, accentuate and contest the wider discursive configurations underpinning their respective settings. The study does therefore not pretend to be comprehensive: the texts constituting the corpus of the project have been chosen because they in some way or another are concerned with themes of social struggle, and they have, in particular, been selected for their outspokenness on identity issues. They thus represent the more critically engaged strands of Scandinavian and French crime fiction.

One of the key questions this book will explore is how the 'subversive potential' that Gorrara identifies manifests itself in French and Scandinavian crime fictions, and whether in fact French crime fictions offer a much more radically subversive potential than their Scandinavian counterparts because of the constraints imposed by pervasive republican universalist discourse which they are forced to find strategies to critique. At the same time, the book will investigate the ways in which the social critique offered by Scandinavian crime fictions can be situated within a consensus formed around the 'Nordic model'. Subsequently, it will explore the primary concern of the Scandinavian variant of the crime fiction genre in that social model's erosion rather than in – as is the case with French critical crime fiction – its very philosophical and ideological premises.

Structure

The book is divided into three thematically organised sections, each consisting of two separate chapters. Part I addresses the critical potential of crime fiction, tracing it from its early form emerging in Sweden and France in the 1960s and 1970s up to the present day, focusing in particular on how individual and collective identities are negotiated in relation to normative state discourse. The focus of Part II is on how crime fiction has been employed to discuss and negotiate questions of gender and sexuality. Finally, Part III considers identity issues relating to ethnicity, investigating representations in French and Scandinavian crime novels that employ the genre as a site for critical engagement with identity issues relating to immigration and multiculturalism.

What the comparative approach of the present study aims to show is that, while the enthusiasm with which the *polar scandinave* has been met in France perhaps has proven to be more revelatory of the problematics and concern of the home-grown *polar*, there are strong reasons for examining the transcultural interplay between the two traditions. Embracing its twelve literary case studies from a comparatist and diachronic perspective, the book explores French and Scandinavian crime novel traditions in terms of points of commonality as well as points of difference. While there are global concerns for the critically engaged crime novel pertinent to both settings (advanced capitalist society, globalisation, immigration, economic crises, etc.), there are also divergent, culturally specific targets of critique and textual ways of approaching them. The cultural specificities and common-sense assumptions persistently reveal themselves in the comparative analysis and become especially visible in the novels' approach to and discussion of identity issues.

Of particular import is an exploration of the connection between conventions of the crime narrative and the society that it represents, that is, of how form and content are interdependent and develop in conjunction with each other. This relationship is not fixed, but rather subject to change both over time and in accordance with the narratives' cultural habitats. While in a classic whodunnit, à la Agatha Christie, the resolution is about the restoration of order, the novels examined in the present study are either preoccupied with exhibiting, documenting and exposing social order or – in exemplars which might be seen as deploying a 'postmodern' aesthetics – directly concerned with destabilising the existing order and the assumptions underpinning it, as well as with destabilising the conventions of the genre. An essential part of the study is, therefore, to establish what precisely are viewed as constituting privileged issues within the social contracts of Scandinavia and France. Ultimately, the study aims to affirm that the formal variations and deviations of the French *polar* and the Scandinavian police procedural are rooted in – but also creatively exploited in order to challenge – their two distinct social and ideological settings.

Part I

The Structure of Crime Fiction Revolutions

1

Social and Literary Models in Crisis

Introduction

In 1967 Swedish journalist and writer Per Wahlöö (1926–75) explained in an essay the aim of the crime fiction novels he was then in the process of writing with his wife Maj Sjöwall (1935–2020):

> We ... had this special idea together: to use the crime novel in its pure form as a scalpel to slit open the belly of the ideologically pauperized and morally debatable so-called welfare state of the bourgeois type ... to simply find out where the responsibility was for what and if there was, indeed, anything to be responsible for.[1]

The use of the crime novel as a means of dissecting society and formulating social critique was unprecedented in Sweden at the time when Wahlöö was writing. Sjöwall and Wahlöö's critical engagement with the Swedish welfare state as presented in their police procedurals not only challenges the contemporary political consensus; it is also intertwined with a rewriting of the generic conventions of crime fiction. This rewriting advances questions about literature's role in society.

A parallel literary movement of politicised leftist crime writing sees the light in France with the post-May 1968 *néo-polar*. Its founder, Jean-Patrick Manchette (1942–95), likewise establishes 'une écriture au scalpel', a 'scalpel'-based, implicitly surgical form of writing, setting forth concerns about advanced capitalism, consumer society and political organisation within the French Republic while simultaneously contesting the formulaic structures and para-literary position of the genre.[2]

This chapter investigates the emergence of the socially and politically engaged crime novel in Scandinavia – specifically in Sweden – and France in the 1960s and early 1970s through readings of novels by Sjöwall/Wahlöö and by Manchette. It considers these novels as articulations of – and responses to – particular socio-political paradigms in their respective national contexts. One unifying theme dominating these writings is the turn from viewing crime as an expression of an individual aberration to understanding crime as a manifestation of a societal malaise. Rather than staging the detective in the role of protector of a social order that is disturbed by the individual and aberrant malefactor, the *néo-polar* and its Swedish counterpart set out to investigate the constellations and dynamics of power and to problematise the political status quo. This implies a persistent interrogation of the prevailing polity and its institutions – the Fifth Republic in the case of Manchette, and the post-war social-democratic welfare state in the case of Sjöwall/Wahlöö. This evolves in the fictional narratives in both cultural contexts into investigations of the state as an inherently criminal institution offering protection only to those who fully comply with its rationale. Thematically, the writers focus on processes within state institutions, predominantly the legal system, the police and the political establishment, as well as on the ways in which the press often colludes with the police and political interests.

However, before the analysis turns towards the fictional texts themselves, the status of these almost simultaneous literary occurrences will be contextualised within the history of modern crime fiction narratives. After a brief discussion of how the genre has shifted and developed to embrace different sociocultural stages of modernity, this section thus situates the writings of Sjöwall/Wahlöö and Manchette as pivotal literary events – and generic turning points – in their French and Swedish contexts. These writings announce the advent of a new category of crime fiction that is critically engaged on multiple fronts.

The crime fiction genre as modern form

Detective fiction emerges in the mid-nineteenth century and develops in close relationship with industrialisation, technological progress, colonialism, urbanisation, capitalism and the bourgeoisie as ruling class. In other words, it develops alongside modernity itself. As well as accompanying, reflecting and charting societal changes, detective fiction also, as Ernest Mandel remarks, surfaces at 'a particular stage of the evolution of literature'.[3] If Charles Baudelaire is celebrated for his radical conceptualisation of modernity in *Le Peintre de la vie moderne* (The painter of modern life, 1863) and for his characterisation of it as a condition rooted in the constantly shifting individual temperament's relationship to the similarly mobile environment, that is, as a *social*

16

condition, it is unsurprising that he should also be the translator and advocate of Edgar Allan Poe's detective stories for a French audience.[4] Poe's short stories 'The Murders in the Rue Morgue' (1841), 'The Mystery of Marie Rogêt' (1842) and 'The Purloined Letter' (1844) are published in Baudelaire's translation in 1856.[5] These stories are generally considered as the texts establishing the genre of modern crime fiction and can be viewed as a transitional literary manifestation at the crossroads between the pre-modern and the modern.[6] As Kim Toft Hansen notes, '"The Murders in the Rue Morgue" materialises a condensed format of the Western rational modern detective story.'[7] Toft Hansen further characterises Poe in the following terms:

> Directionally, Poe builds a literary bridge between past and future, between a metaphysical sensibility [Romanticism] and a rational frame of mind [Modernity] which does not unerringly make him the father of crime fiction, but a hub of attention passing on erstwhile historical roots.[8]

In his analysis of the association between modernity and crime fiction, Jacques Dubois emphasises capitalism and the rule of the bourgeoisie as the conditions upon which the genre establishes itself. Dubois also highlights the three colonial powers France, Britain and the United States as the genre's birthplaces: 'The genre is born in three countries in which liberal capitalism is shaking up the old world and creating the conditions for the emergence of a new culture that establishes its coherence straight away and is still ours.'[9]

Linking the surfacing of the detective novel to the paradigmatic shift from 'the old world' to modernity suggests that other and later significant shifts from one era to another might also have an impact upon the genre's essential features. Therefore, it is productive to investigate the modern crime fiction narrative as a transitional, pivotal literary form in relation to later mutations of the genre, which frequently appear at historically critical moments when societies are in rapid transformation. Accordingly, Ernest Mandel points to another significant sociocultural shift in America in the 1920s and 1930s, coinciding with the emergence of the hard-boiled novel. He argues in *Delightful Murder* (1984) that whereas crime fiction in its early nineteenth-century manifestations mirrored 'the rising need of the bourgeoisie to defend rather than attack the social order', the genre in the interwar period 'represented a typical transitional phenomenon', signalling a shift in focus from a systemic defence to a systemic critique:

> This evolution of the crime story, of course, means that it can no longer function as a literary genre helping to persuade its readers to accept the legitimacy of bourgeois society. Its integrative function has declined, and it has actually become disintegrative with respect to that society.[10]

This shift from an 'integrative' function for the crime story, that is, one supportive of the social order and of its restoration, to a 'disintegrative' function – one of critique – is a significant marker for twentieth-century crime fiction, and one that coincides, moreover, with radical shifts in the economic and cultural bases of society.

The present chapter's rationale, then, is that certain crime fiction narratives in the 1960s and 1970s – in this case, Sjöwall/Wahlöö's and Manchette's – represent yet another turning point in the genre, linked in turn to a shifting of socio-historical tectonic plates moving at the moment when these authors are producing their texts. In the same manner that detective fiction materialises as a literary companion to modernity in the nineteenth century, these crime fictions, it is argued, surface as a response to the paradigm of postmodernity in its early manifestation. Likewise, rather as postmodernity is both continuous and discontinuous with earlier phases of modernity, the rewriting of the genre that begins during the mid-1960s and early 1970s offers form and content that are both analogous to and disparate from previous variants of the genre. From its inception in the nineteenth century, the crime fiction genre is anchored to modernity, and develops in close connection with modernity through the twentieth century, as industrialisation, capitalism, colonialism, nationalism, socialism, along with modernity itself, become increasingly associated with the 'post-' prefix.

The title of this book's first part alludes to Thomas S. Kuhn's *The Structure of Scientific Revolutions* (1962), which argues against viewing history in terms of a 'development-by-accumulation' or a 'process of accretion'.[11] Instead Kuhn argues for viewing the development of science as the result of scientific revolutions, described as 'the tradition-shattering complements to the tradition-bound activity of normal science'.[12] The development of the crime fiction genre is here considered from a similar perspective, from which new generic occurrences are viewed as expressions of paradigmatic shifts linked to contingent literary and socio-historical turning points. This evolution of the crime fiction genre as one undergoing periodic yet 'non-accumulative' revolutions thus takes account of the genre's emergence in the mid-nineteenth century, the appearance of the hard-boiled detective fiction in 1920–1930s' America, Sjöwall/Wahlöö's welfare-state crime fiction and Manchette's *néo-polar* in the 1960–1970s, and also of the historical contingency of these developments. These literary turning points can be viewed as generic revolutions bound to socio-historical critical moments where the genre's predilection for dealing with societal transformation is particularly accentuated.

The theme of social transformation is reinforced by the genre's particular thematic preoccupation with topographical/territorial infrastructure. Paris in the 1840s–1850s, Los Angeles in the 1930s–1940s and European metropoles (including Paris and Stockholm) in the 1960s–1970s are all characterised by radically new infrastructural environments, and these are central to crime fiction's engagement with the respective societies in which they are produced. The changing metropolis as a site of existential alienation found in Baudelaire's and Poe's Parisian boulevards and in the 'mean streets' of the Chandleresque *noir* are paralleled in Sjöwall and Wahlöö's depiction of Stockholm, where, for Bergman, 'urban spaces ... represent the disintegrating Swedish welfare state, and the changes that the city is going through, physical reconstruction as well as social degradation, are presented as the result of capitalism, corruption and greed'.[13] In Sjöwall and Wahlöö's novels, new architectural features and a changing cityscape resulting from urban planning executed to the benefit of business interests expose the degeneration of Swedish society, where the sense of community found in the old residential neighbourhoods disappears to make room for new, dehumanising concrete buildings erected for big corporations 'to achieve the fullest possible exploitation of valuable land'.[14] The reshaping of the city is directly linked to social degradation: 'Behind its spectacular topographical façade and under its polished, semi-fashionable surface, Stockholm had become an asphalt jungle where drug addiction and sexual perversion ran more rampant than ever.'[15] In contrast, the immediate post-war city is frequently throughout the series described in nostalgic terms: 'Stockholm had been a different city then. The Old City had been an idyllic little town ... before they had cleared out the slums and restored the buildings and raised the rents so the old tenants could no longer afford to stay.'[16] The city's appearance thus mirrors the transition between old and new, between past and present, offering physical testimony to a society in transformation, to a process at the centre of Sjöwall and Wahlöö's critique. In Manchette's novels the focus is often on another aspect of urbanism, the *banlieue* (the suburban or indeed extra-urban periphery of a large city), providing in its progressive infrastructural degradation and alienation from the rest of French society an apt setting for depicting a period when the economic and social environment changes at the end of 'Les Trente Glorieuses' and becomes marked by unemployment, the oil crisis and the sequels to decolonisation.

Postmodernity and the emergence of the engaged crime novel

In 'Postmodernism, or, the Cultural Logic of Late Capitalism' (1984), Fredric Jameson characterises postmodernism loosely as 'the end of this and that' and more specifically as 'the end of ideology, art, or social class; the "crisis" of Leninism, social democracy, or the welfare state, etc., etc.'[17] According to Jameson, the ideological and cultural crises of postmodernism begin in the early 1980s, but '[t]he case for its existence depends on the hypothesis of some radical break or *coupure*' taking place in the late 1950s early 1960s.[18] Postmodernism, or postmodernity (as Jameson renames it later to distinguish the historical period from the style), is characterised by the fact that 'all kinds of things, from economics to politics, from the arts to technology, from daily life to international relations, had changed for good'.[19] While the crime fictions studied in chapters 2–6 of this book all deal with the 'postmodern' period after 1980, the engaged crime novel emerging in the 1960s can be said to be characterised by a notion of pre-'postness' in various forms, or what, in paraphrasing Jameson, could be characterised as the beginning of the end of this and that.

'Postmodern crime fiction' as a literary subgenre is generally associated with more literary writers such as Paul Auster, Thomas Pynchon, Jorge Luis Borges, Umberto Eco, Gabriel García Marquez and Don DeLillo.[20] The present study, however, prefers a broader understanding of postmodern crime fiction, situating a wider range of crime novels – including those of more popular stature within the mainstream of the genre – within the paradigmatic constellations of postmodernity. This view of postmodernity corresponds with Jameson's conception of postmodernism, which aims 'to grasp it as the cultural dominant of the logic of late capitalism' rather than to present 'a view for which the postmodern is one (optional) style among many others available'.[21] The novels examined in this book – without falling into the category of literary postmodern crime fiction – still use postmodern modes when adapting and redeploying a classic modern genre. The adjective 'postmodern' is thus here taken as referring to postmodernity as a historical if not in fact socio-historical category, rather than to 'postmodernism' as an artistic or aesthetic category.

Both Sjöwall/Wahlöö and Manchette explicitly place their writings within a paradigm of crisis or decline, and their crime fiction narratives can generally be understood in terms of an experience of the collapse of ideologies. The 'incredulity toward metanarratives', to employ Lyotard's conception of the postmodern condition, translates in Sjöwall and Wahlöö's case into a pronounced disbelief in the social-democratic version of the welfare state, which since the 1930s had constituted (and to some extent still constitutes) an essential part of the national 'metanarrative' in Sweden as in Scandinavia more generally.[22] Their crime fictions, as put by Charlotte Beyer, 'reflect a postmodernist scepticism in authority and a mistrust in organisations'.[23] Cracks are beginning to show in the system of the social-democratic welfare project, and Sjöwall and Wahlöö's critique of the post-war consensus is connected by Beyer to the beginning of post-welfarism.

On the French side, as a chiastic response to what Lyotard calls 'la crise des récits' ('the crisis of narratives'), Manchette characterises the *polar* as 'la littérature de la crise' ('the literature of crisis') and as a genre that 'sees the evil in contingent social organisation'.[24] Correspondingly, he lets Henri Buton, principal character of his first crime novel, *L'Affaire N'Gustro* (The N'Gustro Affair, 1971), pronounce the following axioms: 'God does not exist and Marxism is a con-trick.'[25] In a similar vein, when considering culture, Buton asserts: 'It's dead!'[26] These programmatic and sceptical statements are emblematic of the methodical dismantling of religion, ideology and culture taking place throughout Manchette's texts.

The novels of Sjöwall/Wahlöö and Manchette express uncertainty and instability and are themselves of uncertain and unstable status in terms of genre; the medium thus resembles the message. This contrasts with the underlying ideological premises for the classic whodunnit from the British tradition, and for the French *roman policier* or the conventional Swedish mystery novel conceived in the whodunnit's image. The subversive aspect of the writings offers at least in part a critique of generic conventions, operating within the parameters of the history of the crime fiction genre as such, and aligns itself with the writers' overall leftist political agenda.[27] As Pearson and Singer argue, criticism with reference to the traditional mystery novel has seen 'detective fiction as a paradigm and an implement of the hegemonic processes of the Western nation-state, tantalizing readers with aberrant, irrational criminality while assuring them that society ultimately coheres through a shared commitment to reason and law'.[28] Any opposition voiced by crime fiction to a bourgeois belief system, therefore, necessarily entails a revolt against the conventional mystery novel, characterised, according to Sjöwall and Wahlöö, by its 'reactionary and conservative hallmark'.[29] Sjöwall and Wahlöö categorise what they refer to as 'the Golden age detective novel' as 'bourgeois entertainment' written by writers operating consciously in an unreal world.[30] In its place they propose the realist 'crime novel' or the 'procedural novel' based on a strong sense of contemporaneity. This new version of the crime novel can bring the genre out of the 'entertainment industry' where it has been read by 'blinkered readers', and into the sphere of engaged literature.[31] For Manchette, such opposition is expressed as the fundamental epistemological difference between the nature of the mystery novel and the *polar*:

> I decree that *polar* in no way denotes detective novel. *Polar* means violent *roman noir*. While the mystery detective novel of the English school sees the evil in human nature, the *polar* sees the evil in contingent social organisation ... The *polar* is the literature of crisis.[32]

Having rejected the socially and politically conservative model of the whodunnit, the common point of reference for Sjöwall/Wahlöö and Manchette is instead the American hard-boiled novel. Manchette makes the link between the emergence of the hard-boiled *roman noir* and widespread political disillusion in the early to mid-twentieth century. Facing a rapidly expanding and corrupt capitalism in the 'period of triumphant counter-revolution', that is, the period from 1920 to 1950, the hard-boiled novelists used the genre as a means of expressing such disenchantment.[33] Manchette implicitly draws a parallel with the situation experienced in France after the events of May 1968 and the need for the *néo-polar* as a way of articulating political concern. A similar expression of crisis after a moment of elevation is to be found in Sjöwall and Wahlöö's depiction of the post-war social-democratic welfare state. This social construction was supposed to be based on universal rights and opportunities, but the reality is for Sjöwall in fact a capitalist state described as a 'cold and inhuman society where the rich got richer and the poor got poorer'.[34]

The engaged crime novel evolves alongside a new type of readership both in France and Sweden. The novels' popularity is viewed by Evans as a consequence of the fact that the writers are, so to speak, writing the right things at the right time:

What these writers were to allow ... was doubtless the acceleration and widening of the intellectual recognition of the genre, at any rate within France. Why? Because at the same time that they were emerging, successive generations of male and female readers who had followed similar socio-cultural trajectories (higher education of a certain duration, political engagement, interest in the counterculture) were themselves emerging.[35]

Evans's argument is based on the influence of the *néo-polar*, but a similar account can be found in Sjöwall and Wahlöö's own analysis of their readers, who they claim are different from the readers of the mystery novel seduced by its 'bourgeois entertainment'. Their readers 'want something other than charades, they are informed and want informed literature'.[36] Retrospectively in an interview, Sjöwall explains the crime genre's renewal, its use of realism and its political content as the factors that bring it out of its previous cultural ghetto: '[w]e were the first crime writers who were considered to be serious reading. You did not have to hide Sjöwall/Wahlöö inside Kafka when you were on the train.'[37] This statement reveals a presumed tension or barrier between genre and literary fiction, the breakdown of which is a significant feature of a postmodern sensibility.

In the cases of both Sjöwall/Wahlöö and Manchette, the writers actively use the dynamics found in their fictional projects' position between literature and para-literature as an active and creative force. Making reinvigorations and innovative reforms of the genre to resurrect it in new forms, the works of these authors include a conscious intertextual dialogue with the genre's conventions and previous traditions. The focus of the following readings is on how the novels studied – through interplay of form and content – problematise the political underpinning of the post-war welfare state and how they participate as an alternative voice in political, cultural and social debate in France and in Scandinavia.

Jean-Patrick Manchette: the néo-polar and new social realities

Jean-Patrick Manchette published nine crime novels between 1971 and 1981, most of which appeared in Gallimard's Série noire. As an emblematic representative of a generation of writers who took a political position during the Algerian conflict and in May 1968, Manchette offers a clear left-wing critique of advanced capitalism, political conservatism and the morality of the French state; at the same time, this critique is subtended by the disillusion experienced in the aftermath of May 1968. *La Position du tireur couché (The Prone Gunman*, 1981) concludes Manchette's career, in the year that François Mitterrand forms a government that will later cause disillusionment among many on the left in France.

Manchette invents the term *néo-polar*, which has become a sub-categorical expression used to define the French literary movement of politically engaged crime fiction. He links the emergence of this genre directly to the upheavals of May 1968: 'the appearance of a French "new *polar*" (which we'll term *néo-polar*) echoes the explosive reappearance of History on the ripped-up streets of Paris and elsewhere'.[38] Contrary to the later usage of the term as a designator for politically engaged crime fiction, Manchette employs it rather ambiguously, emphasising that the term does not introduce a new school of French *polars*:

> I coined the term 'néo-polar' on the word model of 'neo-bread', 'neo-wine' or even 'neo-president', used by radical critique to designate ersatz forms that, under an illustrious name, have everywhere replaced the same thing. A section of journalists and fans have taken up this label as a term of praise, without seeing any malice in it, which is amusing.[39]

The idea of the *néo-polar* being an *ersatz* – a copy of inferior quality to the original – corresponds with Manchette's ambivalent affiliation with the genre at large, which he theorises in numerous contributions to newspapers and magazines.[40] As well as being the creator of the *néo-polar*, he is simultaneously one of its fiercest critics. His critique associates the crime fiction genre in the twentieth century with the development of different socio-historical contexts which he categorises in terms of revolutionary and counter-revolutionary movements.

The launching of the Série noire by Marcel Duhamel in 1945 had marked a turning point in history of the French crime novel. Its proclaimed aim was to promote translations of 1920s and 1930s novels from the American hard-boiled school to a French readership increasingly fascinated by American consumer goods and cultural products after the Second World War. As emphasised by Duhamel in his famous presentation of the series, the translated novels were controversial and non-conformist and broke away from the French tradition of the *roman à énigme*'s locked room mysteries and ratiocinative sleuths.[41] Where the *néo-polar* breaks radically with the contemporary French crime novel, Manchette demonstrates a conscious preference for the American inter-war crime novel, relating his own writing especially to that of Dashiell Hammett and Raymond Chandler: 'As I was brought up completely on American hard-boiled *polars*, not at all on French authors, it seemed to me completely natural and automatic to follow the path of "critical realists". The polar, for me, was – and remains – the novel of very violent social intervention.'[42] He places the emergence and popularity of the critical hard-boiled novel – 'the great moral literature of our era' – within the socio-historical conditions in the United States 1920–1950. This period is defined by counter-revolutionary, if not fascist, tendencies.[43] Also inscribed in Manchette's project is, however, knowledge of the fact that the era of the *roman noir* is definitively over:

> To write in 1970 was to take into account a new social reality, but it was also to take into account the fact that the *polar* form was outdated because its era was over: to re-use an outdated form is to use it referentially, to honour it in critiquing it, in exaggerating it, to unshape it from every angle.[44]

This chimes with Manchette's wider view on culture in contemporary society, inspired by Herbert Marcuse's theorisation of consumer society's ways of pleasing and preventing any veritable opposition. Another inspiration for Manchette is Guy Debord and the Internationale situationniste's proclamation of the power of commercial commodities over the individual and of modern life as mediatised spectacle.[45] Not only is Manchette using mass-produced genre literature to critique consumer society, but he also employs the hard-boiled novel – an exponent of all things American – as a vehicle for the political rejection of the hegemonic nature of Western capitalism:

> The first problem encountered by the French *polar* is that it is not American ... When art has become a commodity (named culture), economic and political hegemony is also cultural hegemony. In the face of American hegemony, old forms can survive by setting themselves in stone ... but what is created again necessarily defines itself through its relationship to American forms. This is a relationship of imitation and negation.[46]

This bitter-sweet relationship can be situated within a process defined by Robert Deleuse as the 'amer-ricanement' – a subversive synonym of 'Americanisation' playing on the French words for 'bitter' and 'mocking laughter' – of French culture, a theme that Manchette develops throughout his novels.[47]

Nada

Manchette's novel *Nada* (Nada, 1972) is published in Gallimard's Série noire, only four years after the events of May 1968. The publication thus happens in a climate where the feeling still exists that, in Benoît Mouchart's words, 'social movements could still potentially modify the order of things in France, as well as in the West more generally'.[48]

Nada tells the story of a group of left-wing militants who organise and execute the kidnapping of the American ambassador to France, Richard Poindexter. Manchette categorises the novel as 'a piece of commentary on terrorism' understood as a *gauchiste* terrorism in line with that of contemporary far-left organisations such as the German Red Army Faction or the Italian Red Brigades.[49] The immediate real-life frame of reference for the novel is the Gauche Prolétarienne's kidnapping of Renault's chief of labour relations, Robert Nogrette, in March 1972. The action was a direct response to the killing of the Maoist activist, Pierre Overney, by a security guard during a protest in front of a Renault plant, an incident that was followed by mass demonstrations across Paris.[50] Manchette follows the events closely and makes multiple entries in his diary about how they evolve, before he starts writing *Nada* under the provisional title *Le Consul* in April 1972.[51] He refers to this work in progress as 'the work on my anarchists'.[52]

The first third of the novel is devoted to the introduction of the six members of the Nada group and their planning and execution of the kidnapping (chapters 2–12). This is followed by the police investigation while the group keep the ambassador hostage at a remote farm outside Paris. This section ends with the brutal execution of the activists, mostly performed in person by the chief commissioner, Goémond (chapters 13–32). The novel's last part theorises upon the event (chapters 33–42) by providing the retrospective perspectives of Buenaventura, the only member of the group to escape the massacre at the farm; Goémond, who gets suspended as part of the political and media cover-up following the scene of carnage at the farm; and Treuffais, who left the group before the kidnapping.

Sparse in detailed descriptions of its Parisian setting, the narration is structured upon the grid of streets and boulevards connecting the apartments and rooms that the members of the Nada group occupy. The routes navigated to get from one place to another are delineated so that the reader can reconstruct the itinerary with complete cartographic accuracy. The focus on the mapping of the capital and the vehicles mirrors the narrative organisation of the text itself: the textual arrival point is revealed first, then the narrator describes the route leading to this point. Following this principle, the novel's first chapter, consisting of a letter written by one of the policemen who takes part in the shooting of the terrorists, sets the frame for the novel. Here, the gendarme gives his account of the events at the farm, and essentially of the novel's plot, before the story begins: 'Indeed, the Anarchists who kidnapped the US ambassador, it was we who caught them.'[53] The revelation of the novel's 'story' in narratological terms, which in detective fiction traditionally concludes the narration of events, is in *Nada* disclosed in the second sentence of the text. As highlighted by Margaret Atack, the name of the gendarme who makes this revelation, Georges Poustacrouille, evokes that of Gaston Leroux's journalist-detective, Rouletabille, in *Le Mystère de la chambre jaune* (*The Mystery of the Yellow Room*, 1919).[54] Starting the novel with an intertextual reference to a classic among French detective novels, but in the same instance breaking the generic conventions by revealing the criminal act and pointing out the culprit, sets the tone for the novel's meta-literary comment on the genre. The obliteration of classic detective fiction's drive to divulge the actual story calls for a more elaborated use of point of view as a means of triggering suspense. The novel's *récit*, in the form of a polyphonic representation of various narrative paths subsequently leading to Poustacrouille's *histoire*, reinforces this feature. The same technique is found again in the novel's second part, where two of the kidnappers, Cash and Épaulard, attempt to make love – with a not entirely satisfactory outcome. Cash reassures Épaulard that things will work out better the next day, but is corrected by the omniscient and, indeed, prescient narrator who knows that the police are about to storm the house: 'Cash was mistaken; things would not go better tomorrow. Tomorrow, they would be dead' (p. 407). The dynamics of the textual organisation thus lie in the narrator's revelations about what will happen in the future. This is reinforced by the shift of focus from chapter to chapter between the police and the anarchists. By alternating the perspective, the narrator plays with a double sense of sympathy: the narrative's initial focus on the activities of the Nada group invites the reader to take an empathetic position favouring the group's position, whereas the story's polyphonic nature makes the 'true' story interpretable from various points.

The realism of Manchette is in *Nada* characterised by an abundance of details and specifications of brand names, not only of cars (Ford Mustang, 2CV, Dauphine, Jaguar, Cadillac, Ford Consul, Peugeuot 203), but also of guns (Manurhin, Sten), alcohol (Johnny [*sic*] Walker, Martini), cigarettes (Gauloises, Françaises) and so on. In this setting, the characters themselves are also essentialised as 'brands' and referred to by categorical descriptions rather than by their names. Thus, D'Arcy is 'the alcoholic', Buenaventura 'the Catalan' and Épaulard 'the fifty-something', or in the case of Cash, her position (as quasi-prostitute) is suggested by her surname. This accumulation of consumer objects functions as a constant reminder of what Jean-François Gérault characterises as 'the complete invasion of modern life by business maintained by big capital'.[55] This appears as a recurrent theme in Manchette's fiction. The kidnapped ambassador is likewise reduced to a commodity among other commodities, as Épaulard points out to him at the farm: 'you are a servant of the State, at the highest level. You are no longer anything; you are a thing' (p. 401). Cash herself is also aware of the objectification that she is subject to: 'I'm not much more than a small-time whore' (p. 366). The terrorists, appearing without any clearly expressed political motive, also feed off the same system. In the end, money seems to be what drives the action. When Épaulard contemplates the future, it is not the political message that is in focus: 'He couldn't quite envisage the future. He didn't believe that the ransom would be paid, that he would be rich the following week' (p. 412).

Manchette's writing style, which he attributes to Hammett, is referred to by the writer himself as behaviourist: a matter-of-fact representation of environment and characters from an external viewpoint.[56] The narrator generally takes the position behind the camera and usually leaves the reader to deduce underlying motivations from the description of appearances. The text, naked and purged of any extra-artistic decorations – like the map of Paris outlined in *Nada* – thematises the in-between, the *non-dit*, by not mentioning it. Manchette consciously uses the manner of written expression intricately linked for him with the overall function of the *polar*:

> It's also style and writing that I'm talking to you about. That moment when, once more, the intentions of men count for nothing, that moment when their acts alone can be described in the triumphant terms of a

writing in thrall to behaviourism, is indeed that moment of restoration of order under which *from the actions of men results something other than what they plan and accomplish, something other than what they know and want immediately. They realise their interests, but with that is produced something else that is hidden inside, that their conscience was not aware of and that did not come into their field of vision.* Behaviourism as style is the mode of expression of an overheated consciousness that now favours the trickery of reason. And the form of the *polar* is indeed the form of its content.[57]

The narrative strategy defined here corresponds with the description of the anarchists. Their actions are described, but their intentions, the underlying purposes, remain unknown to the reader and, perhaps by extension, also to themselves. Just as the behaviourist style's focus on external factors creates a desire for what is 'hidden inside', the text generates a craving for what is unrevealed, the unknown, but which cannot be comprehended rationally.

At the centre of *Nada*, one finds an ostensible opposition to the repressive power of the bourgeoisie as the dominant class feeding on the global economic order of capitalism. The kidnapping, ending involuntarily with the killing of the US ambassador – a metaphorical figurehead for Western capitalist hegemony – seems to be the only apparent unifying goal for the group of radical activists. Despite the action's symbolic nature, the actual political *raison d'être* for the kidnapping remains obscure. The content of the manifesto written by the group and posted to various national newspapers to be printed as part of the group's demands for the release of the ambassador is never made available to the reader. As the novel's title suggests, an inherent nihilism reigns within the group and its mission, and ideological purposes seem muffled by a general absorption by a system where diffuse violence becomes the only way of critiquing, and despair seems to be the ultimate sentiment.

The spectacle

The final sentence of *Nada* turns the text back to the starting point leaving the reader with other potential post-textual versions of the story. Treuffais, about to be captured by the police in his apartment, where Buenaventura and Goémond have just shot each other dead, calls up a foreign news agency: 'Listen, my old friend, and note this well, said Treuffais, looking at the bodies. I'm going to tell you the brief and complete story of the "Nada" group ...' (p. 449). The immanent possibility of Treuffais's version of the events being covered in an article by a foreign journalist contributes to the novel's polyphonic nature. The ellipsis further emphasises the novel's iterative narrative circularity, an open-endedness where the story can be reproduced continuously from various sources, through different channels and consequently in different renditions. The story's presumed recycling by the mass media, feeding off the terrorists' dead bodies, evokes the first thesis of Guy Debord's *La Société du spectacle* (*The Society of the Spectacle*, 1967): 'In societies where modern conditions of production prevail, life is presented as an immense accumulation of spectacles. Everything that was directly lived has receded into a representation.'[58] The mediated image of the massacre on the farm is thus what is left, and given that the reader knows already how this image can be manipulated from the previous representations of the events by the press, the ellipsis only brings about further alienation. Manchette summarises in his *Journal* a discussion he has had with his wife, Mélissa, about the terrorists in *Nada* whom she has interpreted as 'positive heroes': 'I tried to correct her misunderstanding by demonstrating that they represent, politically speaking, a danger to the public, a real disaster for the revolutionary movement. I demonstrated that the foundering of leftism in terrorism is the foundering of revolution in spectacle.'[59] What in *Nada* can seem an altruistically motivated statement (the kidnapping of Poindexter to get a political message through) turns into a spectacle (the massacring of the terrorists and the killing of the ambassador), with substituted images mediated by the press. This situation, in which the press operates within a capitalist consumer society as an instrument of the state, is summed up by Buenaventura in his retrospective analysis:

> The regime obviously defends itself against terrorism. But the system does not prevent itself from using terrorism: it encourages it and promotes it. The *desperado* is a commodity, an exchange value, a behavioural model like the cop or the saint. The State dreams of a horrible and triumphal end in death ... This is the trap laid for those in revolt and I have fallen into it. (p. 438)

The major components of the regime – law, school, police, church and the political class – are called upon in justification for the massacre of the terrorists. It is against these institutional and ideological centres of power that the Nada group is introduced merely as desperados without a codified agenda. The educational system, represented by Lamour, the head teacher at the school where Treuffais teaches philosophy, is in cahoots with the state apparatus in which Treuffais is deemed worthless, as Lamour explains during a conversation with another colleague: 'This boy isn't worth a sausage. He's a zero' (p. 358). The unbreakable alliance between the different components of the state is reinforced later during the investigation when Lamour is questioned by the police in relation to the kidnapping: '"The French police can always count on me", declared the teaching-establishment head' (p. 410). Above the institutional power grid with its internal hierarchical structures floats the *République* as the ideological denominator and point of reference for all decisions. The over-shadowing mission for the state apparatus personified by the Minister of the Interior is that 'republican order will be maintained' (p. 390). The state as a mechanism operating independently of individual concerns is a theme found throughout Manchette's novels. In *L'Affaire N'Gustro*, the character of Goémond is introduced and the philosophy behind his work as commissioner is explained in his own words:

> The fact that society has to function properly. That individuals must cooperate. If one of them did not cooperate, he had nothing against them, personally, himself, Goémond. But society, by way of a logically functioning automatic mechanism, struck. It was just as well that people like him, Goémond, were charged with oiling the workings of the logically functioning automatic mechanism in question.[60]

The logical reflex that society uses to reconstitute itself after attacks on its integrity is the real force that the terrorists in *Nada* are up against. Their project is doomed because they themselves are part of the same system against which they are fighting. The parallel narration throughout the novel with its shift in perspective from the terrorists to the investigators accentuates this. The impossibility of revolting against a system that you are a part of is summarised in Buenaventura's conclusion, which he records after having escaped: 'leftist terrorism and state terrorism, however incomparable their motives might be, are the two jaws of ... the same con trick [piège à con]' (p. 438). Alluding to a slogan employed by anarchists during demonstrations in May 1968, 'Élections – piège à cons', Manchette takes the expression further: political hegemony cannot be defeated by way of democratic elections, but nor is violent struggle an option if you want to change the system. As an alternative route to opposition, Manchette brings in the intellectual. The group's violent campaign is opposed by Treuffais, the philosophy teacher who leaves the group before the actual kidnapping takes place. His position is commented on by D'Arcy: 'He's an intellectual. He'll continue for his whole life to eat shit and say thank-you and spoil his vote in elections. But modern history doesn't give a damn about shit-munchers' (p. 406). D'Arcy concludes his analysis of modern civilisation by stating: 'I'd rather end up in blood than in shit' (p. 406). The choice between the oppositional symbolic notions of 'blood' and 'shit' echoes the underlying premise for Manchette's fictional project, operating towards the same doomed finality as the characters in *Nada*. Writing engaged crime novels with a political message is not so much a proactive answer as another part of the problematics of culture in modern society, as Manchette concludes in an interview in 1980: 'we keep at our craft, well though we may be stalked by the market, by criticism, and by two thousand years of culture piled upon our heads. You either die from it or are kept stupid by it.'[61]

Sjöwall and Wahlöö: critique of the welfare state

Desperate violence as the only option against a system neglecting its population can also be found in Sjöwall and Wahlöö's crime novels. This is notably the case in *Den vedervärdige mannen från Säffle* (*The Abominable Man*, 1971), published in the same year as Manchette's *L'Affaire N'Gustro*. There are a number of clear similarities in terms of content between the corpora of Manchette and Sjöwall/Wahlöö. However, the latter's employment of the police procedural as form in order to formulate a critique of the Swedish welfare state in the 1960s and 1970s proposes a more integrative mode of analysis to that of Manchette's *néo-polar*. Before turning towards *Den vedervärdige mannen från Säffle* and its scrutiny of the police's role in augmenting violence, it will be useful to contextualise Sjöwall and Wahlöö's contribution to the genre and their own theorisation of the role of the left-wing engaged writer.

Swedish crime fiction before Sjöwall and Wahlöö drew on the British whodunnit tradition of mysteries with a recognisable detective type. Maria Lang (pen name of Dagmar Lange, 1914–91) was the bestselling exponent of this variant of crime fiction in the Scandinavian countries. Her work consists largely of puzzle stories, often centred on a murder to be solved within bourgeois social circles. Set in non-specific regions (in 'the North' or 'the South' or in the fictive town of Skoga) with little description of the locations, the narratives constituting Lang's mystery universe – often compared to that of Agatha Christie – tend to follow an orthodox tripartite structure: crime, investigation, resolution.[62] Like Christie's detectives Miss Marple or Hercule Poirot, Christer Wijk, Lang's police investigator in her later novels, is rationally able to solve the cases by analysing and putting the pieces of evidence together. The novels thus remain closely associated with a tradition that emphasises their belonging to a conservative, pro-establishment trend aiming to restore the consensus that has temporarily, due to an individual's being led into a criminal act, broken down.

It is against this tradition that Sjöwall and Wahlöö write when, with their first novel, *Roseanna* (*Roseanna*, 1965), they introduce the police procedural to a Swedish readership. During the following decade, they produce another nine novels featuring a collective of police investigators in the Swedish national homicide squad led by Martin Beck.[63] In their article 'Kriminalromanens fornyelse' (The Renewal of the Crime Novel, 1971), first published in the Danish newspaper *Politiken*, Sjöwall and Wahlöö offer a manifesto for the genre with a clear message as to the importance of breaking away from golden-age detective stories. This tradition, represented by Lang and her British predecessors, is deemed 'artificial', 'abstract' and 'bourgeois' with 'charade- and rebus-like entertainment'.[64] These authors, according to Sjöwall and Wahlöö, display a lack of realism with which they 'consciously distance themselves from reality'.[65] By comparison, their version of the crime novel has an ability to hold a mirror up to contemporary society in a 'fairly comfortable and easily accessible form'.[66] Accessibility plays a key role in the argumentation: the crime novel can make complex analysis of a psychological or sociological nature available to readers who would otherwise not have consulted or been able to digest the specialist texts in which this type of knowledge is usually presented. By extension, the crime novelist as analyst of society and facilitator of interpreted information serves a didactic function: 'In the modern alienated society, the crime novel constitutes one of the very few channels through which the average reader can be in contact with the data-controlled and strictly shielded system within which he is forced to operate.'[67]

Alongside the notion of the crime novelist as a teacher whose responsibility it is to educate a less capable public, Sjöwall and Wahlöö also identify a new type of crime fiction reader characterised by valorisation of literary quality, realism and social awareness, 'who previously have turned their nose up at the detective novel, judging it to be a kind of pseudo-literature'.[68] This observation made in the early days of the Swedish engaged novel's history is consistent with what is later acknowledged in critical studies of the crime novel's repositioning in the literary landscape as a result of the generic changes it undergoes in this period.[69] It is also consistent with the more general postmodern trend characterised by the collapse of traditional categories of high and low culture.[70]

Sweden under the surface

The ten-novel series that Sjöwall and Wahlöö put together under the title *Roman om ett brott* (*Story of a Crime*, 1965–75) was a meticulously planned project aimed to be used as a vehicle for the author-couple's political message:

> Our aim with the Martin Beck series is to bring to life an analysis of a welfare society of the bourgeois type – an analysis in which we try to view its criminality in relation to its political and ideological doctrines. This is the fundamental idea in a long novel of about 3,000 pages broken into ten individual parts or, indeed, chapters, to analyse crime as a social function, its relation to contemporary society and to the moralistic life forms of various kinds surrounding this society.[71]

The writers' emphasis on viewing each novel of the series as constituting a part of one coherent narrative enables them to pan in and out from the specific to the general or from the example to the broader analysis of society. Each of the ten novels focuses on an individual type of crime while considering it as an element of an overarching crime: successive Swedish social-democratic governments' flirting with capitalism and their failure to maintain the ideals of the welfare state. More specifically the aim was to show how the Social Democrats had broken away from socialism and let the Swedish working class down.[72] The subtitle *Roman om ett brott*, where 'brott' simultaneously means 'crime' and 'break'/'rupture' illustrates this ideological substratum and its 'criminal' nature. The theme that society in its current guise is a breeding ground for criminality is stated bluntly in *Polis, polis, potatismos* (*Murder at the Savoy*, 1970): 'all varieties of crime flourished better than ever in the fertile topsoil provided by the welfare state'.[73]

The critique of the national political project is inserted into a broader global perspective. From the beginning of *Roman om ett brott*, Sjöwall and Wahlöö thematise a discrepancy between internal and external awareness of various aspects of a national imagery. When American librarian Roseanna's dead body is fished out of the water in the opening scene of *Roseanna* (1965), the scene is being observed by onlookers; the *mise en scène* unfolds 'as the neighbouring children and a Vietnamese tourist looked on'.[74] The plot begins at a time when international media were reporting the aerial bombing campaign in North Vietnam and the arrival of the first US troops in the spring of 1965. In the relatively unknown provincial Swedish setting of Borenshult, the atypical presence in the mid-1960s of a south-east Asian tourist serves the function of a subverting gaze. What does the Vietnamese tourist see and, perhaps more importantly, what does the Vietnamese tourist understand of the events taking place? Implicitly in the scene, there is a notion of the sight having to be explained both to the tourist, who because of linguistic and cultural barriers has restricted access to understanding the event, and to the children, unlikely to comprehend the intrusion of a dead body into their childhood universe in small-town mid Sweden. While the Martin Beck series calls for self-analysis and introspection, there is also an open invitation to the outside world. This is also an implied comment on the crime fiction genre's ability to generate intercultural awareness by accentuating aspects of the Swedish nation other than the version that official promotional discourse tends to reveal for an international audience. The Borenshult scene takes place during a postcard-idyllic Swedish summer, where the discovery of the murdered Roseanna metaphorically becomes synonymous with the disturbing reality concealed in the mud under the surface. With this image, Sjöwall and Wahlöö use crime fiction as an alternative mechanism for the production of a national image both for internal and external observers. What is later to be conceived of as the first Nordic Noir novel thus already touches upon questions about the national and the global, which are to constitute key features of the Nordic variant of the crime fiction genre and its reception in the twenty-first century.

The historical context for Sjöwall and Wahlöö's crime fiction project is a Sweden that had enjoyed a peaceful political evolution after the Second World War, high living standards, low unemployment, social reforms and reduction of class differences. During post-war economic growth, social-democratic governments – uninterruptedly dominating cabinets 1932–76 – introduced universal health care, free education, retirement benefits and child support. *Folkehemmet* (the People's Home) implied an egalitarian ideology within the institutional framework. Sjöwall and Wahlöö's critique of what they clearly regard as an embellished picture of the Swedish paradise is harsh. It is aimed directly at the top of the political hierarchy, personified in *Terroristerna* (*The Terrorists*, 1975) in the caricatured portrait of the unnamed prime minister who – as the national icon of the failed social-democratic project – is symbolically murdered in the novel. Sjöwall makes it clear in later interviews that the character's resemblance to Olof Palme, the then prime minister of Sweden, was intentional:

> We have never had such a talented PR man in Sweden. It is still hopeless when you go to the old Eastern Block and they talk about the fantastic 'Swedish model' that Palme created. He did this extremely well, to make people believe that Sweden was a successful capitalist-socialist society.[75]

Charting main protagonist Martin Beck's 10-year career progression from first detective inspector to chief of the national homicide squad, the long 'novel' offers a chronotope of Swedish society in the decade from 1965 to 1975. Each individual segment takes place the same year as it is written and provides an instantaneous picture of Sweden at that particular time, taking into account contemporary events (the Vietnam War, the Cold War, the situation in Eastern Europe) and contemporary topics of debate (unemployment, pollution, the pornography industry, sexuality, dissolution of traditional family structures).

As noted by Dawn Keetley, critical commentary on Sjöwall and Wahlöö's writing agrees that the first three novels seem distinctly apolitical in relation to the rest of the series.[76] Their focus in the first novels on the pathological nature of sexual crimes as an expression of individual violence does indeed contrast with the strident and confrontational analysis of the welfare state found in the later novels, culminating with *The Terrorists*, the last novel. In her analysis, Keetley argues that 'sexual crimes can be political, although the political conditions that shape what is manifest as individual pathology are deeply buried within the text'.[77] However, the seemingly apolitical ambience in the cycle's first three novels is also part of Sjöwall and Wahlöö's strategic employment of the crime fiction genre to lure their readers into participating through their reading in an engaged critical analysis of the Swedish state. They explain this in an interview after the publication of *Polismördaren* (*The Cop Killer*, 1974):

> It was entirely consciously that we in 1963 decided to write books aimed at readers of crime fiction, and that we in the first three novels described the crimes and their investigation as being as good as apolitical. From the beginning, we had planned that the mask was going to fall with the

fourth or fifth book. It did, and the sales figures did indeed decrease. But they have come back up to their previous levels.[78]

There was, then, a clear and conscious political agenda underpinning the series of novels, even if it was not a discernible element – as far as the authors' explicit statements are concerned – of its early constituent parts. It is important however to situate these early texts within the overall political thrust of the whole, and within the notion of a critique of the post-war social compact, as the following reading will attempt to do.

Roseanna

On 8 July 1964 the naked body of American librarian Roseanna McGown is found in the canal lock outside Motala in mid-central Sweden. *Roseanna*, the first novel in *Roman om ett brott*, follows the investigation of Beck and his team in the homicide squad over six months as it leads to the perpetrator's arrest. Following conventional principles of organisation, the opening of *Roseanna* is comparable to that of a classic mystery novel inasmuch as it is based on a double narrative characterised by Todorov as 'l'histoire du crime' (the story of the crime) and 'l'histoire de l'enquête' (the story of the investigation).[79] The discovery of the body, which in the classic detective story disturbs the prevailing (and naturally ordained) order, is however inserted into a scene emblematic of an already dysfunctional society:

> When the canal opened for traffic that spring, the channel had begun to clog up. The boats had a hard time manoeuvring and their propellers churned up thick clouds of yellowish mud from the bottom. It wasn't hard to see that something had to be done. As early as May, the Canal Company requisitioned a dredging machine from the Civil Engineering Board. The papers were passed from one perplexed civil servant to another and finally remitted to the Swedish National Shipping and Navigation Administration.[80]

Things turn out to be more complicated than this. The ensuing long paragraph – in apparent contrast, both in content and style, with the rest of the narration in *Roseanna* – is a Kafkaesque passage with chiastic structuring and repetitions of the various names of the official bodies involved in the operation of getting the dredging machine in place: the Canal Company, the Civil Engineering Board, the Swedish National Shipping and Navigation Administration, the Harbour

Commission in Norrköping. However, the novel's opening functions as a metaphorical construction at various levels, both for interpretation of the first novel in itself, and of the series in its totality. It is also relevant as a commentary on the crime fiction genre's usefulness as medium for social critique. The operation of unclogging the canal and dredging up the body mimics the police work of bringing evidence to the surface and getting to the bottom of the case, a process made difficult by the amount of irrelevant paper work and bureaucracy facing the investigator: 'the records of the inquiry and reports had already begun to accumulate on Ahlberg's desk. They could be summed up in one sentence: a dead woman had been found in the lock chamber at Borenshult.'[81] The metaphor is additionally reinforced by the fact that the vessel's name is 'Grisen' (The Pig), alluding simultaneously to the pigs wallowing in water and mud and to the pejorative use of a term that in colloquial Swedish denotes 'police officer'.[82]

Originally functioning as a metaphor for the investigator, the dredging machine subsequently acquires the attributes of the impenetrable administrative procedures surrounding it, and becomes part of a metonymic constellation where the machine itself slows down and hinders the investigation. Beck's colleague Ahlberg's nightmarish frustrations over the slowness of the police investigation later in the novel relate to the double-sided image of the dredger, which can reveal and conceal at the same time: 'We have almost no chance there, and maybe not even in Boren if the dredger has buried everything there by now. Sometimes I dream about that damned apparatus and wake up in the middle of the night swearing.'[83] The juxtaposition of police and dredging machine reveals a theme ultimately predominant throughout Sjöwall and Wahlöö's series: the police as a bureaucratic and problematic institution. By using the police procedural as a vehicle for their literary and political project, Sjöwall and Wahlöö engage in a process similar to that of the dredging machine. Under the surface, the police procedural is employed to reveal what is hidden in the deep behind the powerful ideologies of an institutionalised organisation.

Sjöwall and Wahlöö's introduction of the police procedural to a Swedish readership coincides with a radical restructuring of the Swedish police force. The reform, implemented on 1 January 1965, comprises a significant reduction in the number of police districts and centralisation to a unitary national body. The series follows this development and its consequences closely, with the writers basing the narrative on thorough journalistic investigation into police procedures. The description of the policing profession, which Sjöwall in an interview explains as 'the key to [their] true subject' of describing the development of Swedish society, progresses from a rather positive picture of the police corps in the first three novels.[84] Here there is a sense of mutual dependency and an understanding of the police and the public working together for the benefit of society in general; when it comes to solving the case in *Roseanna*, the 'great detective', that is, the public, is called in for support.[85] This picture however changes through the cycle's middle part, which contains detailed descriptions of the processes leading to the police becoming an autonomous 'state within the state despised by the individual citizen'.[86] With constant references to the reform, the alienation of the police officer from the public, corruption, police brutality and violence, the politicisation of the police as a result of centralisation, and the aim for personal power and profit for those at the top of the hierarchy, the narrative evolves into a fierce institutional critique.[87] It culminates with the carnivalesque scene in the series' penultimate novel, *Polismördaren*, where roles are turned around, and policeman Elofsson is shot and on the ground:

> How could this have happened? For twenty years he'd been driving around shouting and swearing, pushing, kicking, hitting people with his truncheon, or slapping them with the flat side of his sabre. He had always been the stronger, had always had the advantage of arms and might and justice against people who were weaponless and powerless and had no rights. And now here he lay on the pavement.[88]

The ambiguity created by the use of free indirect speech here is a distinct feature throughout the series. The bi-vocal projection of narrator and character in the same passage provides an explanation for the situation and for Elofsson's questioning of it. There is a clear indication of continuity over the course of the series, the latter stages of which are characterised by expressions of concern about policing, similar to those existing at the cycle's outset; these are concerns regarding policing as an institution, rather than merely as practice, as the mention of 'rights' suggests.

Den vedervärdige mannen från Säffle

In *Den vedervärdige mannen från Säffle* (*The Abominable Man*, 1971), the cycle's seventh instalment, Sjöwall and Wahlöö explicitly deal with declining police legitimacy as their thematic focus. This central theme is interwoven with descriptions, analysis and critique of dramatic changes in the Stockholm cityscape and fundamental shifts in the social infrastructure of the welfare state.

The novel's opening lines present the image of a man sitting in front of a newspaper crossword. An implicit analogy between an empty crossword column and an unsolved crime, where the clues in both cases are there to be interpreted so that a solution can be found, again sets the narrative up within a classic detective paradigm.[89] This is supported by the neatly sequential establishment of the crime mystery's important actantial roles in the novel's introductory chapters, systematically presenting the perpetrator (first chapter), the victim (second chapter) and the main investigator in the guise of Martin Beck (third chapter). This seemingly orderly structure, in which the participants are positioned in their appropriate places and set up to operate according to a clear set of narratological rules, is however disturbed as it becomes apparent that both perpetrator and victim are also members of the police force.

The story unfolds as follows: on 3 April 1971, Chief Inspector Stig Nyman is brutally murdered in his sickbed at Sabbatsberg Hospital in Stockholm, his throat and abdomen slit open with a bayonet. In the ensuing pursuit of the killer, Beck and his colleagues dig into Nyman's career, first in the army and then in the police, and discover that he is behind a series of ruthless and corrupt instances of maltreatment. The reports of complaints filed against him, however, have all passed unnoticed through the system and have been closed and stamped with 'no action'. The killer, Åke Eriksson, himself a policeman, is one of the victims of Nyman's brutality, his diabetic wife having died in a cell at the station due to neglect under Nyman's watch.

Nyman's true identity as a brutal human being and corrupt professional is revealed later when Beck's colleague Kollberg narrates his experiences of having been trained by Nyman in the army during the war. When Beck asks Kollberg to specify the nature of Nyman's training sessions, he gives the following example:

> Like how to cut off a pig's penis without its squealing. Like how to cut the legs off the same pig also without its squealing. Like how to gouge its eyes out. And finally, how to cut it to pieces and flay it, still without a sound.

Beck, not knowing how this is done, is enlightened by Kollberg: 'It's easy. You start by cutting out its tongue.'[90] This image of the pig evokes Nyman's own mutilated body with its 'gaping wound in the throat, the blood, the entrails welling out of the belly' (p. 104). Subtly establishing the link between the policeman and the pig, the image becomes a part of the connection between the profession and the animal, present throughout the series.

The mutilation of the pig is just one of many examples of Nyman's cruelty and violent conduct. Beck's long interrogation of Harold Hunt, Nyman's colleague and long-time 'faithful sidekick' (p. 76) contains a list of accusations of what Nyman has taught Hunt: 'to commit perjury', 'to copy each other's reports so everything'll [fit together]', 'to rough up people in their cells', to 'cut down strikers [with sabres]', to 'ride down student protesters', to 'club unarmed schoolchildren at demonstrations', to 'drive into crowds [on motorcycles] to break them up' (pp. 80–1). The omniscient narrator does not treat Nyman as a unique exemplar of the police force. Indeed, the narrator launches a direct criticism of the prevalence of police violence: 'The number of injured policemen was negligible when compared with the number of people annually mistreated by the police' (p. 51). Nyman is thus the incarnation of the new type of policeman (Nyman = Newman) that the police force consists of following nationalisation. The reason why he has never been discredited is linked to institutional power, corruption and an internal code of protection within the police. However, it becomes apparent that the police are an institutional set-up operating in an ideological and ethical vacuum with no external points of reference. While the police force might be 'impregnated with esprit de corps' (p. 69), this sense of collective identification resides in empty grounds; it cannot be measured against anything. As Kollberg notes: 'The police stick together. That's axiomatic' (p. 69). However, he has to ask, '[b]ut stick together against whom?' (p. 69). The meaninglessness of axioms is further expressed by another policeman, Hult, in terms of the collapse of the entire value system around them: 'Forty years in uniform in this city ... and now there's hardly anything left to protect anymore' (pp. 82–3).

The disintegration of the investigator's position in the crime story is of a pathological nature. Not only is Nyman malfunctioning as a policeman, he is also, before he is killed, symbolically sick and in hospital, an association linking a bodily pathology to a professional one. As a comment on this association, the extradiegetic narrator lets Nyman, before he is murdered, reflect on his treatment at the hospital and 'the [medical] examinations – which the doctors ironically refer to as the "investigation"' (p. 6). While Nyman is an extreme case hyperbolically symbolising the unstable and problematic nature of the police force and the society that it protects, the pathology of the profession runs as an underlying theme of the series. Sjöwall and Wahlöö's novels thus highlight the inherent flaws within the existing order, which will inexorably degenerate into chaos, and of which crimes are primarily a symptom rather than a cause. As a symptom of the failing universal authority and truth, Beck and the other members of Sweden's national homicide squad are often unwell, have flu, diarrhoea and nausea that make them tired and despondent. The investigators' physical condition is intrinsically connected to their work situation from the beginning of the series: '[i]t had been an uneventful and dreary day, full of sneezing and spitting and dull routine'.[91] Michael Tapper moreover sees their bodies as 'metaphors for the sick and decaying society'.[92] Their illness thus functions as metaphor for the societal malaise that they, as part of the police, help maintain.

The disturbance of the classic triangle of perpetrator–victim–detective is further linked to an ethical questioning of the righteousness of the legal system and society in general. As Beck's colleague Einar Rönn comments: 'as it was often these days ... he felt sorrier for the criminal than for the victim' (p. 17). Disputing the very moral code by which deviance is defined within society, the narrative transfers sympathy to the killer, who within the novel's textual logic is the real victim. The killer is moreover not only a victim of society, but also of the physical infrastructure of society, specifically, of the urban restructuring of Stockholm.

The crime and investigation are woven into the city. The personification of Stockholm as a 'large city in its anxious sleep' (p. 1) during the night when the murder of Nyman takes place parallels the state that Beck is in when he receives the phone call from the crime scene while in his bed. The city at night, characterised by its 'meaningless, mechanical monotony' (p. 3) is also metonymically mirrored by the (at this stage) nameless killer who is described as a 'sleepwalker' (p. 2) and who in similarly mechanical movements travels through the capital to the hospital, following the monotonous changing of traffic lights and speed limits. This synchronised existence expands into a more complex interdependent relationship between the urban space and its dwellers who have experienced, and become victims of, the same circumstances. The Swedish capital's physical appearance has been undergoing considerable transformation, described in terms of anti-social destruction in the name of capitalist imperatives, with devastating human consequences:

The centre of Stockholm had been subjected to sweeping and violent changes in the course of the last ten years. Entire districts had been levelled and new ones constructed. The structure of the city had been altered: streets had been broadened and motorways built. What was behind all this activity was hardly an ambition to create a humane social environment but rather a desire to achieve the fullest possible exploitation of valuable land. (p. 45)

The juxtaposition of the anthropomorphised city and its inhabitants compares the '[v]iolence [that] had been visited on the natural topography itself' (p. 45) with the devastation of the social environment characterised by 'more and more violence and blood' (p. 83). This change in the fabric of Stockholm coincides with an infiltration of capitalism, which creates new class divisions, commented on here by the narrator: 'In the course of the preceding five years, restaurant prices had as good as doubled, and very few ordinary wage-earners could afford to treat themselves to even one night out a month' (p. 11). Instead, the restaurants survive on 'the increasing number of businessmen with credit cards and expense accounts who preferred to conduct their transactions across a laden table' (p. 11).

Significantly, as becomes apparent later in the novel, Åke Eriksson has also been a victim of urban planning, which has forced him out of his old residence, demolished to give way for new profitable constructions. Not unlike the ending of Manchette's *Nada*, the novel closes in a climactic carnage when the desperate Eriksson barricades himself in his new flat at the top of an apartment building from which he shoots and kills multiple police officers. Symbolically, his new apartment is the culmination of the injustices put on him by the system: the death of his wife while wrongfully in police custody, dismissal from his job, the tearing down of his old apartment building, forcing him to move into the new one that he cannot afford, and, as a consequence, the removal of his little daughter by the child welfare services. When the police finally move in on Eriksson to put an end to the shooting, Gunvald Larsson, one of Beck's colleagues, describes him as a 'poor damned lunatic' (p. 209), and then implicitly explains the individual's psychological state and criminal acts as a symptom of larger societal malaise: 'This is an insane city in a country that's mentally deranged' (p. 209).

In strong ideological terms, Sjöwall and Wahlöö's novels point to economic liberalism's powerful intervention in welfare state politics, using the portrayal of working-class or underprivileged citizens driven into desperation to show how the welfare state has failed in its project. *Den vedervärdige mannen från Säffle* (like other novels in the series) also questions notions of justice within a system where the police are corrupt and official channels no longer function optimally. Sjöwall and Wahlöö's employment of the police procedural as a vehicle for their Marxist critique is a rewriting – in support of the proletariat – of the syntax of the classic golden age detective story, which previously had confirmed and supported the dominant bourgeois ideology. While not all successive Scandinavian crime novels express critique as sharply formulated as Sjöwall and Wahlöö's, 'their novels', as Nestingen affirms, 'have proved deeply influential on crime fiction [in Scandinavia] since the 1980s'.[93] Bergman rates this influence in similarly strong terms by arguing that 'a typical Swedish crime novel [in 2014] is that of a police novel presenting some degree of criticism of the disintegration of the national, Swedish welfare society – in explicit as well as implicit and allegorical form'.[94]

Conclusion: Sjöwall/Wahlöö and Manchette

The early politicised crime novel represented by the writings of Sjöwall/Wahlöö and Manchette emerges in Sweden and France at around the same historical moment as an expression of politically leftist and formally rebellious contributions to the crime fiction genre. The comparable purpose in the novels from these two traditions is transgressive revolt. They are anti-establishment, resistant, counter-hegemonic and operate against the political system in power. They explicitly engage critically with previous crime fiction traditions, and mount opposition against literary institutions. Inasmuch as these novels are written at a time of general political and aesthetic protest in the 1960s and 1970s, they are a product of their time. However, these exponents of the genre function as catalysts in various ways; the combination of aesthetic innovation and political agitation has implications for the genre's cultural legitimisation, the development of the genre itself and for critical engagement with crime fiction.

In both contexts, the critique is directed at the police as a corrupt institution, but the texts also investigate the roots of this corruption, seen as being inherent to the organisation and foundation of the state. Both Sjöwall/Wahlöö and Manchette engage in discussions about how collective identities are constructed and not least about how they find expression within the national state. A point of commonality is their general left-wing critique of consumerism, capitalism and the ways in which class differences are accentuated by the state's endorsement of capitalism. However, the parallel readings also reveal differences in the approaches to the state from two distinct national and socio-political contexts, reflected in the writers' use of and engagement with the crime genre and its conventions.

Manchette and Sjöwall/Wahlöö have been trendsetters for crime fiction that challenges the status quo in their respective national genre traditions. References to Sjöwall and Wahlöö as 'founders of the modern Swedish crime novel' or indeed as the starting point for the Nordic Noir wave are a staple in both academic research and journalistic articles about the publishing phenomenon.[95] Manchette is similarly regarded as inspirational, and seen as 'the symbol of a new generation of writers of *noir* detective fictions'.[96] These writers, considered prime movers of a crime fiction genre employed as a medium for social critique, are however in two different positions in terms of their place in genre history. Manchette writes his novel within a relatively long and well-established tradition of crime fiction influenced – since the establishment of Gallimard's Série noire in 1945 – by American hard-boiled writers and their themes of inequity and corruption within the police and society at large. Sjöwall and Wahlöö's starting point is a Swedish version of golden age detective fiction that up until their arrival on the scene has not taken this international development of the genre into account. This might partly explain why Manchette makes more radical revisions of the genre than his Swedish colleagues. Modelling his *néo-polar* on the hard-boiled tradition, Manchette frequently changes the perspective from the detective to that of the perpetrator, or in other ways blurs the traditional roles of detectives, victims, suspects and perpetrators. Sjöwall and Wahlöö employ a more orthodox template. While their police procedurals expand the perspective from the individual to the collective investigator, their tripartite narrative structure (crime–investigation–resolution) maintains the traditional point of view of the investigatory body, and the authors form their critique from within this perspective. This noticeable difference in perspectival orientation between the French marginal protagonists who operate outside the institutionalised power structure and the Swedish protagonists who are part of the power structure is significant. This is especially true in light of the genre's history: where the Swedish police procedural with Sjöwall and Wahlöö as its founders becomes the preferred Scandinavian subgenre par excellence, the *roman noir* and the *polar* establish themselves as the favourites of French writers with a socio-critical agenda. Interesting, also, is the fact that the pronounced distinction between the *roman policier* and the *roman noir/polar* in France, which Manchette ardently argues for, is continuously and frequently evoked by French writers of *noir*.[97]

Seen in this light, it is notable that Scandinavian crime fiction in critical writing and in international media has become synonymous with social commentary and critique, whereas the French *polar engagé* (the engaged crime novel) has been viewed as an enclave in a broader crime fiction category, which also includes more conformist and traditional approaches to the genre. In this perspective Sjöwall and Wahlöö have enjoyed a considerable renaissance in recent years – in particular after the boom in Scandinavian crime fiction publications and translations after the success of Stieg Larsson's *Millennium* trilogy – as progenitors in a local Swedish context of a contemporary Scandinavian phenomenon. In contrast, as Gorrara notes, 'by the mid-1980s, the radical political protest of the néo-polar had run its course'.[98] This is also commonly commented on in French criticism, where the *néo-polar* has been accused of being 'a flash in the pan, a fashion, a media phenomenon apparently now completely outdated and without influence'.[99] However, these comments notwithstanding, the current French *polar engagé* might still be more radical in its critique of contemporary society and its policies than its Scandinavian counterpart, despite the latter's emblematically radical origins in Sjöwall and Wahlöö's Sweden.

One of the main points of this chapter has been to demonstrate that at the start of the study's period of examination (the 1960s and 1970s), the French crime novel in the form of the *néo-polar* and its Scandinavian counterpart in the form of its highly committed early Swedish manifestation are engaged in similar projects, responding to particular conditions of citizenship and social models that prevail in their respective settings during these decades. As crime fiction is anchored to and develops in conjunction with modernity, the genre deals with places that are undergoing rapid transformations related to both physical and social infrastructure. Written towards the end of a period generally described in terms of economic prosperity, high consumption, urbanisation, higher standards of living and a developed system of welfare benefits – 'Les Trente Glorieuses' in France and the 'golden age of Social Democracy' in Scandinavia – the works of Manchette and Sjöwall/Wahlöö are situated within a pattern of decline, and they point to the fact that cracks are beginning to show in the system.[100] In the 1960–1970s, both crime fiction traditions engage critically with the fact that the post-war settlement is compromised by its predication on bourgeois values, and their criteria for reproach are in particular connected to class issues and the individual's relationship with the state. From this starting point at the end of an era of social cohesion showing signs of stagnation and crisis, the next chapter leaps forward to the twenty-first century and will examine how individual and collective identities are negotiated in crime fiction within a paradigm increasingly defined by its post-ness in various forms: post-industrial, post-modern, post-colonial, post-socialist, post-national, post-welfarist, post-golden age.

2

Individual and Collective Identities in the Twenty-first Century

From the era of general political and cultural contestation in the 1960s and 1970s, the present chapter turns towards more recent discussions of social transformations and their expression within the crime fiction genre. The explicit theme of (radical) left-wing protest and the omnipresence of class struggle in the writings of Manchette and Sjöwall/Wahlöö have, in the respective contexts of both France and Scandinavia, become subdued. However, popular twenty-first-century crime narratives still foreground social concerns, and especially those of justice relating to identity issues more globally. In this chapter's first section, this change in orientation within the genre is first contextualised within the framework of identity politics and social theories, and then the specificities of identity debates are investigated in the respective cultural contexts of France and Scandinavia.

Dominique Manotti's *Bien connu des service de police* (2010) and Arne Dahl's *Europa Blues* (2001), discussed in the chapter's second section, are novels rooted in – and making explicit allusion to – the generic traditions established by Manchette and Sjöwall/Wahlöö. The French *polar* and the Swedish police procedural, however, have been thematically and aesthetically reshaped since the establishment of these traditions. Manotti's and Dahl's engagements with notions of national identity intersect with concerns about multiform other identities presenting challenges to the concept of the homogeneous nation state at the beginning of the twenty-first century.

The age of identity politics

In discussions of the 'postmodern turn' in the social sciences, a key focus is the weakening of the nation state and a move from universalism to particularism. Sociologist Krishan Kumar argues, accordingly, that postmodernity promotes a shift away from traditional class-based practices of the nation state and encourages a 'politics of difference'.[1] Kumar specifies that under postmodernity '[t]he "collective identities" of class and shared work experience dissolve into more pluralized and privatized forms of identity' and that 'the idea of a national culture and national identity is assailed in the name of "minority" cultures'.[2]

Questions of identity have accordingly come to be at the centre of debates in the social sciences and cultural studies. The 1980s and 1990s saw the emergence of new disciplinary fields such as postcolonial studies, gender studies, queer theory, among others. Previously well-defined, stable identities of race, class, nationality, gender and sexuality have been contested and, increasingly, alternative practices for identification have been rehearsed both at grass-roots level and in academia. From a cultural studies perspective, Stuart Hall comments on this phenomenon:

> [I]dentities are never unified and, in late modern times, increasingly fragmented and fractured; never singular but multiply constructed across different, often intersecting and antagonistic, discourses, practices, and positions. They are subject to a radical historicization and are constantly in the process of change and transformation.[3]

Echoing (and referring to) Hall's article, Zygmunt Bauman comments on the 'spectacular rise in the "identity discourse"' occurring in the 1990s within both popular and academic discourses.[4] This upsurge, according to Bauman, takes place in all areas of justice, culture and politics, where '[e]stablished issues of social analysis are being rehashed and refurbished to fit the discourse now rotating around the "identity" axis'.[5] Bauman concludes by identifying the contemporary 'avalanche' of identity discourse as 'the side-effect and by-product of the combination of globalising and individualising pressures and the tensions they spawn'.[6]

From a political science perspective, Bauman's observation is joined by the political philosopher Nancy Fraser's reflections on how justice is – and used to be – imagined. In Fraser's understanding there has been a shift 'away from a socialist political imaginary, in which the central problem of justice is redistribution, to a "post-socialist" political imaginary, in which the central problem is recognition'.[7] Fraser further specifies:

> With this shift, the most salient social movements are no longer economically defined 'classes' who are struggling to defend their

'interests', end 'exploitation', and win 'redistribution'. Instead, they are culturally defined 'groups' or communities of 'value' who are struggling to defend their 'identities', end 'cultural domination', and win 'recognition'.[8]

Linking literature to socio-political climates and discursive configurations, the development of the crime fiction genre vividly illustrates this shift in the socio-political imaginary. Furthermore, as crime fiction inherently deals with notions of justice and injustice, the genre is perhaps a site where this paradigmatic shift becomes particularly visible. Whereas Manchette and Sjöwall/Wahlöö write firmly within the paradigm of 'redistribution', dealing with unbalanced power relationships stemming from rich/poor divides, and political or cultural hegemony conditioned by the flow of capital, crime fiction writers in the late twentieth and early twenty-first centuries have increasingly put emphasis on exploring and discussing various forms of individual or collective identities within the paradigm of 'recognition'. The problematics of this shift are arguably acutely present in recent discussions in France and Scandinavia, respectively of the universalism held to underpin the French republican social contract, and of the decline of the homogenous society with which the Nordic welfare state was supposedly associated. Before turning to readings of what might with this contextualisation in mind be designated 'post-socialist' or 'postmodern' novels by Dominique Manotti and Arne Dahl, it will be useful to examine the particularities of the nature of identity discourse in the French and Scandinavian settings.

French universalism and its critique

Debates in France have in fact centred on a so-called 'crisis of universalism', 'a crisis', according to American gender historian Joan Wallach Scott, 'defined through the rhetoric of universalism taken to be uniquely French and therefore a defining trait of the system of Republican democracy, its most enduring value, its most precious political asset'.[9] While Scott analyses the crisis of universalism in France through a case study of the debates on political parity in the 1990s, the crisis is closely linked to issues of identity more generally and how these are legally and publicly expressed within the parameters of French republicanism.

Scholarship from the last three decades has commented on this crisis of French identity, nationhood and citizenship and described it in terms of the difficulty within France of operating between two non-compatible ideologies, persuasively summarised by Nathalie Debrauwere-Miller as 'the eternal debate dividing French society between the rhetoric of Republican universalism … and the recognition of identity-based particularism'.[10] Schematically described, there exists on one hand an overpowering consensus evoking the republican model based on universalist principles and categorising all ethnic, gender, sexual or religious sub-identities under the umbrella concept of *le citoyen* (the citizen), within a legal framework prohibiting moreover the collection or publication of statistics relating to ethnicity or any other particularity of identity.[11] This official unifying identity of an abstract individual is persistently referred to and nourished in public discourse whether from the political left or right, as Schor affirms, 'Whether one reads *Le Monde* or *Le Figaro*, *Le débat* or *Esprit*, one is constantly reminded of France's identification with universalism.'[12] On the other hand, demands have been arising from an increasingly pluralistic and multicultural French society where individuals and groups negotiate for a different view on the reality of a complex France. Naomi Schor describes the debate between these oppositional ideologies as the 'French culture wars', defined as 'wars that oppose the upholders of the Republic and the advocates of a French multiculturalism and democracy'.[13] While the universalist idea stemming from the Revolution of 1789 'stubbornly remains a key phrase in France's discourse of national self-representation and identity', there is – as Schor argues with references to the 1980s and 1990s – a consensus among scholars that France experiences what she refers to as a 'spectral universalism'. She defines this as 'the shadow of a formerly vigorous and dynamic ideology that once functioned as a powerful force that ensured social cohesion, now reduced to an empty rhetoric in whose cosy and familiar terms present-day ideological battles are fought'.[14]

In France, the problematics of the 'rhetoric of universalism' became wholly apparent at the beginning of the 1980s and crystallised increasingly in the 1990s in debates about rights of identity groups whether relating to gender, sexuality, religion or race/ethnicity. The period simultaneously saw a political recodification of the principles of republicanism designed to meet challenges such as increased globalisation, immigration and France's status in the European context.[15] A further issue to consider, intertwined with the conception of *le citoyen*, is the sharp separation between public and private spheres in France often highlighted in debates about minority rights, as well as the vigorous insistence on *laïcité*, or state-enforced secularism, evoked when religious and cultural issues are on the agenda. The fundamental issues in these debates warrant some attention as they constitute an important backdrop for the French crime novels studied in the remaining part of this book.

One context in which the republican discursive framework was highly visible was that of the debates leading up to the gender parity law passed on 6 June 2000, requiring all political parties to list an equal number of male and female candidates. The feminist movement contesting the existing gender hierarchy in French politics in the 1990s did so precisely on the basis of a rigorous argument about the universal rights of the citizen, while at the same time aiming to renegotiate key republican values, or, as Lépinard puts it, simultaneously to 'subvert and endorse core Republican doctrines'.[16] The conservative strand of the criticism of the parity law argues that the special treatment of women and division of *citoyens* into different categories was a threat to republican universalism. While perhaps marking a shift in the political culture from universalism to a more pluralistic culture recognising differences and inequalities, the parity law simultaneously accentuated the arguments in France entailed by the abstract construction of the universal subject proscribed by the Republic.

Another point of criticism of the concept of the universalist rights of the French citizen is what Pierre Bourdieu in his intervention in the debate about gay rights refers to as 'the force of orthodoxy', characterised as a codex of white, male, heterosexual, bourgeois hegemonic values:

> [The force of orthdoxy] thus provides an objective base, and formidable effectiveness, to all the strategies of the universalist hypocrisy that, turning responsibilities upside down, denounces any demand on the part of the dominated for access to common treatment and right as a particularist or 'communitarian' rupture of the universalist contract .[17]

Similarly, sociologist and queer activist Marie-Hélène (now Sam) Bourcier contends that the ideology of French universalism has been at the heart of what has made it difficult for different identity groups to have a voice in French society: 'subaltern minorities cannot really speak or achieve any form of social transformation in the French public space'.[18] In the article about the introduction of queer studies to France, Bourcier shows how this problematic historical interpretation of French universalism pervades all areas of public life, in academia, in culture and in the public sphere generally, and, for example, makes it challenging for scholars in France to introduce new academic study areas concerned with identity issues such as queer and postcolonial studies. Bourcier argues that an important key to an understanding of queer politics in France 'is the fact that "French queer" took up the tool of identity politics in order to fight a form of republicanism and universalism which, while supposedly inclusive, egalitarian and neutral, effectively excludes minorities'.[19] Therefore, the attempts to 'queer' France in the late 1990s are linked with activism and highly associated with a 'critique of the dominant epistemological regimes of knowledge and power in the (social) sciences'.[20]

In political and public debates, multiculturalism as a political approach has been precluded in France for being 'out of hand as at odds with the principles of republicanism', and for being incompatible with the principle of cultural and civic assimilation at the centre of French integration politics.[21] A premise for civic universalism is the relegation of difference to the private sphere, whereas under the philosophy and politics of multiculturalism, as Katharyne Mitchell explains, 'diverse ways of being in the world are recognized as legitimate, and the qualities of "out-group" members … reconstitute the notion of civil competence *within* the public sphere'.[22]

The separation of the state and the church in 1905 and the principle of *laïcité* have been evoked as measures aimed at securing equal treatment of different religions in the name of universalism. However, the same universalist principles have also been accused of being a means to discriminate against the Muslim part of the French population, notably in the heated debates leading up to the 2004 legislation prohibiting the wearing of the full-face veil in public spaces. More recently, in an intervention after the attacks on the cartoonists at *Charlie Hebdo* in January 2015, Jacques Rancière adds to the critique by pointing at how universalism has become a stick with which to beat the Muslim population. He argues that the drift of French thought to the right feeds on universalist values, monopolised and manipulated into a justification for xenophobia and racism by the Front National. In relation to the ongoing debate on the principle of freedom of speech after the terrorist attack, he argues:

> Grand universal values are used all the better to disqualify part of the population, opposing 'good French people' who support the Republic, *laïcité* or freedom of expression, against immigrants, almost by definition communitarian, Islamist, intolerant, sexist and backward.[23]

The above examples from public and academic debates in France demonstrate how the notion of republican universalism continues to play a dominant role as a backdrop for understanding French society and cultural life. Whereas the particularism–universalism paradigm permeates any debate on identity issues in France, the discursive context for discussing identity in Scandinavia is strongly associated with the idea of the welfare state.

The Scandinavian welfare state in crisis

The welfare state put in place in the 1930s and maintained by Scandinavian social-democratic governments during the post-war period is comparable in legacy to the French Republic inasmuch as it represents a dominant force in national self-understanding, self-image and self-representation. Simultaneously, the 'Nordic model' has been an internationally acclaimed social model, and Sweden especially has been regarded as a 'paragon welfare state in its realisation of universalist principles and an institutional welfare model'.[24] However, since the early 1990s, the Scandinavian welfare state has been undergoing profound transformation, and in the outside world, 'recognition of the "Nordic brand" is being undermined [and] losing its marketability, which in turn poses questions for the future of the idea of "Nordic exceptionalism" as a central part of Nordic identity'.[25] For the present study, it is of significance that the welfare state and the attributes of the welfare state – whether at its peak or in its declining form – are the points of reference in relation to identity issues, most distinguishably in discussions of immigration, diversity, national identity and citizenship. These issues have taken centre stage in public and political discussions in the Nordic countries since the 1990s, that is, since the moment when debates on various identity issues began in a similar manner to intensify in France.

From an international perspective, the social and political construct of the post-war Nordic welfare state has been seen as a successful model to strive after. There is an abundance of academic publications, especially from the social sciences, dealing with the phenomenon of the Nordic model, which has, according to historian Peter Baldwin, 'commonly been regarded as the embodiment of the highest stage of the welfare state's evolution'.[26] The Nordic welfare model has hence warranted adjectives such as 'universalistic and decommodifying', 'peace-loving and rational', 'different, progressive, egalitarian, solidaristic … compassionate and charitable', 'extraordinarily stable', 'distinctly modern [and] highly efficient'; it has also frequently been described with 'an image of the nation as a family'.[27]

From an internal perspective, it is significant too that there exists in addition to a national identity a pronounced understanding of a supranational regional identity. As Ole Wæver puts it in his analysis of debates about European integration in the Nordic countries: '[i]n the case of "smaller" countries like the Nordic, a sub-regional category like Scandinavia/Norden enters between state/nation and Europe'.[28] The construction of Danish, Norwegian or Swedish national identity is thus cushioned by a relationship with what is frequently phrased in terms of a Scandinavian 'brotherhood' or fraternity. For France, on the contrary, there is no bolstering identity interface; the collective above the state/nation is Europe.

Characteristically, issues of modern Scandinavian national identity are expressed in politico-economic terms and are closely related to the Scandinavian models for social policy.[29] In his much-quoted (and also criticised) publication *The Three Worlds of Welfare Capitalism* (1990), political economist Gøsta Esping-Andersen identifies three western welfare regimes: the 'liberal', the 'cooperatist' and the 'social-democratic', where the latter category is exemplified by the Scandinavian countries. Typical of the form of Scandinavian welfare statism, Esping-Andersen contends, is a high degree of fair economic distribution: '[r]ather than tolerate a dualism between state and market, between working class and middle class, the social democrats pursued a welfare state that would promote an equality of the highest standards, not an equality of minimal needs as was pursued elsewhere'.[30] Under this regime, a homogenous society was secured by moderating the gap between rich and poor by means of income regulation and proportionate taxation. The crisis of the Scandinavian welfare state is thus often expressed in terms of a change in market conditions and an intrusion of neo-liberal tendencies destabilising the economic egalitarianism prevalent in Scandinavia, and in terms of the effects of globalisation and Europeanisation.[31] Corresponding to what might be termed a social-democratic ideology, historically 'diversity in Scandinavia has primarily been seen as a question of social class'.[32]

In addition to the economic equality promoted by the social-democratic governments, the state church has had a homogenising effect on the Scandinavian region. The dominant status of the Lutheran variant of Christianity has thus been highlighted as 'perhaps the most important explanation of the similarities among the Nordic states and, in particular, of the Nordic type(s) of welfare'.[33] Kildal and Kuhnle further point to 'the early fusion of the Church and state bureaucracies' as a factor underpinning 'a more unified and stronger public interest in and responsibility for welfare matters in general'.[34] Often this type of connection is made between the welfare state and Lutheranism, which 'has contributed to a certain understanding of work ethics and equality'.[35] Others go as far as suggesting that 'Protestantism, more than social democracy, shaped universalism and the Nordic model of welfare.'[36] However, processes of secularisation taking place in Scandinavia in the twenty-first century – most significantly illustrated with the (much-debated) separation of the Lutheran church and state in Sweden (in 2000) and in Norway (in 2012) – have been seen as necessary in order to accommodate multicultural and multifaith societies.[37]

Another key factor that is often highlighted as an important and unique aspect of the Scandinavian welfare state model is the high level of equality between genders. This aspect of the welfare state is frequently expressed in absolute terms as an essential hallmark of the 'Nordic brand': '[t]he ambition of gender equality has been more explicitly expressed and applied in the Scandinavian countries than in other countries in Europe'.[38] The social-democratic welfare states are foreshadowed earlier in the twentieth century by initiatives to acknowledge and secure equal rights for women. Scandinavian women were among the first in the world to obtain suffrage (for Norwegians this happened in 1913, for Danes in 1915 and for Swedes in 1921), a record comparing favourably to that of France, where women had to wait until 1944 for the vote, and until 1965 for the right to open a bank account in their own name. The successful claims of feminist grassroots organisations in the 1970s and 1980s led to what Norwegian political scientist (and feminist activist) Helga Hernes has called 'the women-friendly welfare state' and 'state feminism'.[39]

The relationship between the Scandinavian welfare state and gender equality seems evident: social services, such as provision of child care, extended possibilities for parental leave, and care for the elderly, have played an essential role in creating the necessary conditions for women's participation in the labour market and thus also in opening up possibilities for female input in political decision-making. The modern gender relationship based on the 'dual breadwinner model' is however being contested.[40] This is frequently expressed in terms of challenges to the welfare state's social policies as a condition for gender equality. Borchorst and Siim thus point to several areas where the Scandinavian countries have not managed to secure equality between the genders: the gender pay gap conditioned upon a private–public gender division of the labour market, old age pensions and the tackling of immigration.[41] Additionally, Diana Mulinari's study of immigrant women in Sweden, based on an intersectional analysis, determines that the Swedish welfare state constitutes a case of 'gendered racism'. She demonstrates how the dominant Swedish discourse places all immigrant women in the same category as being '"different", "passive", "traditional"', lacking democratic traditions and with backgrounds in "patriarchal" cultures', and that ultimately 'the specificities of the Swedish race formation [constitute] a regime [that] produces discourses of belonging and boundaries against the other through a narrative where national pride is symbolised in the welfare system'.[42] The introduction of market-oriented solutions in place of public regulation has equally had an impact on gender equality in Scandinavia: 'the picture of woman-friendly policies as simultaneously inclusive and competitive has been challenged by neo-liberal discourses about the need for welfare reforms during an era of globalisation'.[43]

The Nordic model as a successful and desirable construction is beginning to fall apart with symptoms appearing in various areas. This also affects the Scandinavian sense of place in the world and self-esteem. Somewhat analogous to the concept of *l'exception française*, which captures the sense of both political and cultural exceptionalism in the French national imaginary, there exists a similar notion of uniqueness associated with the Nordic model, functioning both as a reference for a Scandinavian self-understanding and for the outside world's view of the region. Christopher Browning contends that '[c]entral to the Nordic brand have been ideas of Nordic "exceptionalism" – of the Nordics as being different from or better than the norm – and of the Nordic experience, norms and values as a model to be copied by others'.[44] Browning further defines the 'Nordic brand' in political terms referring to the Nordic countries' image during the Cold War era as 'peaceful societies and bridge-builders', valued for their 'internationalist solidarism' and 'egalitarian social democracy'.[45] The brand is wholly reliant on a well-functioning Scandinavian welfare state, which begins to disintegrate in the early 1990s as a result of the international transformations brought about by the collapse of Communism in Eastern Europe and the end of the Cold War.[46] The banking crisis of the early 1990s and subsequent high rates of unemployment also had an effect on the early stages of the shift in welfare policies.[47] Financial and demographic globalisation, however, remain perhaps the most commonly employed explanation for the crisis of the Scandinavian societal model.[48] Mikko Kuisma further argues that '[t]he "Nordic model" is not well equipped to deal with the blurring of the boundaries between internal and external – domestic and foreign' and is 'rather ill-suited to facing the challenges of multiculturalism'.[49]

Within this new political climate, public and private discourses have changed. Accordingly, the influence of neo-liberal tendencies has had an effect on how notions of national identity and cultural diversity are expressed and how the Other is represented. As the Norwegian social anthropologist Thomas Hylland Eriksen has argued in relation to the shift in politico-economical ideology and correspondingly to the way minorities and their rights are discussed: 'it is no wonder that immigrants were praised in the 1970s, when the collectivist ideology of social democracy still held sway in Scandinavia, for their strong family solidarity; while in the new century, they are criticised for it since it impedes personal freedom'.[50] Swedish anti-racism scholars and activists Tobias Hübinette and Catrin Lundström express the national identity crisis of the post-welfare state in considerably more radical terms in their articles about Swedish 'white melancholy', a notion expanded on in reference to the neighbouring Scandinavian countries as well.[51] In the context of the Swedish 2010 general election, which secured the anti-immigrant, right-wing populist *Sverigedemokraterna* (Sweden Democrats) 20 seats (out of 349) in parliament, Hübinette and Lundström describe the presence and manifestation in Swedish national discourse of a general mourning for the loss of what they refer to as the 'Swedish whiteness' – 'the master signifier for Swedishness'.[52] Significantly, they argue, this mourning is double-sided, consisting of a longing for either the 'good Scandinavia' or the 'old Scandinavia'. They continue:

> [I]t is ... as much about the humiliating loss of Sweden as the most progressive, humanitarian, and anti-racist country in the world as about the mourning of the passing of the Swedish population as being the most homogeneous and whitest of all white peoples.[53]

While Hübinette and Lundström represent a certain political activist branch of Swedish academia, notions of loss, mourning or lament are frequently expressed sentiments echoed in much research on Scandinavian welfare models and national identities, whether from social sciences or humanities. Sociologist Staffan Marklund thus already in 1988 described the Nordic welfare states in terms of a 'Paradise lost'.[54] At the beginning of the 1990s, when the golden age of the welfare state was definitively over, the effects on the Scandinavian *folkesjæl* ('People's soul') are clear: 'Nordic identity is in crisis', as Ole Wæver spells it out in the first sentence of an article commenting on 'Nordic nostalgia'.[55] This mourning of the loss of the protecting and nurturing welfare state, and the subsequent existential rootlessness of Scandinavians, has become an integrated feature of the socially aware Scandinavian crime novel from the 1990s, and is perhaps most manifestly expressed in Henning Mankell's Wallander figure, described by Michael Tapper as an 'incarnation of Swedish melancholy'.[56] McCorristine's notion that 'Mankell's novels are haunted by the lack of secure orientation in contemporary Sweden' is further illustrated in the collective title that Mankell gives his Wallander texts, 'Novels about the Swedish Anxiety', consolidating the sense of neuroticism related to Wallander's existential attempts to navigate an incomprehensible and complex reality.[57]

The core of the Nordic model relies on some of the same principles as the French Republic, but whereas French universalism from the outset was an essential foundation stone of the nation, the Scandinavian concept was formed through practical political exercises. Kildal and Kuhnle argue that in Scandinavia 'universalism has come about more through pragmatic, reformist consensus-building policy-making than through a historically embedded, clear visionary programme'.[58] The lack of historical foundation might have an effect on the ways in which the so-called 'crisis of universalism' is experienced in Scandinavia. Additionally, it might also explain the low level of critical engagement with the ideological basis of the welfare state. In contrast to the (relative) absence of reflection on core ideological principles of the welfare state, symptomatic, it can be argued, of welfare policies and institutional adjustments taking place in the Nordic countries in the 1990s, there exists in France an ardent and continuous debate on the ideological foundation and governing values of the French Fifth Republic during the same period.

This apparent absence of engagement with the ideological underpinnings of the Scandinavian welfare states within political discourse, however, finds a counterweight in popular culture where these debates have flourished more freely. This is one of the key foci of *Crime and Fantasy in Scandinavia* (2008), in which Andrew Nestingen conducts an analysis of changing Nordic societies through the prism of popular culture from the region. As the basis for this analysis, he reiterates observations from the social sciences, ascribing the crisis of the welfare state to a transition from a sense of 'transparency' to one of 'opacity' caused by a number of significant changes taking place in the Scandinavian countries since the 1980s, including a political change in a neo-liberal direction, the Scandinavian Social Democrats' shift towards the centre of the political spectrum, Europeanisation, strengthening of anti-immigrant parties and their influence on immigration politics, and easy movements of capital and culture via new technologies such as the Internet.[59] As part of Scandinavian popular culture, the crime fiction genre, Nestingen argues, has become perhaps the most influential site for an engagement with and discussion of the societal effects of the decline of the social-democratic welfare state, not least when measured in sales statistics. In this context, it is noteworthy that the Scandinavian variant of the genre sees a substantial upsurge in the early 1990s – when Mankell's crime novels are among the first to receive international recognition – at the same time as the Scandinavian welfare state begins to crumble.

French identity, provisionally summarised, can be said here to be based on an ideological contract grounded in the powerful notion of republican universalism, criticised for not being capable at a foundational level of embracing a new diversified society, whereas in Scandinavian countries there is a solidarity contract based on a Lutheran, social-democratic understanding of society, suffering from an incapability to accommodate contemporary complexities. In both cases, there is a sense of crisis and undermining. In France, this civic conception of the nation has, significantly, been the subject of recent debate in the public sphere; this is less the case in Scandinavian contexts.

The following readings centre on the ways in which more recent crime narratives in the French and Scandinavian settings deal with the experience of national identity crises. Further, they explore how the texts problematise normative and homogenising notions of national cohesion in contemporary multicultural realities.

Dahl and Manotti

Whereas Manchette and Sjöwall/Wahlöö write in a period that can be characterised as the 'beginning of the end of this and that', to paraphrase Fredric Jameson, the French writer Dominique Manotti (alias Marie-Noëlle Thibault, 1942–) and Swedish writer Arne Dahl (alias Jan Arnald, 1963–) both deal with a period during which France and Scandinavia have undergone significant socio-economic and sociocultural changes under late capitalism.[60] The parallel reading of Dahl's *Europa Blues* (*Europa Blues*, 2001) and Manotti's *Bien connu des services de police* (Known to Law Enforcement, 2010) marks a rather significant jump in time from the 1960s and 1970s to a different contemporary reality, characterised by neo-liberalism and globalisation. Ideologically and thematically, however, these two authors, in order to express concerns about the organisation of society, explicitly draw upon the critical left-wing crime fiction traditions established by Sjöwall/Wahlöö and Manchette.

In both textual universes there is critical commentary on the state and its underpinnings: Manotti engages explicitly with republican universalism, whereas Dahl – while critiquing certain points of Swedish statism – offers a commentary on how the points of reference for a Swedish national identity, having abandoned the sense of Nordic exceptionalism, have shifted in the post-Cold War period towards a 'more positive reading of Europe' to employ Browning's characterisation.[61] Furthermore, both novelists write firmly within a 'post-socialist' perspective in Nancy Fraser's terms, and these readings thus mark the shift from the 'paradigm of redistribution' to the 'paradigm of recognition', where the pronounced focus is identity.

*Dominique Manotti: discussing identities within
the framework of the French Republic*

Dominique Manotti, formerly a lecturer (until 2002) in modern economic history at Paris VIII-Vincennes-Saint-Denis, publishes her first *roman noir* – *Sombre Sentier* (*Rough Trade*, 1995) – in the year of Manchette's death. The two writers' fictional universes, however, overlap historically around the symbolic year of 1981. The election of the Fifth Republic's first socialist president, François Mitterrand, coincides with the publication of Manchette's final (non-posthumous) crime novel, *La Position du tireur couché* (*The Prone Gunman*, 1981), set in the years immediately preceding Mitterrand's election (1979–81).[62] Manotti's first crime novel is similarly set in Paris in 1980. It depicts the working and living conditions of undocumented Turkish immigrants in the Sentier district of Paris, during a time marked by pre-election hopefulness on the left. Indeed, Manotti evokes this mood in an interview, describing her first novel as 'a very optimistic book in that it was borne on the hopes of the 1970s', adding that 'the other novels are much darker because they correspond with the Mitterrand years'.[63]

If Manchette's body of works can be defined as post-1968, Manotti's *romans noirs* can be seen as articulating the climate of growing disaffection on the political left following Mitterrand's election and the shift in economic direction towards a market-oriented approach, the so-called *tournant de la rigueur* (introduction of austerity policies). *Sombre Sentier*, representing, according to Manotti, 'the last great social struggle preceding *Mitterrandisme*', is followed by *À nos chevaux* (*Dead Horsemeat*, 1997) and *Kop* (Kop, 1998) to form a trilogy featuring commissaire Théo Daquin.[64] This cycle and the following novel, *Nos fantastiques années fric* (Our Marvellous Money Years, 2001), engage retrospectively with the 1980s and, as the last title suggests, with the decade's fixation on money as the dominant societal value. On a personal level, for Manotti – who was a member of the French Communist Party and a political activist during the 1960s and 1970s – embarking on a career as a crime writer is intrinsically connected with the sense of the collapse of social alternatives to capitalism: 'The choice of fiction imposed itself automatically, doubtless because the general atmosphere of disenchantment was already pervasive ... In fact, literature marked my break with political struggle.'[65]

Manotti's conception of the *roman noir* is close to that of Manchette; it is something radically different from the traditional *roman policier* concerned with the psychology of the individual:

> The *roman noir* roots crimes in the social circumstances in which they are committed. It's no longer the isolated individual who is the criminal; it's the world of suffering, poverty, violence and corruption in which we live that produces criminal individuals, this world that law and justice cover without providing any organisation for it.[66]

This vision evidently also influences the nature of the narration and has an impact on how characters are constructed and displayed, as Manotti points out: 'in my characters, the role of psychology is slender, but the role of social relations is significant'.[67] Within the post-1980s paradigm of disintegration of ideological alternatives to capitalism, the crime fiction genre however also needs to undergo a revision, according to Manotti: '"Noir" needs to be reinvented. What needs to be written is the *roman noir* of globalisation, of capitalism triumphant without a formal adversary, without limits'.[68]

Manotti is not only an author of *romans noirs*. Her academic articles as historian, her polemical blog interventions on her website (*www.dominiquemanotti.com*) and her frequently published journalistic articles are all part of her textual production. In many cases, it is a question of the same topic being covered from different angles: the crime fiction method approach only constitutes one approach to a certain theme. One example is her continued engagement with themes of police violence in confrontations between young *banlieusards* and the police, and of the framing of innocents within the legal system, dealt with both in *Bien connu des services de police* and in her website's outspoken blogposts beginning with 'Bien connu… 1'. Seven short texts written in March 2015, her posts constitute a non-fiction polemic centring on court cases where the police escape legal prosecution. Manotti makes this connection between her work of fiction and reality in the introduction:

> The news too regularly offers situations close to those I had related in my novel *Bien connu des services de police*. A novel that police officers and judges encountered in various debates had declared much too forced, even based on caricature. Well, the same mechanisms are reproduced, at more or less regular intervals.[69]

Manotti views fiction as a supplement to the work of the historian. In this light, revisiting historical periods and events of the past in crime fiction is not 'a criticism of the work of historians because it couldn't be done without historians'.[70] However, she states that 'the novel ensures that it becomes an element integral to reflection'.[71] The *roman noir*'s ability to create a space for reflection happens in a different register to that of the journalistic article or the academic paper, both unable to answer, or even properly discuss, questions such as those that express Manotti's political disillusionment: 'How did the French left become converted into a money-worshipping cult?'[72] Crime fiction cannot necessarily answer such questions satisfactorily, but it can engage with them and problematise them: 'if I've lost hope in action, I still write in order to understand'.[73] The following reading will aim to highlight precisely Manotti's problematisation of political questions through crime fiction – here, specifically the question of police misconduct vis-à-vis marginalised groups within the Republic.

Bien connu des services de police

The *banlieue* is the setting for *Bien connu des services de police*, in which marginalised identities – including those of women, and sexual and ethnic minorities – are read through the prism of French republican norms. The novel problematises these in a critique focusing on the police as an institution that interprets these norms in ways that suit its own expedient purposes. Ultimately the novel can be said to reflect on the question that Manotti highlights herself in an article in *Libération*: 'how has French society managed for so long to avoid seeing, observing, acknowledging the moral, social and political problems presented to it by the way its police operate?'[74]

Bien connu des services de police does not take the form of a traditional detective narrative: there is no identifiable crime to be solved, no distinguishable detective figure and no real resolution at the end. Rather, the story – as a *reportage* – simply follows life at the police station in the fictional *banlieue* setting of Panteuil, more precisely described as referring to 'une ville du 9-3', that is, in the department of Seine-Saint-Denis, north of Paris.[75] The name of Panteuil can also be read, as has been suggested, as the combination of Pantin and Montreuil, both in the departmental arrondissement of Bobigny.[76] Manotti furthermore emphasises the documentary aspect by labelling the novel as 'a chronicle of everyday life in a police station'.[77] The novel is set in the summer of 2005, but written five years later, and thus can be read as offering an interpretation of the circumstances leading up to the riots in the *banlieues* during October and November of that year. The photograph on the front cover of Gallimard's *Folio* edition of the novel, depicting a police officer in front of a burning car, further highlights this link.

The two newly appointed officers at the Panteuil station, Sébastian Doche and Isabelle Lefèvre, find themselves exposed to the inconsistencies, brutality and corruption of their police colleagues. The violence is directed both outwards at the young Maghreb population of the *banlieue*, but it exists also within the police force itself, where Lefèvre is sexually harassed on her first day at work by a superior male colleague. The incident evokes memories of her being sexually assaulted as a little girl, originally prompting her desire to become a police officer: 'being a cop was also sheltering yourself from that kind of violence'.[78] The violence that Lefèvre meets in the photocopying room at the *commissariat* – the station – immediately defies the image of the police as a sheltering protector from violence.

Doche and Lefèvre's role as observers functions in a double motion where they operate both as outsiders, idealistic new police officers, and as insiders who themselves become part of the system they are observing. The overpowering feeling of being unable to escape the operation to which Doche and Lefèvre contribute manifests itself as a physical malaise. This becomes symptomatic of a more existential, even quasi-Sartrean, 'nausea', that again becomes representative of societal malaise:

> Doche feels ill, very ill, somewhere between wanting to vomit and wanting to cry … Being a cop to find a place for yourself in a supportive group and in an ordered world. And in a single day, he finds himself once again alone, in a state of complete disorder. (p. 47)

The paradigmatic axis of order, group solidarity and well-being is thus rapidly replaced by disorder, solitude and ill-being at both a personal and a societal level.

The condition experienced by Doche is also reflected in the physical surroundings. The novel's first chapter, Balzac-like, telescopically zooms in, first on the *quartier*, then on the exterior of the police station, before the third-person narrator enters the building itself. From the outside, the 'commissariat' appears strikingly non-accommodating and unfriendly: 'Tinted reinforced glass, no windows, a protective grille on the ground floor: it looks more like a fortress than a public building' (p. 24). It is easy to establish a metonymical analogy between the appearance of the building and the police profession: when Doche and Lefèvre are guided through the station, they express their surprise at seeing the decrepit and dirty interior: 'Why is everything so dirty? On the outside, it looked almost new', to which their guide replies that 'it's dirty because it's a dirty job, that way we can feel at home' (p. 27). Subsequently, the two newcomers are symbolically shown to the 'locker rooms' with the remark 'get into uniform' (p. 27), implying that Doche and Lefèvre have ultimately no option but to adopt the collective identity of the police. Even a very slight step away from the norm is promptly corrected, as Lefèvre comes to experience when they re-emerge from the cloakroom: 'Your attire is in breach of the rules. Fix and tie back your hair: no strands sticking out. And tomorrow, wear the regulation shoes' (p. 28). Important also, however, is the fact that the acquisition of this collective identity denotes a growing contradiction between exterior and interior.

Manotti spotlights the national identity crisis in contemporary France by thematically treating aspects of what Schor calls 'spectral universalism'.[79] In the novel, a particularly conservative strain of republican discourse is represented by the views of the majority of the police officers in the novel, but especially by 'la commissaire' Le Muir, who, having inherited a 'sense of colonial nostalgia' (p. 34) from a father who fought as a colonel in the Algerian war, not only refuses to recognise, but directly opposes, the multicultural and multi-ethnic reality of the *banlieue* constituting her police district. Le Muir's driver, Pasquini, performing the role of her sidekick, is a *pied-noir* – a white colonial immigrant from Algeria – who shares both her nostalgia for French Algeria and her attitudes towards the problems in the *banlieue*. Whereas they are united by a colonial nostalgia figured as being nourishing (p. 34), their idea of the *banlieue* community is clearly based on French superiority and segregation, a vision also reflected in the nickname given to the commissioner: 'La Muraille' – 'The Wall' (p. 62). Echoing a past colonial agenda predicated upon financial gain, their agreed proposition to counter the current situation in their district is 'cleaning out of the zone' ('nettoyage de la zone'), 'expulsion' and 'destruction of tenements' (p. 36). This has to be executed, not because of the safety hazard that the buildings impose, but in order to make room for 'urban regeneration projects' and 'potential investors' (p. 36).

The juxtaposition of the colonial past and the postcolonial present of the *banlieue* is further reinforced by Le Muir's ironic use of biblical imagery, inverting perceived notions of good and bad. She is conscious of the radical aspect of her suggestion when she invokes a divine force to solve the problems of the *banlieue*:

> So I'm waiting for an act of divine intervention, a miracle, a disaster, any of these will do. A fire, an earthquake, a volcanic eruption, the mass departure of Africans deciding to go back to their homelands by crossing the Mediterranean on foot just like Moses crossed the Red Sea. (p. 37)

The imagined exodus in which a series of fantasised instances of divine intervention culminates represents a desirable outcome for Le Muir while at the same time echoing – in reverse – the actual trans-Mediterranean exodus towards France in the wake of the Algerian war of the *pieds-noirs*. But the first in this litany of acts of God finds an echo in the targeting the following week by arsonists of a building accommodating Malian families, leaving seventeen people (including six children) dead – an incident recalling similar acts in which Pasquini has been murkily involved in the past. There is thus seemingly a continuity between the macroscopic historical imaginary of the colonial legacy and its localised symptoms.

The blurring of the boundaries between fictional construct and reality by way of inserting true (and recognisable as such for readers of French newspapers) details into the narrative adds another dimension to the polyphonic nature of Manotti's novel. To this extent, the political rhetoric of Le Muir unambiguously points to that of Nicolas Sarkozy during 2005 when the novel is set. Le Muir's 'nettoyage de la zone' is a re-articulation of the controversial remark made in June 2005 by Sarkozy who was then minister of the interior in Dominique de Villepin's government: 'Starting tomorrow, we're going to take a power hose to clean out [nettoyer au Kächer] the Cité des 4000. We'll put in place the necessary personnel and the time it will take, but it will be cleaned out.'[80]

The Le Muir/Sarkozy association is further established through Le Muir's close connections with the unnamed minister of the interior, and that she is an essential part of 'the informal task force put in place [by him] to develop the security programme he intends to use as one of the central planks of his presidential candidacy' (pp. 71–2). In her speech to this group (pp. 72–4), Le Muir again recalls Sarkozy by making a version of his 'security policy' a significant part of her agenda. This is not least the case when she insists on the word 'insecurity', a trademark of Sarkozyan rhetoric, from Sarkozy's appointment as minister of the interior in 2002 to the time of his presidency: 'let us not kid ourselves, today, it's the fear of insecurity, of being unsafe, strongly correlated to the fear of the foreigner, the terror of the ghetto, at one and the same time ultra-reality and fantasy, that are the basis of social cohesion' (p. 73).

Le Muir's answer to this imagined sense of insecurity also alludes to Sarkozy's. One of her pronouncements engages with the security question: 'in the ghettos, power does not rest on law, but on force' (p. 72). The perception of security and of the exclusive right of the police to enforce it, is, moreover, as important as security itself: 'Our police must be perceived, above all, as the exclusive legal holder of the right to use force' (p. 72). The actual implementation of the politics of (in)security in Panteuil happens in the form of groups of 'Bacmen' (i.e. from the 'anti-crime brigade') patrolling the *quartier*, frequent 'systematic identity checks on Beurs [second-generation Arabs] and Blacks' (p. 81) and increased surveillance generally.

Manotti, rewriting Sarkozy's enunciations into the words of Le Muir, engages critically with the political discourse of the Sarkozy *mandat*, expressed here in a speech that the president gave on 29 November 2007:

> Security is a strong preoccupation among our citizens. It is derived from republican values. Police officers, you are the guarantors of respect for

republican principles, you are guarantors of the freedom of everyone to come and go and you are guarantors of social peace.[81]

Taken to its logical extremity, the novel's establishment of a subtle but powerful link between Sarkozy's rhetoric and political ambition and that of Le Muir creates a hyperbolic association between seemingly 'innocent' oratory and the image of immigrant children dying in a fire. Indeed, the symbolic context of 'nettoyage' shifts from that of political tough-guy bravado invoking high-pressure cleaning to one of purification through fire in the concrete end result of the arson attack.

As a benevolent counterpart to Le Muir, the novel introduces the character of Noria Ghozali. The mirroring of these two strong female personalities is supported by their wearing identical clothes: 'Le Muir is wearing a beige trouser suit' (p. 33) and '[Ghozali] is dressed with a certain elegance in a beige linen trouser suit' (p. 55). The Manichaeism of this mirroring is an essential part of the novel's narrative argument and runs through much of its imagery: Ghozali stands in contrast to the police environment's (physical and symbolic) dirty aspect in being described as 'a pure flower of the *banlieue*' (p. 55). Ghozali's appearance moreover adds another layer to the novel's multiple interpretations of the relationship between investigator/investigated when she starts looking into irregularities within the police station of Panteuil. In her capacity as investigator within the police intelligence service (RGPP), Ghozali is in the first instance leading an inquiry into a case of police misconduct: officers have been pimping Eastern European 'sans papiers' (undocumented migrants) in a multistorey car park. Her investigation, however, gradually moves upwards within the hierarchy, where she firmly challenges the abuse, personified by Le Muir, of political power and corruption within high society.

Ghozali's Algerian Arabic background – and the fact that her French identity is expressly a product of her ancestry's colonialised existence – gives counterweight to Le Muir's colonial heritage. Investigating the *banlieue* from the outside, according to her professional role, Ghozali has however an insider perspective on life in the suburban *quartier* as a 'Beurette' – a female second-generation Arab – who has grown up in a similar environment herself. Whereas Lefèvre perhaps assumes the role of a female victim and is being exploited because of both her age and her gender, Ghozali's confidence and determination become a prism through which attitudes towards gender, class and race are challenged, as in the following interior monologue channelled by the novel's narrator: 'She remembers having slowly become aware that the racist, macho and violent cop was much better accepted by all her colleagues, in a more spontaneous and natural manner, than she was herself, a woman, an Arab, too young, too ambitious' (p. 92).

The image of the police as the barrier protecting society has a problematically symbolic texture in *Bien connu des services de police*. Doche and Lefèvre's situation as both insiders and outsiders is mirrored by the novel's preoccupation with thematic constellations concerning inclusion and exclusion in relation to the French nation state and the question – frequently raised during Nicolas Sarkozy's 2007 election campaign and throughout his presidency – 'what does it mean to be French?'[82] In Panteuil, we meet a cross-dresser, abused women, Arab women, Romanians and Malians. All of these representatives of minorities provide us with a microcosmic image of a France made up by a multitude of diverse cultural, ethnic, gendered and sexual identities. The 'clients' at the Panteuil station also reflect a heterogeneous population, as Doche notices on his first day at work where he meets 'men, women, of all states in life, of all colours' (p. 29). The police, on the other hand, become a force defending a society based on a uniform, heteronormative, white and male-centred identity. In the courtroom, we follow the thoughts of police officer Ivan who escapes a prison sentence by wrongfully blaming a young Arab for his own crime of having kicked and disfigured a female colleague. Ivan captures this image of privilege during the court case: 'all these men who look like one another, the same physical solidity, the same way of walking, talking, a mixture of connivance with authority and bitterness at feeling unloved by "those from outside"' (p. 172).

Inclusion and exclusion, the feeling of being on the inside or the outside, are linked to concepts of homogeneity and heterogeneity. The diversity of 'those from the outside' opposed to the uniformity of those on the inside mirrors France's difficulty in maintaining a (male-centred, heteronormative and ethnically homogenous) republican universalism in a society with growing cultural diversity, where advocacy for particularism is increasingly amplified. The police force, forming the impenetrable membrane between these two ideals of community, performs a function opposite of what is expected in the novel. This is emphatically demonstrated in the prologue where a group of men collects protection money from illegal Eastern European prostitutes and sodomises them brutally in a multistorey car park. At the end of the scene we learn that the men are in fact police officers from the 'anti-crime brigade'. The distinction between 'criminal' and 'anti-criminal' no longer exists. The same can be said about the quotation in the novel's epigraph from the *Déclaration des droits de l'homme et du citoyen*: 'To guarantee the Rights of Man and of the Citizen a public force is necessary; this force is therefore established for the benefit of all, and not for the particular use of those to whom it is entrusted' (p. 9). Through its ironic employment of the iconic quotation, Manotti's novel implicitly argues that the ground on which present-day France is built bears no meaning: the statements from the declaration are traduced in the everyday activities of those who represent the institutions of the Republic. Le Muir in her capacity as commissioner explicitly confirms this manipulation in her circumstantial rejection of the declaration: 'When you're in the field, remember that policing is not and has never been done by the rights of man' (p. 74).

The 1789 declaration as the novel's thematic gatekeeper is not only associated with the role of a corrupted police force, but it accentuates the novel's critique of the French republican model founded on longstanding, if unquestioned, ideals and iconic expressions that derive from the French Revolution and the Third Republic. Within the critical optic of Manotti's novel, the past has from the outset been troublesome in that the major historical point of reference – the 1789 revolution and the social contract ultimately resulting from it – has had constitutional, discursive and social consequences privileging certain segments of society over others. Ultimately, the book's title reveals an ambiguity which resembles the novel's thematic preoccupation with interior/exterior contradictions: 'bien connu des services de police', as well as being a standard designation for 'known to the police', could equally be interpreted as what might well be expected *from* the police.

Manotti's novel is, then, an(other) example of how French crime fiction plays an essential role in discussing matters that are difficult to engage with in the public sphere in France. Articulating an explicit critique of the dysfunctionality of the French police and not least of the 'mafia omertà' with which it protects itself, the novel highlights and engages with an issue that the author explains as follows in her *Libération* polemic: 'All those who take part in the functioning of the policing establishment (police hierarchy, prosecutors) are familiar with its reality, but the total of its malfunctionings can explain the fact that this information does not intrigue – as it should – "civil" society.'[83] Manotti herself raises the point of the crime fiction genre's ability to counter a general silence over matters such as police misconduct and concludes her article in the following terms: 'The authors of *romans noirs* still have great days ahead of them.'[84]

More generally, formal and informal understandings of the relationship between a state and its citizens impact upon crime fiction's critique of society. As well as in the French setting, this can be seen in the Scandinavian context, as the following reading of Arne Dahl's police procedural indicates. However, an important initial observation can be made here: Manotti's rewriting of the *roman noir* is one manifestly breaking away from the *roman policier*. As the author has pointed out in an interview: 'the lesson of the detective novel is: "Sleep well, good people; we're taking care of law and order."'[85] *Bien connu des services de police* is demonstratively not a *roman policier*, but a novel that explicitly accuses the forces of order of being racist, sexist, chauvinistic and violent in the name of a republican universalism past its sell-by date. While Dahl's novels certainly contain a social critique and treat issues of marginalised identities, the police remain for the most part a compassionate and inclusive institution working for the benefit of the general public and the individual. To a certain extent, Dahl's novels, therefore, conform to Manotti's definition of the *roman policier* as a genre endorsing the police and reassuring the public.

Arne Dahl: rewritings of genre, history and identity

Swedish author Arne Dahl has to date written three crime fiction series. The first of these (1999–2008), known in English as the *Intercrime* series, is for the most part set in Stockholm where it follows the investigations of the 'National Police Special Unit for International Violent Crimes', or in short 'the A-Unit'. This group of seven investigators is comprised of both old and young people, of both genders, some Swedish, a Finno-Swede, a Chilean refugee and a gay man, thus presenting a microscopic version of a multicultural society. In this respect, the four-novel *Opcop* series (2011–15), in which a pan-European team of investigators operate out of Holland, supplements the first series by including a further aspect of well-functioning cooperation grounded in cultural diversity. Structurally, methodologically and ideologically, Dahl's first series can be viewed as a palimpsestuous rewriting of Sjöwall and Wahlöö's *The Story of a Crime*, insofar as it employs the writer-couple's template and allows parts of their original text to appear via continuous intertextual references. Peter Kirkegaard thus assertively refers to Arne Dahl as the 'true heir' of Sjöwall and Wahlöö, justifying this label by the author's use of the police procedural subgenre and the collective police team as protagonist, in addition to the novels' realism and humour and their social engagement in their analysis of the Swedish *folkhemmet*.[86] Dahl's own comments on Sjöwall and Wahlöö as the 'biological parents' of his fictional style are bolstered by explicit allusions to Sjöwall and Wahlöö's series in his crime novels.[87] Dahl thus, for example, adopts a ten-novel structure for his first series, following Sweden over a decade from 1997 to 2007, and humorously concludes it with the appendix novel entitled *Elva* (Eleven, 2008). Echoing Sjöwall and Wahlöö's declared intention with their series, Dahl furthermore comments that '[t]he theoretical objective was extremely clear. 10 books in 10 years, pick up everything you can about our age, about a humanity that has chosen a neo-liberal route after the breakdown of social democracy.'[88] Dahl thus borrows the methodological framework from Sjöwall and Wahlöö and follows their ideological path. However, he adjusts the content of the writing to a contemporary reality three and a half decades after the source template.

In her reading of Dahl's first Opcop novel *Viskleken* (Chinese Whispers, 2011), Kerstin Bergman discusses Dahl's 'transition from a national to a transnational European perspective' from the first to the second series.[89] While this shift is apparent – not least with the symbolic change from the Stockholm-based national crime unit to the inter-European Opcop unit located in The Hague – this latter transnational perspective is however already prominent in the first series. This is particularly true of the fourth *Intercrime* novel, *Europa Blues* (2001), which offers insight into various issues relating to a particular Swedish self-image in the European context, and draws lines from Sweden's involvement (as a neutral party) in the Second World War to present-day internationally organised crime. In the novel's rewriting of a national past, *Europa Blues* joins other Scandinavian crime novels preoccupied, as Karsten Wind Meyhoff formulates it, with 'digging into the secrets of history in order to expose the complex reality behind the official, homogeneous version of Scandinavian history from the 1940s until today'.[90]

Prevalent in *Europa Blues* is the theme of the (de-)construction of a national Swedish identity, also a subject of investigation in Sjöwall and Wahlöö's crime fiction cycle. However, while Dahl's predecessors viewed this as part of the dismantling of an all-inclusive national welfare state from an internal perspective, Dahl's novels offer a further enquiry into Swedish identity, engaging with international history and cultural, financial and demographic globalisation. Dahl thus joins other authors like Henning Mankell, whose Wallander novels

(1991–2009) chart the processes of globalisation and their effect on Swedish society.[91]

If, categorically put, Sjöwall and Wahlöö point to the dangers of the Swedish welfare state's flirtation with capitalism, and Mankell expresses 'the melancholic lamentation for the loss of a Golden Age, the post-war welfare state and its promises', Dahl's crime novels can be said to represent conscious, post-nostalgic attempts to navigate a new neo-liberal reality.[92] The following reading of *Europa Blues* focuses on the text's preoccupation with identity constructions – be they national, cultural or genre-related. Re-mappings of European cartography and rewritings of the historical past play a role in these constructions, linked in turn to the novel's explicit insistence on generic and cultural reconfigurations.

Doppelgängers and identity theft

Europa Blues weaves together (at least) four different cases that the A-Unit are charged with solving: the remains of a Greek gangster are found in the cave of the wolverines at the zoo in Stockholm; a 10-year-old girl is shot in the arm while on a walk with her father; a distinguished near-nonagenarian Jewish neuroscientist is murdered at the Jewish cemetery; and eight Eastern European girls disappear from a refugee station. The already international nature of the crimes, as indicated by the victims' origins, further expands temporally and spatially when it becomes apparent that they are linked both to atrocities committed during the Second World War and to a contemporary inter-European network of criminals. The many layered contents of the cases then also become entangled with the personal stories of the investigators, and most importantly with that of detective inspector Arto Söderstedt, who, after having inherited a large sum of money from a distant uncle, is enjoying a sabbatical with his family in Tuscany. As it becomes clear that the family gap year is in fact financed by blood money derived from the uncle's time as an SS officer in Buchenwald, the essential question in the investigation becomes related not only to the archetypal pursuit of revealing the identity of the criminal ('who are you?'), but also to an introspective question ('who am I?).

Söderstedt's discovery of his own genealogical identity (at odds with his politico-ethical identity) is only one of the novel's many affirmations of the non-fixity of identity. The investigation in *Europa Blues* centres on the exposure of a complex system of false identities, of people who are not who they pretend to be and of people who are mistaken for being someone else. The doppelgänger – a literary figure that is a staple of detective fiction – is central to this, as is identity-related crime in the form of identity theft.[93] The novel's most striking example of the latter is the respected public persona of the Jewish Professor Emeritus Leonard Sheinkman, concealing the true identity of a Swedish doctor who operated (with Söderstedt's uncle) as an SS officer in Buchenwald, where he experimented on, tortured and executed prisoners. Having stolen and been living under the identity of one of his Jewish victims, the old professor is murdered with the same method that he used when torturing captives in the concentration camp. In Sheinkman's case the perpetrator takes on the role of the victim; in Söderstedt's case the investigator becomes the investigated (through his family history), and, as is often the case in crime fiction, the decoding of identities interlinks with the action of detection. The text's employment of pathetic fallacies further consolidates these themes of pretence and deceptiveness. Metonymically mirroring the characters' false appearances, the surrounding environment participates in similar games of disguise. The description of the first days of May when the investigation begins thus alludes to the characters' concealment of their true identities: 'The kind of day that looks so inviting from indoors but turns out to be a slyly masquerading winter's day.'[94]

The motifs of the doppelgänger and concealed identities link to a more fundamental doubleness relating to the alleged neutral position of Sweden during the Second World War. In an analysis of contemporary Scandinavian crime novels, Karsten Wind Meyhoff argues that 'the opposition between East and West [during the Cold War] gave all the nation states a strong and convenient identity between the two blocks', and after 1989 'a strong need for understanding the fabric of the national societies and for investigating ... cultural myths ... emerged'.[95] In the case of Sweden, the post-1989 collapse of the nation state's stable geopolitical identity and what the historian Dan Stone has called the 'return of memories' is further complicated by the scrutiny of the official image of Sweden's acclaimed wartime neutrality.[96] This scrutiny takes place a few years before the publication of *Europa Blues* in 2001 and includes the exposure of pro-Nazi sentiments among influential elements of Swedish society (including King Gustav V), of the country's export of iron ore to Germany during the war, of the acquisition of gold from Nazi Germany by Sweden's central bank, and of the fact that German troops were allowed passage through the country from occupied Norway to Finland.[97]

Dahl's novel engages explicitly with these issues in the first instance by letting the A-Unit's Paul Hjelm critique an official national discourse of solemn distance from wartime sufferings:

> The Holocaust is an abstraction that you talk about using big words from a podium but will never approach properly. We were not part of it, we will never be able to understand, we do not have anything to do with it, that is for you to take care of. Swedish ahistoricity and false neutrality in unholy unity. We *were* most definitely part of it. We *had* most definitely something to do with it. We *can* most definitely understand it. And there *is* no way around it.[98]

The repetitive structure of the passage – first with the negation in a comma-separated list, and then with the confirmatory and punctuated list with italicised emphasis – questions the nature of statist discursive control ('from a podium') and the rights to the use of the pronominal 'we'. Hjelm's reconfiguration of the official stance becomes particularly forceful because he re-employs the rhetorical mode of the political speech by imitation and irony in his own version of the speech in the second part of the passage. The creative rewriting of state discourse applies by extension to the entire fictional text. *Europa Blues*, then, as a crime novel constitutes a different mode of rewriting and opposing the imposed inclusive 'we' of the first part of the cited passage.

It is, however, important that Dahl's text was written and published at a time when Sweden was witness to a significant political will to investigate and actively publicise the less polished truth about the country's involvement with Nazi Germany.[99] As such, the text can also be seen as a timely fictional contribution capable of supplementing and further nuancing contemporary debates contesting previous dominating master narratives. In the closing lines of *Europa Blues*, Söderstedt finds himself personally entangled in both history and place after learning the truth about his uncle: 'Everything was wonderful. And everything was false. He was standing on top of bodies in order to see Paradise. And he wasn't alone. He was an entire continent' (p. 360). The individual is nested, *matryoshka*-like, within the collective, just as the local (national, regional, European) nests within the global. The novel's prevailing idea of recursion also works in the dimension of historical time, where the novel's present-day network of organised crime nests within a network of National Socialists dating back to Nazi Germany in the 1930s and 1940s. Evidently, this necessitates the question of how the next historical layer will look:

He was quite convinced about the return of fascism, but suspected it would probably take place in a much more subtle, indirect way – it would sneak in by a back route while we kept watch over its more obvious, simplistic manifestations – and then we would suddenly find ourselves face-to-face with a person but see them as an object instead, an item, a potential' return. He was convinced that economism was the first step towards the new fascism. (pp. 124–5)

It is more than a case of containment, however: it is useful also to see the relationship between individual and collective as a dynamic network of mutually interdependent components. As the individual human subject is linked dynamically to the collective, so the individual story or case history is linked intertextually to a much larger narrative.

Individual and collective voices

The collective protagonists in Dahl's novels – the team of investigators in the A-Unit and later in the Opcop group – take turns in having the narrative point of view. As has been demonstrated, Hjelm frequently expresses anti-authoritarian attitudes towards both statism and neo-liberal tendencies; another example is Sara Svenhagen, who engages in a longer critical questioning of Swedish asylum and immigration politics in an interior monologue (pp. 39–40). The political identity of the members of the A-Unit seemingly fits the profile of a left-wing agency. This suggests an equivalence between capitalism and crime.[100] The organic nature of the police procedural's collective protagonist, however, does not equate to a univocally homogenous critical voice in the novel. Rather, the novel's narrative forte is precisely its multiplicity of voices and dialogicality, where discourse takes the form of an ongoing interaction.

The voicing of criticism in *Europa Blues*, then, is not confined to the individual characters of the A-Unit but rather emerges from the interaction between the characters and the third-person omniscient narrator, an interaction rendered more complex by the use of irony. An example from the novel's beginning in which a 'dialogue' takes place between the narrator and – in this case not-so-socially conscious – Hjelm illustrates this. Walking up to the zoo, Hjelm engages in a line of thoughts about the most linguistically elegant expression in Swedish to designate 'the year 2000' and summarises in a long rambling interior monologue the different positions in the debate: 'tjugohundra' (twenty hundred) versus 'tvåtusen' (two thousand). His thoughts are interrupted by the omniscient narrator who critically comments on the irrelevance of Hjelm's thoughts:

> That was what was playing on Detective Inspector Paul Hjelm's mind in this, the year two thousandth year of Our Lord – a year in which the kingdom of Sweden had been singled out by Amnesty International for a sharp rise in police violence; a year in which the police had regularly turned their batons around to strike with the hard end; a year in which Kosovans and Albanians had been sent back to their war-torn homelands with five thousand noble Swedish kronor in their pockets. (pp. 21–2)

Hjelm picks up his internal monologue again after the interference. Seemingly as a reaction to the narrator's problematisation of his linguistic musings at a time where more ethically pressing matters ought to be on his mind, he wonders: '[f]or a short moment it seemed to him as if *somebody* had taken over his thoughts' (p. 22). What in the first instance appears to be Hjelm's realisation of the critical state of his profession and country as prompted by the narrator's intervention is nevertheless turned around once again in Hjelm's own conclusion to the paragraph. Here, it becomes apparent that the critique has not reached its target within the novel's parameters; instead of engaging with the concerns of the narrator, Hjelm 'wondered where all the good old-fashioned sexual fantasies had gone, those fantasies the latest research said should grip us at least fifteen times a day' (p. 22).

While the police investigators in *Europa Blues* regularly offer their critical interpretations of current affairs and political matters, they are complex figures, not merely used as vehicles for the novel's critical agenda. The structure demonstrates the way in which the narrator functions as a transcendent manifestation providing a strong critical voice, but ultimately not controlling the individual. This dialogical design is fundamental for the novel's stance not only at the level of utterances, but also in its understanding of interhuman relationships more generally.

The struggle over and negotiation of meaning at speech level is complemented by the fact that various languages and the interpretation of these play an important role in the novel's plot. Adding thematically to the polyphonic narrative structure, multiple explicit references are made to the aetiological myth of the Tower of Babel. Likewise, multiple signifiers from different languages with similar connotations appear. For example, the respectively Swedish, English, German and Italian nouns *järv*, *wolverine*, *Vielfrass* and *ghiottone* appear in different contexts in the novel, but in all these contexts the symbolic rapacity of the animal is a common reference. Ultimately these terms allude to the same connoted concept of human evil in all languages. Translation and interpretation, moreover, play significant roles in the investigation, and the resolution is only found when connections between words and expressions from different languages (Ukrainian, Yiddish, German, Italian, English and Greek) become apparent. Vocal and bodily metaphors merge when Hjelm begins to realise how linguistic riddles fit together: 'Something was calling to him. Something was starting to come together. The edges of a wound slowly growing closer. All the different languages which had turned up during this case ... It was like the Tower of Babel' (p. 176). Realising the investigation's enigmatic resemblance to the Babel legend, he is inspired to seek the solution in the 'richness of European languages' (p. 176) underpinning the case.

The linguistic perspective is further widened to include culture more broadly when the wolverine leitmotif is subtly established by literary clues in the form of frequent references to James Ellroy's *The Big Nowhere* (1988). Hjelm appears culturally illiterate in the world of crime fiction and does not understand the allusions to the American novel in which wolverines play a significant role. He is thus left wondering on multiple occasions: 'Ellroy? ... Which Ellroy? (p. 29), 'Who the hell is Ellroy?' (p. 67). Solving the cases also makes his own narration fall into place in an intertextual grid: 'He pulled a book from the shelf. It was called *The Big Nowhere*. The author was James Ellroy' (p. 289).

Resolution is found, then, through the unlocking of a code rooted in a lack of fixity of meaning. And just as there is no one definitive monolithic (or monologic) language for expressing the reality underneath the apparent mystery, there is no one single representational form at play in the narrative. Dahl's series is in fact characterised by generic hybridity, and flags this explicitly through the recurrent motif of other aesthetic forms within the prose narrative. A key example is jazz.

Jazz in Europa Blues

There has been a longstanding association between jazz and crime fiction, not least because many of the genre's tropes stem from the American hard-boiled tradition contemporaneous with the pre-eminence of jazz as popular musical form. In *Jazz et polar* (2007), Bob Garcia analyses the relationship between jazz and the *roman noir*, focusing on the subversive nature of these two artistic expressions.

Citing a large corpus of both Anglophone and French crime novels, Garcia establishes that whereas allusions to jazz are very rare in the *roman à énigme*, this musical genre is a significant reference point in the *roman noir* in which 'jazz underlines the seedy and often sordid side of the story'.[101] The function of jazz in its original American form as 'a music of revolt, the symbol and anthem of a deracinated and declassified population' compares with that of the *roman noir* 'which swims against the tide of the established order and denounces its malfunctions'.[102] Furthermore, both expressions are considered inappropriate by the cultural establishment. Garcia designates as 'polar-jazz' the crime fictions that both concretely and symbolically employ jazz as background music for the narration, a category into which most of Arne Dahl's crime novels can be said to fall with their frequent references to well-known jazz compositions.[103]

Dahl's use of jazz as supplement to his textual universe has received some attention from scholars, albeit with different emphases. Kerstin Bergman comments that the Swedish jazz trio e.s.t.'s composition 'Promonition' (2008), the musical accompaniment to Dahl's novel *Viskleken*, 'primarily [works] as a relaxing transition phase, constituting a break of sorts for the novel's characters between fast-paced events'.[104] In an article on the use of jazz in *Europa Blues*, Peter Kirkegaard and Tore Mortensen emphasise the comparable syntactical relationship between musical and linguistic form.[105] Rather than merely being a narratological feature, the use of jazz in Dahl's novels relates, it shall be argued here, to a more profound metafictional questioning concerned with the identity of a Swedish crime novel as part of a complex global (or at least Western) network of texts and genres.

The novel's title, *Europa Blues*, emphasises the theme of cultural corruption or productive hybridity. Striking some of the same chords as the title of James Ellroy's novel *White Jazz* (1992), Dahl's title plays with the introduction of the black American blues genre into the European setting and thus with both generic and geographical transgression. Just as black American writers have employed detective fiction – a predominantly white Euro-American popular form with its origins in the imperial nineteenth century – to explore black identity and convey a social message about societal injustices, the articulation of the jazz/crime fiction confluence in Dahl's novels brings another layer of complexity to perceptions of cultural identity.[106]

The generic relationship between jazz and the type of crime fiction that Dahl is concerned with is explicitly commented on when Hjelm reflects on the high culture/low culture opposition and on his own musical preferences: '[a]fter a jaunt into the world of opera, like some kind of slightly depraved Inspector Morse, he had gone back to jazz' (p. 17). The (ironic) employment of 'depraved' to describe Hjelm in comparison with Colin Dexter's detective figure draws attention to a supposed hierarchical structure not only in the realm of musical genres, but also in that of crime fiction. It is however unclear from the passage whether depravity comes from the interference of a low-cultural musical form into the realm of classical high culture, or whether the invocation of Morse suggests that Hjelm is a contaminated and hybrid protagonist, less generically pure than his classic British counterpart.

The above example occurs in the third chapter of *Europa Blues*, in which Hjelm is on his way from the Astrid Lindgren Children's Hospital, where he has visited the girl who was shot, to the zoo where the body eaten by the wolverines is being examined. Stuck in a traffic jam, Hjelm listens to Miles Davis's album *Kind of Blue* in its entirety, and as he passes 'Dramaten', Stockholm's Royal Dramatic Theatre, he has a vision of Ingmar Bergman entering the building. Notions of temporal and spatial dimensionality intermingle here with questions of cultural identity: 'His route – from Astrid Lindgren to Skansen via Ingmar Bergman, practically a trip through the heart of Sweden – was the exact same length as Miles Davis's *Kind of Blue*. That was that' (p. 21). The juxtaposition of the jazz album and twentieth-century Swedish iconic cultural figures offers a comment on the flexibility of culture as something that can easily move between different geographical contexts, and contract and expand in time (from minutes to centuries) and space (from the confined extent of the car to the Western world). Just as textual identity within the optic of *Europa Blues* is an intertextual identity, cultural identity must also be understood as an intercultural identity. Intrinsically, transnational exchanges and encounters of aesthetic forms and cultures in the novel promote a benign and productive counterpart to monetary and criminal exchanges across borders.

The police and the societal body

As discussed earlier, the malfunctioning human body constitutes a recurring trope in Sjöwall and Wahlöö's *Roman om ett brott*, where it appears as metaphor for the corruption and disintegration of the social body of the Swedish welfare state. This correspondence between body and state established by Beck and his colleagues continues to find expression in the typical middle-aged, depressed male protagonist who has become a staple of the Swedish crime novel (Henning Mankell's Wallander, Åke Edwardson's Erik Winter and Håkon Nesser's Van Veeteren are three prominent examples). However, the physically and mentally suffering hero seems, as Kerstin Bergman points out, 'almost to have died with the last Wallander novel [*The Pyramid*, 1999], as there are very few traces of him in the Swedish police procedurals in the 2000s'.[107] Nevertheless, Dahl establishes another type of metaphorical analogy where, inversely, anthropomorphic bodily characteristics are transferred onto society. This is made explicit in Dahl's first novel, *Misterioso* (*The Blinded Man*, 1999), in which Hjelm's superior in a conversation with his colleague makes this overt analogy between the human body and society:

> [T]he skin of this societal body, so loosely held together, is law enforcement. We're way out on the periphery, closest to the crimes, the most exposed of all. If the skin is cut open at the right place, the entrails of the societal body will come pouring out.[108]

The police are in a precarious membrane-like position. In *Mistorioso* there is a sense of the police performing the role of barricade against external forces. This image shifts in the *Opcop* series, where the use of the societal body metaphor expands into a European body of nations whose psychological and physical state is defined by internal instability and deterioration. At the end of *Viskleken*, the European investigation team is wrapping up the case and examining the traces on the digital wall. What they contemplate on the whiteboard is described by the narrator as '[a] completely mad and completely logical map of a continent in mental shambles. An unlikely constellation of connections between dying body parts. A nervous system drugged by money. A horrifying diagram of spiritual decay and cultural varnish.'[109] Significantly, this alternative map of Europe appears on the Opcop group's new digital whiteboard, which Hjelm's German colleague suggests should replace his old, printed atlas. The globalised world image can no longer be captured in traditional maps with fixed borders, but is better represented as a flexible flow map that can encapsulate the constantly changing complex geographies of international networks and migration. *Viskleken*'s mini-narrative thus describes a post-Westphalian and post-1989 Europe characterised by a large degree of transnational interference and exchanges in all areas.

The narrative allegory of the psychologically unstable and intoxicated European societal body, which does not bode well for the continent's future, is however countered by the existence of the Opcop group. In a world where the state economy has become deregulated and is partly in the hands of international criminal networks, there is a sense of solidarity and optimism embodied by the pan-European police unit. While the novel deals with the 'post-national' and with the destabilisation of old national categories of understanding, the overarching sentiment expressed in the conclusion to *Viskleken* pinpoints the inclusive and post-nostalgic creed voiced by Dahl's texts: 'we have saved a small but important European country [Latvia]. Most of all, we have shown that we as Europeans are able to work together without too much trouble. That is what points forward in all of this.'[110]

In the first instance, *Europa Blues* represents a timely fictional contribution to the revisions of historical memory taking place in Sweden around the time of the novel's publication. Re-examining and revealing elements of 'neutral' Sweden's participation in crimes committed by Nazi Germany is, however, not the novel's only critical function. Emphatically insisting on a postmodern reality, the novel creates a universe characterised by nation states no longer treatable as distinctive organic wholes, and where a social-democratic Swedish self-understanding is in the process of being transformed by neo-liberalism and economic globalisation. The ideology of the text then sets up parallels between neo-liberalism's commodification of interhuman relationships and the objectification of the Other that took place in concentration camps during the Second World War.

At plot level, the different cases in *Europa Blues* are linked to the Tower of Babel as symbolic representation of human hubris, narcissism and madness. Mimicking the biblical myth's confusion of languages, the novel includes a multitude of different voices, perspectives and modes all contributing to the creation of a polyphonic text, reflecting through its ambiguity at different levels the doubleness on which the novel thematically centres. Generically, the text situates itself in a field of intertextual conversation by explicitly drawing on and engaging with other crime fictional texts (Sjöwall and Wahlöö; Ellroy). The dialogical interrelationship is more than textual as it comes to represent the novel's fundamental idea of connectivity between texts, genres, cultures, nations, peoples and histories. The text's stylistic expression of a transgressive hybrid genre thus resembles the transgressive hybridity of identity that it represents.

Solving the cases depends on Hjelm's skills as translator and interpreter, in the same way that his own complex social identity is reliant on his skills in navigating different generic connections and cultural references. For Hjelm, for Söderstedt, and even for Sheinkman, it might not even be relevant to talk about *identity* as indicator of their respective modes of individual being within society, as these are expressions of non-static processes of constant negotiations and renegotiations. Rather, as Bauman has suggested, '[p]erhaps ... it would be more in keeping with the realities of the globalising world to speak of *identification*, a never-ending, always incomplete, unfinished and open-ended activity in which we all, by necessity or by choice, are engaged'.[111]

Conclusion: globalised identities, localised narratives

Manotti's and Dahl's texts deal with changing spaces and notions of national identity and citizenship in an increasingly globalised world. In *Bien connu des services de police* the spatial transformation is internal, consisting of the alteration of the cityscape in terms of both infrastructure and demography, whereas *Europa Blues* has an extroverted perspective, focusing on how Swedish identity is informed by a broader European and global transformation. The respective internal and external foci of Manotti's and Dahl's novels mirror to a certain extent how debates on identity issues are shaped in the two national contexts. Whereas French debates on nationality, ethnicity, gender, sexuality, and so forth centre on inherent interior problematics of the socio-political model of the Republic, the crisis of the Swedish welfare state is explained by way of heterogeneous external forces (internationalisation, Europeanisation, technological development, geopolitical transformations, global culture, neo-liberalism, etc.) disturbing the fundamentally 'good old' ways of the welfare state.

The parallel reading also highlights different ways of viewing the police's role in society and its position in relation to the national culture's dominant ideology. In Dahl's crime novels, the power of the collective is emphasised by the A-Unit and the Opcop group as collaborative entities protecting humanitarian values and accommodating diversity. The police procedural, as archetypical Swedish crime fiction template, serves the purpose of showcasing some form of stability by reflecting a microcosmic ideal of communal Scandinavian integrity, existing despite the failures and moral corruption of some individuals and elements within the state. In Manotti's novel there is no nostalgia: the grounds on which the current French state is built are shown to be fundamentally flawed and to have been so from the outset; the country's institutions are corrupt at all hierarchical levels to the extent that any positive development of society is reliant on the good nature of individuals regardless of their position within the state's administrative apparatus.

A key issue emerging here concerns the relationship between form and content: the question arises of why crime fiction should be a suitable medium for discussing identity issues. In relation to this, the observation might be made that crime narratives symbolically imitate in their very form the concepts of universalism and particularism. On the one hand, the genre's global and rigid form, a normative model, demands that the writer conform to a set of universal rules in order not to break the contract with the reader; on the other, the individual work of crime fiction is singular in that it contains both national or sometimes very local specificities, often reflecting also a particular approach to the genre.

PART II

Gender and Genre

3

Gender and Sexuality in the femikrimi *and the* polar au féminin

The *roman noir* seems an obvious genre in which to discuss issues concerning gender and sexuality, because of its history of essentialising women – and men – in static stereotypes, and a new generation of writers have used it precisely to engage with such stereotypes. Criticism analysing this phenomenon has been particularly occupied with the masculine dominance of the *noir* genre and the contestation of this universe by female writers. Véronique Desnain, commenting on the emergence of female crime writers in France, observes, for example, that 'fixed rules offer great potential for deconstruction and parody. It is therefore no surprise that female authors should have homed in on a genre [*noir*] which has until recently been fraught with macho clichés and androcentric preoccupations.'[1] It is no surprise either that feminist theory and feminist readings of crime fiction have also engaged in this critique. But, as this chapter will argue, feminist perspectives can also be of particular benefit in the critical analysis of crime fiction's engagement with wider issues of identity. Methodologically, the criticism in this chapter is aligned with issues of concern regarding identity politics by investigating the ways in which questions of female identity are approached by texts employing conventions of the *noir* genre.

National traditions have pigeonholed female writers concerned with contesting a previously male-dominated genre in categories accentuating a gender opposition to the genre's conservatism: the *Frauenkrimi* (Germany), women's detective fiction (US and UK), the *femikrimi* (Scandinavia) and the *polar au féminin* or *polar féminin* (France). Characteristically, but not unproblematically, these are categories formulated by media in the individual national contexts – perhaps under transnational influence – to describe the sensational novelty of a new publishing phenomenon. Actual definitions of these localised categorisations, however, prove harder to find, and both critical academic discussion and media representation have, in order to designate a work as 'female' or 'feminine', variously focused on the gender of the writer, the investigating protagonist or that of the perceived readership, frequently mixing these three entities into a jumbled pell-mell where the fictional texts get the least attention.

The first part of this chapter investigates this tradition by examining how the *polar au féminin* and the *femikrimi* have been analysed and represented in their respective national contexts. It seeks to demonstrate parallels and divergences in their reception by including theory, literary criticism and media commentary to establish whether there is a distinct national discourse surrounding novels addressing questions related to gender and identity. The chapter can thus be seen as a development of Nicola Barfoot's work in *Frauenkrimi/Polar féminin: Generic Expectations and the Reception of Recent French and German Crime Novels by Women* (2007), in which one conclusion drawn from her analysis is that French literary criticism tends to avoid dealing with a 'discourse of subversive intentions'.[2] Importantly also, however, this chapter offers a critique of the paradigm through which gender-focused criticism, specifically feminist criticism, approaches crime fiction, arguing that the categories it employs – female author, female writer, female reader – are problematic (notably in their exclusivity) and frequently reductive.

The second part of the chapter then aims to demonstrate how texts by crime writers from France and Scandinavia employ the genre as a vehicle to discuss gender and sexuality issues. Novels by Norwegian author Anne Holt are approached through thematic readings alongside the work of French author Maud Tabachnik in order to answer the following questions: how are questions of gender issues addressed in the texts? How is diversity in terms of sexuality discussed? How are normative gender perceptions approached in the novels? What constitutes gender socially and culturally in the Nordic and French contexts, and in which ways are identity formulations present in the texts?

French critical engagement with the polar au féminin

Gill Plain, identifying a shift in late twentieth-century Anglophone crime fiction away from a focus on security and stability, both when it comes to narrative resolution and in terms of the characteristics of the detective figure, reasons: 'we might argue that feminist and lesbian crime fiction's refusal of androcentric bourgeois methodologies was instrumental in bringing about this change'.[3] Despite a seemingly global movement revolting against generic rigidity and employing crime fiction to explore identity issues, these changes to the genre do not necessarily occur simultaneously in different national contexts; they have moreover taken varied forms. Likewise, national criticism examining this development is informed by both international trends and specific national discursive configurations.

In the American tradition of feminist criticism involved with women's detective fiction emerging in the early 1980s, particularly concerning the works of Sara Paretsky and Sue Grafton, the categorisation is frequently associated with destabilising activism and gender politics as two (if not indeed three) sides of the same coin. As Maureen Reddy remarks, 'feminist literary theory, feminism as a social movement and feminist crime novels have grown up together'.[4] The feminist readings that have dominated American criticism of female crime writings have in turn been linked with analysis of these works' contestation of male-dominated generic conventions – often with a political agenda characterised by Glenwood Irons as 'unwrit[ing] the idea of Woman in order to challenge it and make a brand-new genre'.[5] However, research on the female subject – whether author or protagonist – in crime fiction has not developed within feminist studies in France to the same extent as it has in the United States. By contrast, as Deborah Hamilton argues, 'in France, it is for the most part male critics who have politicized the *roman policier*, creating an explicit, self-conscious identity for the genre as progressive, based on its association to a universalistic, liberal republican model'.[6] Perhaps as a result of this, French writers adhering to the generic conventions of the French post-war *roman noir*, inspired by the American hard-boiled novel, remained, as Hamilton points out in a later article, for some time oblivious to the changes in traditional gender roles in the real world: 'the passivity of the female characters and the reductive polarisation of traditional female stereotypes as vamps or virgins … contrasted sharply with a growing diversity of women's roles and the blurring of boundaries that traditionally defined male-female relationships'.[7]

One of the earliest studies in French of female representation in the crime novel is Anne Lemonde's *Les Femmes et le roman policier* (1984), in which the absence of well-defined female characters in twentieth-century crime fiction is considered:

> Whether one dwells on the female reading public, on women authors or on characters who are exploited women (and this is indeed the case) in

the crime novel, it's hard to say that a feeling of unease emerges. Female roles are curiously distributed, spread out here and there, difficult to trace, to schematise, without any really convincing features.[8]

Lemonde's intervention can be seen as a starting point for critical engagement with problematics of gender in French crime fiction. It might also be seen as symptomatic of subsequent French criticism in that several critical categories that could productively be considered separately are discussed as constituting one unitary phenomenon.

Another factor identified by critics as having played a role in preventing serious critical discussion of gender issues is constituted by conditions within the publishing industry. The French publishing landscape's two major crime fiction 'collections', Librairie des Champs Elysées's Le Masque and Gallimard's Série noire – launched respectively in 1927 and 1945 – have symbolically divided writers and reading audiences based on subgenre and gender. Le Masque, which published the first French translations of Agatha Christie, has, as Barfoot argues, 'had a somewhat ladylike image, highly susceptible to ridicule'.[9] Desnain notes that this imprint, having published women writers since the 1930s, 'was seen as specializing in more "gentle" non-violent whodunnit narratives and therefore ideally suited to female writers'.[10] By contrast the Série noire's translations of American hard-boiled novels have been regarded as more prestigious by French critics and media with prominent literary figures such as Raymond Queneau and Jean-Paul Sartre praising this collection.[11] A lack of critical interest in novels by female writers is explained precisely by the fact that they are writing in a less respected subgenre. The masculine *noir* universe, as opposed to the supposedly more feminine one found in the *roman à énigme*, symbolised respectively by the two iconic French crime fiction collections, is therefore reflective of an oppositional division based on gender (of both writers and readers). This hierarchical order has immanently informed critical discussion of the emergence of the *polar au féminin* in France. In her analysis of the influence of the Série noire in her – much quoted but rarely referenced – 1994 PhD thesis, 'The French Detective Fiction Novel 1920's to 1990's: Gendering a Genre', Hamilton demonstrates precisely how the politics of French detective fiction aesthetics has been predominantly masculine, and how – through imagery and textual description in marketing material from other publishing houses – women's roles and women writers have been marginalised.[12] Although separate from the actual fictional articulation of questions of gender, this underscores the importance of the publishing industry in shaping representation of gender and other identities.

From a publisher's point of view, Patrick Raynal argues that the change in the crime fiction landscape comes from a new editorial openness towards female writers previously ignored by the publishing business. Raynal – editor-in-chief of Gallimard's Série noire from 1991 to 2004 – explains in 1996: 'I opened the pages of the Série noire to about ten women', aiming to 'change the macho image clinging to the skin of the *roman noir*'. The shift in the industry, however, has not been enough to encourage female writers of crime fiction: 'they still send me very few manuscripts ... I hope that will change.'[13] Raynal's statement bears witness to the shifting landscape in the mid-1990s of French publishing's attitudes towards writers' gender. The boom in the *polar au féminin* and the media attention that it attracted occurred simultaneously with the burgeoning interest in foreign literature being translated into French; for example, crime fiction from the Nordic countries. These changes in attitude in the field of literary production are furthermore emphasised in the multitude of new publishing houses – and new 'collections' within existing ones – created in the 1990s and 2000s, accommodating specialised niche crime fiction genres.[14]

A number of critics have been concerned with writing the history of female crime writers in France, concurring that critical discussion in the 1980s and 1990s focuses on the sudden appearance of female writers and has largely ignored earlier female writers of the genre.[15] Despite earlier publications by women, it seems, however, that the gender/genre dichotomy between the *noir* and the *roman à énigme* had to be broken in order for female writers to be acknowledged as serious contenders on the market. Michel Abescat, journalist for *Le Monde*, acknowledges that even though there have been women writing crime novels in French literary history, 'what is really new is the arrival of women in the universe of the *roman noir*'.[16] That the hierarchical gendered division is discontinued when female writers start writing *noir* is frequently stressed in media engagement with the new publishing phenomenon, as this quotation from an article in *Lire* implicitly suggests: 'It's not at all a question of detailing a drawing-room mystery; they are pounding the muddy paths at the heart of *noir*.'[17]

In French media coverage, the *polar au féminin* is treated as a publishing phenomenon like the *noir nordique*, and new female authors' considerable impact on the literary market in terms of sales figures is frequently commented on: 'the *polar* girls are shaking up tradition and making advances on the bestseller lists ... invading the market'.[18] There is also here a universal template applied to the 'sensational' emergence of the subgenre. When French media in the early 1990s start commenting on the *polar au féminin*, its approach was centred on the occurrence of female authors and not on the way in which the texts themselves discuss gender identity issues. In the first instance, the emphasis is mainly on the influence and superiority in terms of numbers of female writers from the Anglophone world: 'If "authoresses" have always been in a minority in the French-language crime novel, it is not the same story in Britain or the United States where no one bothers to keep count of them any longer.'[19] Media treatment of the emergence of a French *polar féminin* then focuses almost solely on female intrusion into a market traditionally dominated by male writers, and often there is a presumed equivalence of the female writer with the female detective. The vocabulary surrounding the representation of the 'new' female authors re-utilises tropes from the *noir* genre's depiction of women, evoking the possibly dangerous potential behind female beauty. Journalistic headlines such as 'Détectives en talons aiguilles' (Detectives in High Heels), 'De quelques femmes à la plume meurtrière' (Women with Killer Pens), 'Polar, les femmes renouvellent le genre en beauté' (Women Re-beautify the *Polar* Genre) reinvest associations of the femme fatale in the image of the female author of crime fiction.[20] The dominant metaphor employed by the press to describe the feminine renewal of the genre is consequently that of a violent (armed) attack on the genre: 'Les filles à l'assaut du polar' (Girls on the *Polar* Assault), 'Polars: les femmes attaquent' (*Polar* novels: Women on the Attack), 'Les nouvelles armes du polar se dégainent au féminin' (*Polar*'s New Weapons Whipped Out in Womanly Style), or 'Polars – sale temps pour les durs à cuire!: La mort des machos' (*Polars* – Rough Times for Tough Guys! The Death of Macho Men).[21] This lexical field, apparently situating the woman author as a mirror image of the hard-boiled detective, is also repeated in titles for articles about individual writers: 'Avec Maud Tabachnik, chaque mot est une balle' (For Maud Tabachnik, Every Word is a Bullet).[22]

Indeed, Maud Tabachnik (1938–) is an interesting case in point: she is emblematic of female crime writers who use the genre as a vehicle for feminist activism.[23] Tabachnik, who lets some of her female characters enact vengeful mutilation and murder of men as a way of contesting patriarchal societal structures, has – like many other socially critical crime fiction writers – also entered public debate and produced a considerable amount of non-fictional commentary. In a gender-political article from 1997, Tabachnik takes as her starting point the expression *cherchez la femme* (look for the woman) in order to determine that the role of the female fictional character in crime fiction is a figure who 'par définition' and 'par détermination' is guilty.[24] The author then categorises female characters found in crime fiction in a number of classes: the 'femme fatale' as the immediate adversary of the principal masculine character; the 'oie blanche' described as 'the young woman, natural blonde, in love and silly'; the 'women-mother figure'; 'the secretary'; and the 'woman-victim' (often because she has 'asked for it').[25] Her analysis of crime-fiction tropes extends into a depiction of French society, where language itself articulates a consensus whereby women are considered victims and it is unthinkable to conceive of women as persecutors: 'men are misogynistic, so why shouldn't women be misandrist? Need I add that this word is not in the dictionary?'[26] Highly aware of the identity issues at stake in crime fiction, Tabachnik thus situates her own crime writing as a female response to male dominance by problematising and transcending the fixed female typology.

Tabachnik's engagement, both in her fictional writings and in her polemical journalism, provides an example of how some French female crime writers intentionally employ the genre, and the critical potential of its conventions and typologies, as a platform for subversive feminist writing with a pronounced political agenda. Some mainstream media commentary may stress the femininity rather than the feminism of contemporary French crime fiction written by women, but even where this is the case, metaphors of combat and struggle are used. It is noticeable that this 'subgenre' – which clearly assumes that the *polar* as mimetic fiction has the potential through its own conventions and typologies to provide critical insight into those of the society it represents – is one that is engaged in a combative critical struggle, and, as a closer reading of Tabachnik's fiction shows, it engages through its subject matter and themes in a transgressive critique of a society seen as repressively patriarchal, and of conventions of genre and gender that reinforce patriarchal norms.

Scandinavian critical engagement with the femikrimi

While French critical engagement with the emergence of the *polar au féminin* is particularly concerned with the contestation of patriarchal structures immanent in the *noir* genre, critical discussion of the *femikrimi* adopts a different perspective. This can in part be understood as an effect of the generic development in the Nordic countries, where the mystery novel dominated the market until the politically engaged police procedural took over in the mid-1960s. Arguably, the general absence of the *roman noir* in the post-war Scandinavian tradition has generated a less pronounced experience of a gendered paradigmatic shift in the genre compared with the French tradition.

In Scandinavia, female crime writers attracted media attention later than in France. It was not until the late 1990s that categorisations such as the Danish 'femikrimi' or the Swedish 'deckardrottningar' (queens of crime fiction) started appearing in the press. This, however, does not mean that crime novels concerned with the representation of women and gender identity issues were not published before then. This is especially true of Norway, where female writers – Kim Småge in the early 1980s, followed by her compatriots Karin Fossum and Anne Holt in the early 1990s – began publishing novels with a thematic insistence on gender issues. Following the success of Liza Marklund (1962–) and later Camilla Läckberg (1974–) in Sweden, women writers have had a strong influence on the market, as Kerstin Bergman asserts in 2014: 'There are many strong trends in Swedish crime fiction from the past decade, but *the* most notable trend is unquestionably the influx and presence of so many women crime writers.'[27]

Scandinavian female authors generally write within the police procedural tradition with a female criminal investigator as the recurring protagonist: in Norway, Kim Småge's Anne-Kin Halvorsen and Anne Holt's Hanne Wilhelmsen; Swedish authors Åsa Nilsonne's Monika Pedersen and Helene Tursten's Irene Huss; and Danish author Sara Blædel's Louise Rick, to name but a few. Another popular profession for the protagonist is journalism (examples are Gretelise Holm's Karen Sommer, Liza Marklund's Annika Bengtzon or Elsebeth Egholm's Dicte Svendsen). It could be said that these writers, as Bergman argues with reference to Marklund, 'use the procedural genre in a tabloid newspaper environment, portraying a team of investigative journalists working at the crime desk'.[28] As a contrast, it is interesting to note that not many female protagonists in the *polar au féminin* function within the framework of the police institution. As Desnain concludes: '[French female writers] present women who are at once victims, survivors and avengers. Few of the characters written by women are professional investigators.'[29] Desnain further gives an explanation to the choice of the *noir* genre by French women writers: 'the lone wolf of

American fiction is not dissimilar to the disenfranchised women who must resort to cunning rather than official challenge in their search for justice and who are constantly confronted with obstacles put in their way by a male-centred society'.[30] Perhaps because Scandinavian writers remain more faithful to a subgeneric template (the police procedural) that does not have quite the same masculine characteristics as the *noir* genre, they produce texts that are less overtly challenging and controversial.

If there is in Scandinavian criticism an interpretation of the *femikrimi* as a contestation of male hegemony, the position is usually argued in literary historical terms with reference to the American feminist crime novel functioning as an intermediary between the hard-boiled tradition and the Scandinavian *femikrimi*:

> The Anglo-American hardboiled feminist crime fiction is historically a prerequisite for the new Nordic *femikrimis* ... but they [the American female detectives] preserve the identification with the male detective, the lone wolf, who ... lets his identity and sexuality merge with the detective function.[31]

The accentuation of the femininity of the Scandinavian female detectives in comparison with the masculinity of the protagonists of Sara Paretsky and Sue Grafton is comprised in the lexis itself: the prefix 'femi-' can both be read as 'feminine' and 'feminist'. 'In a *femi-krimi* the detective's gender forms part of the genre convention, because a *femi-krimi* in brief can be determined as a crime narrative created by a female author with a female protagonist and a gender-political agenda.'[32] The genre's typology defined here by Hejlsted can seem reductive.[33] Nevertheless, these three ingredients in Hejlsted's definition seem to be the main focus points for Scandinavian media engagement with the *femikrimi*.

In academic criticism, the welfare state with its general equal opportunities for men and women is often highlighted as one of the reasons for the emergence of the *femikrimi*. Nestingen and Arvas, for example, read the phenomenon within 'the context of the broad egalitarianism of the Scandinavian states' – the culmination of a socio-political movement giving Scandinavian women voting rights early in the twentieth century was developed under the social-democratic governments during the post-war period and was further reinforced by 'strong feminist movements and state-feminist policies since the 1970s'.[34] Interesting, also, is the line Nestingen and Arvas draw back to the pan-Scandinavian literary and theoretical movement *Det moderne gennembrud* (the Modern Breakthrough) in the 1870s and 1880s, where gender politics was a prominent theme, discussed openly through the medium of fiction. The concerns of this naturalist and realist movement, the authors argue, 'have been taken in new directions through revisions of the socially critical crime novel's gender politics'.[35] While the emergence of the French *polar au féminin* is frequently discussed within a paradigm of *limitations* for women (masculine genre conventions, essentialising and stereotypical roles attributed to women in the *noir* genre, lack of publishing possibilities, etc.), the critical discussion surrounding the emergence of the Scandinavian *femikrimi* is contrastingly often developed in terms of *opportunities* provided historically by the egalitarian nature of the welfare state. Perhaps because of this socio-political background understanding of the emergence in the late 1990s of the *femikrimi*, academic engagement with the genre has been particularly occupied with writing the early history of female crime writers and with pointing out that there has been a strong presence of female authorship dating back to the nineteenth century.[36]

While Bergman in her analysis of the increasing success and proliferation of Swedish female writers makes a note of the fact that 'Sweden is still a patriarchal society', the factors that constitute the most important threat to the country's gender egalitarianism are also what threatens the welfare state more broadly: 'The last decades have also witnessed intensifying privatization of the public sector (education, health care, care of the elderly, infrastructure), a development that brings with it not only growing class differences, but also increased gender inequalities.'[37] This development is seen by Nestingen and Arvas as something imposed from the outside world which is having an impact on the Scandinavian countries' literatures: 'with the European Union adhering to neoliberal policies in key areas, the Scandinavian welfare states continued to alter old policies for new market-based and consumer-oriented thinking during the first decade of the twenty-first century'.[38]

Despite there being a clear political context for its engagement with gender issues, the *femikrimi* did not – at least in Sweden – emerge from a grassroots awakening of feminist consciousness. In fact, the Swedish *femikrimi* was brought to life somewhat artificially by the intervention of the Swedish crime fiction journal *Jury*. Having looked with envy on the success of Norwegian female writers and recognised, given the popularity of translated female crime writers, that there was an obvious market for crime writing of this kind, the journal set out to identify and cultivate home-grown talent.[39] In 1997, *Jury* established the Poloni Prize to be given to 'promising female crime fiction writers', and Liza Marklund was the first winner, awarded for her novel *Sprängaren* (*The Bomber*) in 1998. This year marks the ignition of the phenomenon: *Sprängaren* became a huge sales success, *Jury* launched a creative writing course for female crime writers, in cooperation with the publishing house Ordfront, and a further twelve Swedish female crime writers were published. The new 'genre' was marketed as being 'by women, about women and for women', a categorisation that revealed not only a concern with promoting female writers, but also with finding its audience among female readers.[40] Commercial imperatives might thus be said to have played a role in the emergence of the *femikrimi* as a consumer-marketed cultural product with a specific targeted readership: for example, Liza Marklund's novels were sent out as supplements to the Danish women's magazine *Søndag*.[41]

It is clear, then, that to some extent the *femikrimi* is subject to a form of industry-sponsored mediatisation, as might be expected in the case of any literary product, irrespective of genre. In this case, the mediatisation process exploits the novelty of the woman writer, but also associates her with a supposed feminist agenda. So on the one hand, press articles focus on the gender of writers and their success stories, a tendency summarised by Sara Kärrholm in an article where she dubs Camilla Läckberg and Liza Marklund 'two contemporary Cinderellas'.[42] Their Prince Charming – in the form of a readership – has finally arrived. Elsewhere, there is much reference to Danish, Norwegian or Swedish 'queens of crime fiction', a label generally applied to any successful female crime writer from the individual Nordic countries. At the crasser end of this spectrum, this new wave of crime novels received primarily as *feminine* rather than feminist is categorised as 'chick-lit', as when Egholm Andersen uses the term *læbestiftslitteratur* – 'lipstick literature' – in the title of his book.[43] On the other hand, the phenomenon has been received in some quarters as more properly feminist, but at the same time its feminist agenda is still understood to be part of a marketing ploy. For example, Kärrholm states that 'Liza Marklund's feminist position has from the beginning been a considerable part of her trademark.'[44] Even more explicitly, Sarrimo asserts that 'the mediatized feminist position is a possible way of establishing oneself as an author'.[45] With specific reference to Marklund and what she names 'the feminist literature factory',

Sarrimo argues that 'the contour [has] been drawn by a media logic which creates an intensification of intimacy often with commercial incentives. The personal face and the personal experience are important ingredients in this process of increasing intimacy.'[46] A feminist agenda is just one aspect of a self-marketing programme, which, in the case of Marklund, can even be seen in a conscious linking of her authorial identity with that of her protagonist Annika Bengtzon, who shares the 'z' of her forename. As feminism becomes subsumed within femininity, the political becomes subsumed within the personal – the essential component of the appeal to the market.

At the very least, it is problematic to claim that the Scandinavian *femikrimi* has a feminist agenda without contextualising any such agenda within the commercial promotion of the genre. In France, by contrast, despite some media focus on the femininity of authors and protagonists, the fiction examined seems to indicate a much more conscious and considered feminist critique of gender norms in society, particularly with regard to the blind spot in the attitude of universalist republican discourse towards gender issues. These French examples in turn relate the question of gender to wider issues of identity. Perhaps most significantly, as the following readings will confirm, where the Scandinavian *femikrimi* endorses a late twentieth-century liberal consensus on gender, whereby difference is unproblematic, and individuals previously considered 'other' in terms of gender or sexual identities are integrated without controversy within society, the French *polar féminin* offers a much more radical reading of contemporary society, in which gender becomes a means of transgression.

Anne Holt's women: private and public identities

Anne Holt commenced her career as a crime fiction writer in 1993 with the novel *Blind Gudinne* (*Blind Goddess*, 1993), featuring the Oslo-based police investigator Hanne Wilhelmsen as the main protagonist. The novels about Wilhelmsen constitute one of two different series by Holt, the other of which presents another female character, the psychologist and profiler Johanne Vik. Holt situates her fictional discussion of gender roles in these two series within an egalitarian understanding of feminism. In response to a French journalist's question, 'What's your definition of feminism?', she answers: 'Very simply: feminism is the belief that the value of men and women is exactly the same. The value of them as people, the value of their work, of their contributions. As a consequence of which their rights should be the same.'[47] This is, in fact, representative of the kind of feminism that is to be found in the Scandinavian *femikrimi*; that is, a feminism based firmly on equality and rights, which can be seen as being broadly consistent with the Scandinavian social model.

The following reading concentrates on one novel from each of Holt's cycles: *Salige er de som tørster* (*Blessed Are Those Who Thirst*, 1994) – the second novel in the Wilhelmsen series, currently counting ten volumes – and *Det som aldri skjer* (*The Final Murder*, 2004) – the second novel of five about Vik. The analysis examines how these two novels, each with a different type of female main protagonist, explore aspects of public and private identities created as both social and personal constructs.

In the same way that Sjöwall and Wahlöö's characters develop through the *Story of a Crime* series in the 1960s and 1970s, each of Anne Holt's recurring female investigators (Wilhelmsen and Vik) undergoes a personal development mirroring conditions within Norwegian society during a period of social change and globalisation from 1993 to the present day. Anne Holt's novels are all set in contemporary Norway, a country ranking highest in international indexes alongside the other Nordic countries when it comes to gender equality.[48] Anne Holt's novels have indeed been described as '[expressing] renewed faith in Norwegian society and its inherent "goodness", as well as in its ability to become more inclusive'.[49] However, this positive take comes up against counter-arguments not only in the themes accentuated in many of Holt's novels (of violence against women, rape, injustice towards immigrant women, and so on), but also in the way questions of identity intermingle with the structure of the crime narrative.

Det som aldri skjer showcases the investigation of a killer on a deadly search for high-profile, good-looking celebrities. The narrative explores and comments on the media-saturated public sphere and is interspersed with sensationalist press coverage of what becomes known as the 'Celebrity Killer'. The celebrity culture is strikingly contrasted with the narration of the everyday minutiae in the lives of the investigators Adam Stubø and Johanne Vik, who both work and live together. In the novel's opening chapter, the couple have just had a daughter, and Stubø gets himself and Vik's daughter from a previous marriage ready to go the hospital to pick up the newborn baby and her mother. The birth coincides with that of Norway's new princess, and in the mind of 10-year-old Kristiane, the two events meld together:

'Princess Mette-Marit is so pretty. She is on TV. Leonard's mummy said a princess had been born. My sister.'[50] The child's comment sets out the novel's theme of a mediatised public space and its intersection with a domestic, private life. The narration conveys this by having alternating chapters set in the domestic sphere – where focus is on family activities (nappy changing, breastfeeding, care for the older daughter and food preparation) – and in a public sphere dominated by social and professional activities. The private–public divide is blurred when Vik – as a mother on maternity leave – gets personally and professionally involved in the murder cases.

Salige er de som tørster discusses other aspects of private and public identities through the prism of the Hanne Wilhelmsen character. Her investigation of two cases – the brutal rape of a young woman and the serial murders of female asylum seekers – is interposed with the parallel narration of Wilhelmsen's relationship with Cecilie, her lover. Over the course of the series, her lesbian identity undergoes a progressive transition from a strictly private taboo subject to an essential feature of her public and professional persona.

The professional female identities of the respective investigators in both novels intersect with private female identities (as mothers, partners, lovers, neighbours, and so on). Two female victim figures furthermore highlight the blurring of the public–private divide in *Det som aldri skjer*: the celebrity and the prostitute. These are two figures who are interconnected by the fact that they are both *femmes publiques*, that is, public property. It becomes apparent that once a woman has taken on either public identity, that identity becomes a case of professional performance, which excludes the possibility of having a private self. The celebrity's media prostitution is symbolically also an act of undressing and sharing a stylised intimacy with a public audience: when the first murder victim, Vibeke Heinerback, has just been elected Norway's youngest party leader, she gives an interview from her bathtub: 'The papers and magazines were all in raptures about her evening bath. Vibeke raised a glass of champagne to the readers from a sea of pink bubbles, with her smooth, beautifully shaped leg hanging over the edge of the bath' (p. 36). Both female figures have to accept what is coming to them, which ultimately, within the novel's optic, is death. Even after death, displays of intimate parts of life and body continue for public observation and consumption: literally on the police station's noticeboard where 'a poster-sized picture of a bare-breasted, open-legged Fiona Helle screamed at them' (p. 27), and figuratively in the multiple references

100

to the tabloid press's scrutiny of the lives of the murdered celebrities. What separates the prostitute and the celebrity is a hierarchical order based on society's judgement. Whereas there is immense media coverage of the murder of Vibeke Heinerback and TV talk-show star Fiona Helle – a beautiful politician and 'the ultimate example of young Scandinavian success' (p. 35) – the death of a drug-addicted prostitute found in a multistorey car park gets little attention, either from the press or from the police:

> Katrina Olsson was cremated three days later, and no one bothered to erect a stone to mark the remains of the late thirty-something prostitute. The four children she had brought into life before she was thirty would never know that their biological mother carried baby pictures of them in her otherwise empty wallet. (p. 35)

The circumstances of women – whether empowered or powerless – effectively exercise control over the advancement of the plot: the first three murders are committed against women, the murderer is a woman and Vik, despite the fact that she is on maternity leave, becomes the investigator, who by knowledge and intuition 'solves' the murder case. However, the case is dominated by men, with Stubø and Siegmund Berli as the active investigators. All of the main suspects are men and the general assumption is that the murderer is a man, as implied by the insistence on the use of the personal pronoun *he* during the investigation. Vik struggles from the beginning to contest the common way of thinking when asked to give a first intuitive profiling of the murderer: '"it would be a woman," she said slowly. "Simply because we always imagine it to be a man"' (p. 79).

The subtly subversive tone of the narrative challenges the way the police institution works. When the head of the National Criminal Investigation Service, referred to as 'the boss', belittles Vik, it is with reference to the fact that female qualities in ways of thinking do not suit the way the police operate:

> No one knows better than we do that hard work and the systematic processing of all new evidence is the only way to go. We are a modern organization, but not so modern that we would throw weeks of intensive, good police work out the window because some woman feels and thinks and believes that maybe she knows. (p. 314)

The fact is that Vik does have vital evidence, which she is able to analyse on the basis of previous professional experience. It is clearly not the case that she merely 'feels and thinks' that she knows what the true circumstances of the crime are: the narrative subtly and implicitly undermines the senior colleague's claim.

Boredom

In the postscript to *Det som aldri skjer*, Anne Holt acknowledges Lars Svendsen's philosophical essay *Kjedsomhetens filosofi* (*A Philosophy of Boredom*, 1999), which she describes as 'a great source of inspiration and help in writing [the novel]' (p. 343). Boredom is indeed one of the novel's prevailing themes and operates not only as the motive behind the murderer Wencke Bencke's serial killings, but is also more generally employed to describe contemporary Norwegian society:

> Where there is a lack of personal meaning, all sorts of diversions have to create a substitute – an ersatz-meaning. Or the cult of celebrities, where one gets completely engrossed in the lives of others because one's own life lacks meaning. Is our fascination with the bizarre, fed daily by the mass media, not a result of our awareness of the boring?[51]

This collapse of 'personal meaning' is expressed by Vik's daughter Kristiane, whom her mother catches one evening in her room with a knife in her hand:

> Johanne sat down on the bed and carefully loosened her daughter's hand and took the knife. 'You musn't ... It's dangerous ...' Only then she noticed the dolls' heads. The Barbies had been decapitated. Their hair had been cut off and lay like old golden Christmas decorations on the duvet. (p. 259)

To her mother's question of why she has ruined her dolls, Kristiane answers 'Don't know Mummy. I was bored ... I was so bored' (p. 259). The Barbie doll – with the toy's heavily loaded symbolism connected to materialism, celebrity and gendered stereotypes – metaphorically becomes a pendant to the four murders that Bencke has committed. Little girls are supposed to identify with the gendered values symbolised by the doll, and Kristiane rebelliously acts out her boredom by 'killing' the flawed identification objects representing a cultural 'ersatz-meaning'. Similar expectations are placed on Bencke who repeatedly talks about her boredom with life as a celebrity crime writer and the existential emptiness she experiences, to which the only remedy is going to the extreme.

Svendsen asserts that '[i]f boredom increases, it means that there is a serious fault in society or culture as a conveyor of meaning'.[52] The analysis of boredom and how it relates to a Western societal malaise is put into the thoughts of the two main female characters (the murderer and the investigator), who both seem to have an analytical understanding of this modern condition. While the male investigators are looking for clues and evidence in the murder cases, the more profound psycho-societal interpretation of the killings is located within the minds of the female characters. Bencke, as the writer of popular crime novels, also affirms that she is writing her own story: 'I'm writing a crime novel about a crime writer who starts killing people because she is bored' (p. 320). The *mise en abyme* of a fictional 'autofiction' encompasses both *Det som aldri skjer*'s narrator as a projection of Bencke, and a supposed real reader, who finds him or herself mirrored in the novel's fictional readers of Bencke's crime stories. The consumption of the crime novel offers the intradiegetic reader a thrill that is a literary reproduction of Bencke's own thrill deriving from the 'extreme sport' of killing another person and getting away with it. *Det som aldri skjer* thus provides a meta-commentary on crime fiction as a means of entertainment consumed to escape the meaninglessness of modern life. Projection of reality into fiction and vice versa is made explicit when towards the novel's end, in a climactic finale, Bencke appears on a TV talk show and the interviewer asks her with reference to her crime novel career: 'how many people have *you* killed over the years?' (p. 300).

Missing pieces

The polyphonic nature of both novels gives voice to all actants in the cases (investigators, victims, criminals, witnesses and their relatives). This diversity of voices not only creates a dramatic suspense in the novel, by making the knowledge of the narrator and the reader greater than that of the investigator's, it also raises important questions about truth and the legal system's capability of exposing it and seeing justice done. These novels' manipulation of generic conventions thus goes beyond the mere fact of having a crime with no resolution: it directly challenges the legal framework understood as representational code, offering security and the certainty that the criminal will be held responsible. The crime narrative, for Todorov the coupling of 'story of the crime' and 'story of the investigation', thus finds in Anne Holt's novels a third 'story', which we could name the 'public story' – the story as it appears (or does not appear) as a story within the legal system and/or the media – and which is constantly in conflict with the narrative of the investigation.[53] Although the reader and the investigators are aware of who the culprit is, there is no legal or public resolution and the killer either goes free (*Det som aldri skjer*), or justice is seen to be done outside the legal system (*Salige er de som tørster*). By the end the reader has been provided with the information necessary to reconstruct the 'story of the crime', but the public story does not find a resolution. This narrative breakdown is thus closely linked to implicit allegations against social inequalities.

The missing clue in Stubø and Berli's investigation is the dead prostitute. When her body is discovered the police draw a rapid conclusion rendered in free indirect discourse: 'she died of an overdose and no [one] would ever ask after her' (p. 35). The novel makes use of generic expectations according to which prostitutes commonly appear as (female) victims. However, what appears to be an insignificant side-plot – the death of an insignificant character – is the important textual 'trigger', which remains unrevealed to the investigators, but not to the reader. Before killing the prostitute, Bencke allowed her to use her credit card for a day in order to create an alibi for herself for the murder of the second celebrity. The investigating team are incapable of proving that Bencke is the murderer precisely because the dead prostitute does not get the same degree of attention from the police as do the murdered celebrities. Plot and societal representation thus become intermingled. The resolution of the traditional crime narrative (through legal retribution) is ultimately hindered by entrenched class division.

In *Det som aldri skjer* the death of the prostitute and the lack of significance placed on this constitute the missing piece; in *Salige er de som tørster* it is another minority group at the fringe of society that is not given a voice. The first potential witness Wilhelmsen interviews after the rape is an 89-year-old man and neighbour of the victim in the apartment block. After a cup of coffee and inedible stale cake in his apartment, Wilhelmsen classifies the hunch-backed man in an interior monologue as a 'waste of time' and draws the conversation to a quick close.[54] However, when the narrative perspective shifts to the man after Wilhelmsen has left, it becomes apparent that he holds important information and also provides an overview of social change in Norway:

> He had lived in the same apartment all his life, watching as horses and carts were replaced by noisy motorcars, gas lamps disappeared as they

were overtaken by the advantages of electric lights, and cobblestones were covered over by dark-gray asphalt. He knew his neighbourhood well, at least as far as he could see from his window on the first floor. He knew which cars belonged here and who owned them. The red car was one he hadn't seen before. Neither had he known the tall, well-built young man who had driven off in the early hours either. It must have been him. (p. 38)

By failing to apply equal significance to all bearers of information, the investigator becomes representative of a society where all inhabitants are not treated with the same respect and acknowledgement. Again, the police's refusal to listen to a vulnerable population group becomes detrimental to the solving of the case.

As a contrast to this investigative discrimination, subtle textual clues appear, embedded in the narrative, challenging the modus operandi of an inhuman, faceless police apparatus. Public dissatisfaction with the police's lack of progress in solving cases is countered with a metonymic description of the Oslo police headquarters: 'The elongated, curved building sat there at Grønlandsleiret 44, grey and unshakable, seemingly unmoved by all the merciless criticism ... the awnings were pulled down ... making it appear both blind and deaf' (pp. 7–8). The revolt against the non-engagement and impenetrability symbolised by the grey construction comes from the inside: Wilhelmsen, in this case representing a contrast to the police institution's emotionless taciturnity, alters the appearance of the building's eyes to the world. This change is noticed by her colleague Håkon Sand when he comes into her office: 'It struck him as soon as he entered. She had new curtains. They weren't exactly police regulation. Periwinkle blue with meadow flowers' (p. 29). The symbolic subversive action carried out against these 'state-issued rags' establishes the character of Wilhelmsen as a rebel within the police institution. An attempt to extend her insubordination to her closest colleague fails however: '"Sewed some for you as well" ... Police Attorney Håkon Sand accepted the pile of material with enthusiasm, immediately spilling his entire cup of coffee over it' (p. 29).

The overt reaction against conformity and normativity, taking the form of a personal domestication of the public space, does not, however, extend to Wilhelmsen's own private life. The fact that she has for a long time been in a lesbian relationship is something that she does not share even with her closest colleagues. Her sexual orientation and her fear of its exposure to her co-workers is of major concern to Wilhelmsen, while Cecilie, her partner, frequently challenges this closeted existence to the extent that it becomes a source of conflict in their relationship. Throughout the series, Wilhelmsen develops a more and more relaxed attitude to public knowledge of her gay identity. This, however, has more to do with personal development and increased maturity than with the attitudes of her professional environment, where her colleagues generally exhibit open-mindedness and approve of diversity. Wilhelmsen's sexuality is, as Rees argues, in many ways portrayed 'as part of the mainstream in contemporary Norway' to the extent that she can be labelled 'straight queer'.[55] It becomes apparent that identity is both a private and a public construct. Wilhelmsen exhibits protean identities in different contexts, and her lesbian identity is not the only one jeopardising the work–life balance: admitting to her neighbours in the apartment block where she lives that she is a police officer also poses difficulties for her. Personal integrity becomes a central theme as Wilhelmsen's development is intertwined with her interaction with her surroundings.

Democratic negotiation

What is clear from the above is that a mode of representation of women that is sensitive to gender politics is essential to Anne Holt's fictional work. Holt's protagonists are typically complex, multifaceted female characters who juggle private and public identities and who do not fall into a conventional typology of repressed womanhood. While the representation engages with gender issues, it is, in fact, not premised on gender or sexuality per se, but rather on individual characteristics and qualities.

A further feature of Holt's fiction is a noticeable focus on family life and relationships. The individual is firmly contextualised within both intimate and more wide-ranging social networks. These networks, moreover, notably in the case of victims, facilitate an intersectionality of identities: there is frequently an overlap between categories such as immigrant woman, violated woman, lesbian woman and professional woman. A related and important theme is marginalisation, articulated along with social inequalities through exposition within the crime fiction template. As well as the alienation of the marginalised, Holt's fiction – in its focus on boredom and celebrity culture – also expresses the alienation of the supposedly contented (and privileged) mainstream.

If Vik and Wilhelmsen in relation to all these themes become pivots for psycho-social understanding, it is significant that these female protagonists' individual and often alternative views (on the investigation, on the police institution, on relationships) do not stand alone. Conclusions are not solely drawn on the basis of the female characters' own observations and interpretations, but are continuously negotiated through dialogues with their surrounding environment. Negotiation of meaning is an in-built characteristic of the police procedural where the criminal investigator functions as part of a team, and Holt's choice of genre – in keeping with that of the *femikrimi* generally – emphasises dialogue and democratic processes also when it comes to discussing gender issues.

Maud Tabachnik: rewriting/re-gendering the hard-boiled novel

If Anne Holt's work is in some sense representative of an engaged crime fiction that is non-confrontational and consensus-seeking and in which non-normative gender identities are presented as banal and non-threatening, a radically different approach can be found in the work of Maud Tabachnik (1938–), which proposes an uncompromising and destabilising critique of heteronormative discourse on genre, gender, sexuality and identity. Tabachnik's work is, as Gorrara notes, 'always articulated in feminist terms' and expressed through a 'revisionist imagery'.[56] In Tabachnik's novels, this feminist revision of the genre is proposed both through an inversion of masculine–feminine taxonomy and through a textual investigation of various forms of sexuality, and in particular female homosexuality. Using this double approach, then, Tabachnik challenges a heteronormative consensus.

The following reading of Tabachnik's crime novel, *Un été pourri* (A Rotten Summer, 1994), considers how perceived notions of gender, sexualities and power relationships between men and women are refracted through a rewriting of the hard-boiled novel. Significantly, this generic modification of this subgenre takes place within an American setting, the United States being its birthplace. This dislocation places the text within a specific generic tradition and evidently implies a commentary on transcultural transfer in the history of the genre. However, and perhaps more importantly, it also – by way of the conspicuous and unspoken absence of the French context – offers a reflection on how difficult it is to engage with debates on identity issues within the ideological context of French republicanism. Tabachnik employs a manipulated form of the hard-boiled novel to raise a critique of gendered and sexual hierarchies otherwise commonly honoured by the generic template, not least through the reporter Sandra Khan, the 'first serial French lesbian investigator'.[57] Accordingly, the ways in which location, genre, gender and sexuality play together in the text will be given special attention in the following exegesis of *Un été pourri*.

Male dominance: cutting it off at the root

During a very hot summer in Boston, four murders take place. All the victims are male and are found with their throats cut and emasculated in alleyways or parks in the city. While the reader is made aware from the beginning that the murders are committed as revenge acts by two separate women, the plot follows the police's misguided and erratic investigation. As a counterpart to the 'Boston Strangler', who during the early 1960s murdered thirteen women in Massachusetts and to whom the novel makes numerous explicit allusions, the female killers of male victims reverse the habitual notion of female victimhood and male perpetration. Crime fiction in its more traditional forms has been defined by Gill Plain as being about 'confronting and taming the monstrous'.[58] In more than one sense, *Un été pourri* goes against the traditional, by radically letting the monstrous-feminine loose and – with the reader's intradiagetically implicit 'consent' – making a point of allowing female forces of monstrosity to operate in uncontrollable ways.[59]

The murders and their investigation are acted out within a rather limited character gallery spread out over the professions of the press, the judiciary and the police. Various connections between the characters, mostly of a non-professional and sexual nature, interlock with each other to produce a close, almost theatrical, grid between perpetrators, victims and investigators: Sandra Khan, the murderer of the second victim, is the journalist colleague of Thomas Herman; the public prosecutor Augusta Magnusson and her husband Ron are Thomas's best friends; Augusta is having an affair with police detective Sam Goodman, who also becomes Thomas's close friend; Fanny Mitchell, who is responsible for the first murder, works as a secretary at the attorney's office with Augusta; Thomas is pursuing a liaison with Fanny, whom he has met at the attorney's garden party; and in the novel's very open-ended ending, Ron and Augusta are exposed as (potentially) having killed the third and fourth victim.

Sandra Khan and Fanny Mitchell are not inherently predisposed to murder; rather, their actions are provoked by an extreme male brutality against people whom they love. In Fanny's case, her becoming a retributive killer is a result of her childhood experience of seeing her mother being raped by her stepfather, while her mother afterwards is forced to watch the sexual brutalisation of her daughter (Fanny herself) by the stepfather and his drunken friend. Fanny's experience of the legal system's failure to imprison the rapists is further reinforced by the fact that her mother never recovers her sanity after the assault, and in a reversal of justice her mother is the one who is 'sentenced' to imprisonment: 'The poor woman was locked up in an asylum. Because of "the love" of a man.'[60] As for Sandra, she turns into an avenging angel after her lover Joan has been found killed, raped and mutilated. Joan's murderer, Frederick Latimer, whom Sandra kills, has recently also raped the 10-year-old Carmen Sanchez (who is hospitalised and not recovering from her post-sexual assault trauma), but is about to escape legal punishment due to a lack of evidence. There thus exists a clear distinction between the situational and circumstantial male violence against women, which only finds its motivation in primal sexual urges, and female violence against men, motivated by extra-situational considerations, long-time suffering and the incentive to prevent further crimes. The monstrous-feminine in these cases therefore is closely associated with feelings of grief, and its mode of persuasion relies predominantly on pathos.

The novel's first chapter is a thematic preamble introducing one of the text's key textual mechanisms for subverting perceived notions of male perpetration and female victimhood: Mort Newman spots a woman (Fanny) in a bar, follows her in an attempt to rape her, but is himself killed by the woman. The shifting of otherwise firmly established roles is executed very swiftly during Mort's attack after a suspense-filled opening scene: 'The bitch! he raged. I'll kill her! Suddenly he was no longer thinking. Something had just happened in his throat' (p. 13). The murderer thus becomes the murdered, and the penetrator becomes the penetrated, by way of analogy between the male sexual organ and the murderous blade. The fact that this opening scene functions as an embedded narrative within the novel is reinforced by the victim's name, implying that he is just another 'mort', another 'dead man', albeit having set out with the intention of being 'death' personified.

The novel's second chapter introduces an alternative man, Sam Goodman, who investigates the murder of Mort Newman who has been found dead, testicles cut off and placed in his pocket. The killer, referred to by Goodman as the 'découpeur de virilité' (p. 15) – the 'manhood chopper' – is metaphorically paralleled in this initial chapter by Goodman's Jewish mother who exercises a controlling ('castrating') power over her adult son. His mother's attentions result in his becoming less conventionally masculine: he is unable to act unthinkingly on his urges due to this domineering feminine presence, and thus cannot be categorised as the kind of man referred to by Ron Magnusson as 'that class of men who think with their dick' (p. 121). Rather, he is incapable of being anything other than 'the kind mama's boy' (p. 180), a man who is 'good'.

The *femme castratrice* thus in her various forms imposes herself on the species 'Man'. The text in fact applies a nomenclatural system to the species 'Man' through the use of a post-nominal suffix: this can be seen in the names Mort New*man*, Thomas Her*man*, Sam Good*man*. There is a typology of men – readable as a response to male heteronormative discourse's categorisation of women – in which the sign is far from arbitrary. Herman, accordingly, who already after his first encounter with Fanny 'was already practically decided on marrying her' (p. 24), decides to become his name, 'her man'. Goodman, similarly, is addressed by Augusta in the following terms: 'you're clean, honest, reasonable' (p. 182). Fanny's first kill within the novel's time span, Mort Newman, is presumably in her view just a 'new' man in a line of other men who share the same attributes as her stepfather.

When Fanny exacts retribution for her stepfather's crime against her and her mother, she acts according to an unwritten penal code demanding that female victims of male sexual violence be avenged: 'For her, this wasn't a murder, but rather an execution' (p. 175). Khan also takes on the role of executioner in response to the rape, murder and mutilation of her lover Joan, but in her case it is a role she actively appropriates from an executioner expressly defined as being male: 'I thought I'd been assuaged by the death of her torturer, but I was wrong. Because there are as many torturers as men, or just about' (p. 107). An equivalence is thus established between torturers and men – all men are guilty and must be punished. Because this association between murder and masculinity predisposes the investigators to think in certain ways, the idea of a female murderer is unimaginable, and, as was the case in Holt's *Det som aldri skjer*, the investigation in *Un été pourri* moves in circles. Goodman assumes immediately that they are looking for a male killer because 'this is not a women's crime' (p. 63). For Goodman, this stance is linked to an incomplete evolution of gender equality: 'So, a female of the Rambo species going after rapists and sex-maniacs? Excuse me, but in spite of women's liberation we're still not there yet!' (p. 63). Goodman's analysis is somewhat misplaced, however, as it is not a matter of liberation or equality, but of gender inversion. These gender-inverted tropes are highlighted multiple times as a direct consequence of the serial killings, as Thomas Herman expresses in a confidential conversation with Sam Goodman: 'I no longer go out alone at night … Usually, it's women who have this kind of problem' (p. 113). Sam Goodman's elderly mother, when told about the castration of the male victims, articulates a similar opinion of the inverted situation with an added element of corrective comeuppance: 'It serves them right! … It was always women who up until now had gotten themselves murdered by nutjobs' (p. 158). The fear imposed on men inverts the habitual situation for the female part of the Bostonian population: 'Women are less afraid of men at the moment … Especially since it's been the latter who have been getting attacked and raped' (p. 140). This inversion is furthermore accompanied by a lexicon associated with battle or war. The castration of the male victims is thus alluded to by Fanny Mitchell when discussing the case with Goodman as 'the same kind of mutilation that you find in wartime. Vietnam, Afghanistan' (p. 61). This conflict theme is also played out in terms of how the generic template is manipulated.

No more 'private dick'

About a quarter of the way into the novel, there is an abrupt change of narrator (p. 73). The omniscient third-person narrator who until now has conducted the advancement of the plot is replaced by a first-person narrator who is introduced in a Chandleresque bar scene, resembling (for example) the incipit of *The Long Goodbye* (1953). The Philip Marlowe allusion is, however, unexpectedly disturbed by the female gender of the French past participles, and the bar becomes the setting for the first encounter between the narrator, Sandra Khan, and the character who is to become her lover, Joan Shimutz. This encounter, evolving into a passionate love scene between the two women, a description of their 'seven hundred and fifty days' together and concluding with the police announcing to Sandra that Joan has been found raped and murdered, presents a rather condensed version of their relationship (pp. 73–5). The chapter does, however, stand out in the midst of the novel's many otherwise complicated, harmful or violent relationships, as it contains the only trouble-free and joyous sexual liaison in which the two persons involved are mutually satisfied. The implications of framing Khan as both woman and homosexual in the narrative position of the hard-boiled detective is given further layers of complexity later in the novel when it becomes clear that she has killed Joan's murderer and thus also assumes the role of perpetrator. Contesting the prescribed roles within the hard-boiled template, Khan comments knowingly to Sam Goodman later regarding the gridlock of the (male-centred) investigation founded on a presumed normativity: 'You've never thought that you might for once run into someone a bit different?' (p. 194). As protagonist Khan actively rejects categorisation herself and makes a point of it: 'If I were to describe myself, I would say rather that I'm a *provocatrice*. I hate labels' (p. 196).

The introduction of this ambiguous, non-classifiable female ('private') 'I' in the chapter is a prominent example of what Gill Plain has described as the 'death of the detective', brought about by the narrative mode of contemporary crime fiction 'that embraces exactly that which it initially sought to exclude'.[61] The Khan character represents everything that under the conventional paradigm of detection, in Plain's words, would be considered the 'monstrous' and 'deviant' female other; she can thus be seen as a precursor for twenty-first-century paradigmatic constellations of gender representation: '"Woman"' has returned not only as the other, but as the self of the detective, and has exploded this self with her contradictory and multiple desires – with her refusal to adhere to the patriarchal codes of rationality, explicability and order.'[62] It is notable that the position of female subjectivity through the first-person narrator is only effectuated in the form of momentary intermezzos scattered sparingly throughout the text (pp. 73–5, 106–7, 144–9, 189–96, 228–32, 238–45, 275–9). The 'explosion' of the detective self in these textual passages – and the associated transgression of boundaries between the masculine and the feminine, between perpetrator and investigator, between the heterosexual and the homosexual – is also conveyed in terms of a (narrative) struggle 'won' from time to time by the female protagonist emerging from an object position to become subject.

Khan does not merely operate as a conventional *femme castratrice* within a rape–revenge crime narrative. The way in which she mutilates the male body from her position as lesbian protagonist takes on a further symbolic function, encompassing gender, sexuality and genre at various levels. The fact that her male victim is not only 'emasculated' but also has his throat cut and is thus symbolically deprived of both his manhood and vocal capacity suggests that the act of mutilation – effectively an attack on the power of masculine heteronormative sexuality and discourse that is oral, present and thus privileged – is an anti-phallogocentric one, echoing a more generalised critique of phallogocentrism underpinning the text.[63] The alteration of the generic template is additionally, and significantly, complemented by a change in the way the story is told and by whom. The customary dominating masculine voice in the hard-boiled tradition is, after the castration/throat-cutting, replaced by a feminine logos, powerful enough to interrupt the narration in the position of the first person.

The fact that Khan is the only character in the novel to be given a narrative voice and in this manner takes control does, however, not imply a subsequent objectification of the genre's traditional male subject. The female–male inversion upon which the novel is otherwise conditioned is ultimately annulled by the insertion of the female lover as the object of Khan's desire. The definitive symbolic 'emasculation' of the classic hard-boiled detective narrator is thus combined with a dissolution of the imposed binary structure under which the other characters seem to operate. Here lies the novel's use of lesbianism as potential critical tool. This conforms to the idea that Plain puts forward: 'It is the lesbian detective who has pushed the genre to its limits, and who has finally destabilised a formula that otherwise seemed capable of absorbing it all.'[64] To sum up, the novel's subversion and destabilising of patriarchal mythologies happen in two ways: the initial inversion of the traditional pattern of masculine violence and feminised victimhood is subsequently challenged by the breaking down of gender dichotomisation in the female same-sex relationship. Such a break with a feminist revolt solely based on an inversed replication of male supremacy also forms part of Tabachnik's own personal position, as she explains in an interview:

> Anti-judaism, racism and the oppression of women arise from the same reflex of fear, contempt and hatred. Why trample men into the ground? Must feminism ... be the counterpart of male chauvinism? As for consideration of woman as man's equal, I would prefer other terms of reference for her.[65]

Tabachnik's position, like that of her texts, appears then to advocate subversion and transcendence rather than mere inversion of traditional gender roles. While the novel clearly exploits a male–female inversion as a tool for its feminist critique, it also makeas a point of deconstructing the binary structure upon which the inversion is conditioned.

The employment of Boston as the backdrop for *Un été pourri* deserves some comment related to the discussion above. While there has been considerable academic focus on Anglo-American creations of French detectives and the appropriation of French settings for crime fiction plots by American or British writers, there has been little discussion of the converse. However, French crime novelists do adopt American loci for their narratives, as in the case of both Tabachnik and her contemporary Andrea H. Japp (1957–), who set most of their novels in the United States. In the first instance, the fictional displacement of a French crime novel to an American setting inverts, intentionally or not, some of the staples in the history of the French *noir* genre, marked by Edgar Allan Poe's early and emblematic use of Paris as the setting for his Dupin stories, and later by the influence of the American hard-boiled novel on the French *roman noir*. Moreover, returning the hard-boiled crime novel to its original *father*land and blatantly manipulating its generic masculine features is a powerful symbolic manoeuvre. Tabachnik's work thus takes its critique of the conventions of hard-boiled crime narrative back to the genre's place of origin, so that its masculine heteronormative inclinations may be – so to speak – cut off at the root. This latent meta-textual commentary on literary influences contributes to the novel's general mode of inversion and dislocation.

The actual inversion of cross-cultural transfer across the Atlantic, however, only takes the form of a brief, momentary parody of cultural stereotypes, as in the example from a garden party where Thomas Herman meets Fanny Mitchell for the first time and invites her out to 'THE French restaurant [in Boston] where it's essential to have gone at least once in order to know what eating means' (p. 20). Thomas's evocation of the stereotypical gastronomic superiority of France is, however, quickly turned around by Fanny who rejects his invitation by use of another cultural food cliché: 'I'm not really a lover of frogs' legs' (p. 20). Significantly, this is a unique incident in the novel, which – apart from the fact that the text is written in French – is conspicuously bare of allusions to France or French culture of any kind. The brief mocking of and then explicit annulation of the French subject are associated with a sense of liberation from cultural constraints.

Accordingly, in an interview Tabachnik explains the employment of the American setting in the following terms: 'There's also a geographical dimension which gives me an impetus that I wouldn't have here.'[66] It might, then, be a case of being able to engage with issues (e.g. of sexual identity) within an American context that are not as easily approached in a French setting. The choice of moving the narration away from France also brings about a dislocation and accompanying disorientation that reveal the restrictions of social discourse and allow the individual to create different and new identities. As such, the prominently absent France generates a sense of it being a case of *non-lieu*, in a metaphorical understanding of the legal term meaning 'no case to answer'. However, as the reader knows from the fictional female characters' own way of addressing notions of justice, there are methods that can be used to circumnavigate the system's failures. Rewriting the generic template of the hard-boiled novel is therefore also linked with a subversive rewriting of the French cultural template.

Blurring of binaries

As continuously highlighted by criticism, the hard-boiled novel is a particularly suited medium within which to form a feminist critique of masculine dominance because of its accentuated clichés and stereotypes concerning the female gender. This generic characteristic is wholly exploited in *Un été pourri* where a manipulated form of the genre's gender ideology is acted out. The gender binarism, which the hard-boiled crime narrative in its conventional form subscribes to and reinforces, is challenged and transcended by the introduction of a protagonist who is not only female, but who also demonstratively subverts the original genre's notion that 'the roles given to female characters were only those of whores and victims'.[67]

In the first instance, the novel can be said to operate within the same male–female dichotomy as the one it sets out to critique by merely recasting the genders in an inversion of the genre's stable oppositions. However, a further manipulation of this gender-generic tautology takes place through the insertion of the lesbian subject as first-person narrator, disabling the mere reversal of roles and bringing about a blurring not only of the masculine and the feminine, but also of the heterosexual and the homosexual. The violence executed by Khan and Fanny Mitchell destabilises the classic paradigm of the feminine as monster by situating their female 'monstrosity' in radical opposition to a privileged phallogocentric discourse. Foregrounding the symbolic structure of castration is therefore a way of placing Woman in logos/ language.

Conclusion: gender constructions

The categories *polar au féminin* and *femikrimi* – coined in their respective cultural contexts to signal female authors' entrance into a literary market traditionally dominated by male writers – are in part media-constructed entities. They draw attention to a distinct subgenre of women's writing that frequently addresses gender issues through the subjectivity of a female protagonist. However, they also foreground such writing's supposed feminine characteristics and appeal to a feminine readership, rather than its critical engagement with gender problematics from feminist perspectives. The mediatisation process does, however, display some interesting nuances: in Scandinavia, feminist stances are occasionally mentioned in media coverage, but primarily in its marketing. In France, feminine qualities are emphasised, but often in a way that stresses conflict and transgression implicitly in response to supposedly universal but in fact patriarchal norms. French media commentary also stresses the implication of these norms in the generic conventions and structures of crime fiction, which are there to be critiqued and undermined by an ostensibly feminine, if not, in fact, feminist reworking of conventions of genre and gender through the inclusion of female protagonists. The more openly displayed attack on male (generic and societal) hegemony in French media commentary on the *polar au féminin* corresponds to the way in which the works of fiction themselves initiate discussions of gender issues.

Turning to the novels discussed in this chapter, the confrontational and combative approach of Tabachnik's text noticeably contrasts with the more conversational and subtly problematising stance of Holt's fiction. The female murderers in Holt's *Det som aldri skjer* (Wencke Bencke) and Tabachnik's *Un été pourri* (Sandra Khan and Fanny Mitchell) provide illustrative examples of this contrast. Whereas Bencke's motives for becoming a serial killer lie in a personal crisis related to boredom and a revolt against a mediatised world that has made 'fame and fortune' the existential human goals, the revenge acts of Khan and Mitchell represent an overtly critical response to male violence and dominance. Holt's female protagonists generally represent non-confrontational individuals who are well integrated and are able to operate on an equal footing with men both professionally and domestically. If there exists a discussion of gender issues it is predominantly done within the inconspicuous setting of the home, where societal norms and values are renegotiated in an unproblematic manner from the comfort of the sofa or over the dinner table. The 'unproblematic' approach could in fact be said to be the organising principle of Holt's textual universe. Holt's texts thus reflect the general Scandinavian state discourse on gender inequality as something belonging to the past when it comes to sharing both work and domestic responsibilities. Therefore, when there is no apparent and immediate need for transgression of male dominance and traditional gender codes, the Norwegian texts can turn to other considerations when discussing gender issues: for example, the representation of women by the media, intersecting social identities or the difficulty of managing public and private roles. The unproblematic approach also extends to other forms of identities inasmuch as the straightening of the queer, that Holt's homosexual Wilhelmsen represents, explicitly promotes a mainstreaming of non-normative sexual identities.

If Holt's texts foreground a domestication of identity issues, Tabachnik's fiction radically de-domesticates its subject matter. *Un été pourri* draws attention to female stigmatisation and essentialisation by employing dislocation as a means of problematising the conventions of the genre around the question of gender. Removal of the text from its cultural 'home' to America operates in concert with removal of the first-person male protagonist. Removal, absence and replacement thus function as organisational and thematic principles informing the subversion of gender and genre norms. Constructed around an inversion of the male–female dichotomy, which is then wholly deconstructed, the novel rewrites the definition of the woman as 'other', 'deviant' or 'monstrous'. Female monstrosity is contextualised and thereby also validated within the paradigm of masculine violence.

The fact that Holt and Tabachnik display fundamentally different concerns in their treatment of issues relating to gender and sexuality is reflective of different discursive constructions of female identity in the two different cultural settings. This collides with generic perceptions of femininity. Here it is noteworthy that Norwegian and French constructions of gender constellations are mediated through the authors' choice of two different sub-generic variants of the crime narrative: the police procedural and the hard-boiled crime narrative respectively. Where Holt's texts are mainly concerned with personal integrity, Tabachnik's critique is directed at a fundamental societal issue. However, the comparison is more complex when we consider the authors' works in terms of content and form. While the content of Holt's work indeed addresses personal concerns and that of Tabachnik's collective ones, it is a somewhat different matter when it comes to form: in an effective reversal, the form of Holt's work is evocative of collective concerns (the police procedural with its team of investigators), whereas the form of Tabachnik's work stresses personal ones (the hard-boiled crime narrative characterised by its first-person narrator).

4

The Figure of the Prostitute

Chapter 3 set out the geo-culturally specific terms upon which the *polar au féminin* and the *femi-krimi* are conditioned by examining the different ways in which the crime fiction genre is employed to counter and transgress gender roles through the incorporation of female protagonists. The present chapter investigates constructions of gender and sexuality through a reading of a figure usually portrayed in the crime fiction genre as the ultimate example of female victimhood, namely the prostitute. Since its emergence in mid-nineteenth-century urban Europe, the genre has employed representations of prostitutes – not least through the figure's association with urbanisation, immigration, consumer society and globalisation – to mirror social values and practices.

From this follows the idea, expressed by Ruth Rosen, that a culture's notion of prostitution 'can function as a kind of microscopic lens through which we gain a detailed magnification of a society's organization of class and gender'.[1] In addition to being a tool for describing and understanding of identity issues related to gender and class, the prostitute has the potential – because of her liminal position – to engage critically with the social consensus, not least when she is presented within a discourse of criminality. As Christine Schönfeld points out in her examination of the prostitute within the context of modern German literature: 'she is the perfect image for writers who seek to question existing hierarchies, moral codes, or social norms'.[2] Accordingly, the literary projection of the prostitute can assume different positions in this questioning, for instance as a powerful trope through which a critique of heteronormative constellations of sexual relationships and interactions can be channelled. At the same time, from a more traditional, conservative perspective, the prostitute can be seen as a threat to monogamous heterosexuality and the institution of marriage, or, alternatively, as a symptom of increasing sexual equality within the traditional relationship.

The prostitute also moves beyond national confinements. Since the nineteenth century, the circulation of money, people and cultural products has evidently attained different levels, and in the contemporary globalised environment, prostitution is no longer bound to a local market, but moves across both physical and virtual borders. Organised human trafficking and the use of online technology to deliver sexual services are examples that have international dimensions and place the prostitute in a global economy. Consequently, thematic emphasis has in contemporary crime fiction been placed on the transnational dimension of prostitution, frequently framed within a structure of oppositional pairs: masculine/feminine, black/white, Western European/Eastern European, rich Europe/poor Africa. The ambiguity of the prostitute's position as either a devalued female figure or a figure of protest is linked furthermore to the binary structures of modernity – a discourse, which, in Shannon Bell's words, 'dichotomizes the female into the "good" and "bad" woman in all her manifestations'.[3] In crime fiction, the prostitute figure is frequently represented in this Manichaean way. However, crime fiction also has the potential, in its more consciously postmodern manifestations, to counter and deconstruct such binary structures.

The productive critical potential of discourses surrounding prostitution is at the centre of the following readings of Katarina Wennstam's *Smuts* (Dirt, 2007) and Virginie Despentes's *Baise-moi* (*Baise-moi (Rape me)*, 1994), each of which allows an investigation of the prostitute as a literary figure appearing in the respective contexts of Sweden and France. Significantly, these two countries have in the period under discussion witnessed a concerted political focus on the issue of prostitution, with France having introduced a law in 2016 modelled on the Swedish client-only criminalisation model of 1999, with which Wennstam's text engages directly.

In the readings of Wennstam's and Despentes's novels, the investigation of the prostitute collides with themes of globalisation, market economics, immigration, notions of class and gender, traditional family structures and alternative sexualities. However, while both texts employ the prostitute to form a critique of male-centred hegemony, their representations of this figure are radically different, and the readings will seek to highlight and contextualise these divergences. Additionally, it is noteworthy that Wennstam and Despentes in their respective cultural contexts share the status of engaged public figures, and that they are both considered to be in the more polemical and radical end of the crime fiction spectrum.

Katarina Wennstam's Smuts: the European whore
or how Sweden lost her Swedishness

Swedish Katarina Wennstam (1973–) employs crime fiction to approach and discuss topical issues relating to violence against women and attitudes towards the female gender within Swedish society. Considering Wennstam's ways of exploring these issues, Kerstin Bergman points to the fact that the author has 'even stronger feminist ambitions' than the other authors in the 'second generation of Swedish women crime writers', namely the ones following Liza Marklund's generation.[4] These ambitions are also prominent when Wennstam appears in debate programmes on TV and in her journalistic texts, such as her often controversial and critical articles in the national newspaper *Svenska Dagbladet*, in which she continues to question how women are treated within Swedish society.

Before becoming a full-time crime novelist, Wennstam produced two contentious book-length works of reportage: *Flickan och skulden* (The Girl and the Guilt, 2002) and *En riktig våldtäktsman* (A Real Rapist, 2004), which both include the subtitle *en bok om samhällets syn på våldtäkt* (a book about society's view on rape).[5] These reports have the explicitly polemical agenda of shedding light on profound inconsistencies within the criminal justice system, which the author criticises for having a backward, conservative, male-centred view of abused women and their own 'role' in the crimes. In particular *Flickan och skulden* generated media debate in Sweden in 2003 by arguing that 'the status of gender equality [in Sweden] is 30 years behind the times compared with what most people believe' and by '[exposing] a view of women that society will not openly acknowledge, but one which can be extracted from court records and which often leads to the victim being punished more severely than the perpetrator'.[6] One of the central points in the book is that, despite a reform of the Swedish rape legislation in 1984 (according to which the victim's actions could no longer be counted as relevant for the case), the rape victim's behaviour is still taken into account. If she is deemed as having dressed inappropriately, as having flirted or been drunk, as having a dubious reputation, and so forth, she is still – both in court and by the media – accused of having 'asked for it'.

Wennstam's crime fiction trilogy, consisting of *Smuts* (Dirt, 2007), *Dödergök* (Death Omen, 2008) and *Alfahannen* (The Alpha Male, 2010), dealing with prostitution/trafficking, domestic violence and sexual harassment at the work place respectively, is in accordance with the author's journalistic polemics and their critique of the Swedish judiciary:

> My authorship has a clear stance whether I write non-fiction or novels. I am not dissembling about where I stand, and, also, I think that certain of those in power, especially within the judiciary, are aggrieved by the fact that again and again I put the criminal justice system in the spotlight.[7]

At the centre of the following reading is Wennstam's first crime novel, *Smuts*, which employs the recently introduced Swedish law on prostitution and its implications as the backdrop for the plot. This so-called *kvinnofrid* law, prohibiting the purchase of sexual services (and thus criminalising the client rather than the seller) came into effect on 1 January 1999. The 'Swedish model' for prostitution, however, comes under scrutiny in *Smuts*, which exposes a conflicting image of Sweden being controlled by sexist and sometimes misogynistic men in powerful institutional positions.

Underneath the new man, the Neanderthal

Set in Stockholm, Wennstam's novel follows the successful lawyer Jonas Wahl and his wife Rebecca, a TV producer for the national broadcaster, who live a perfect and peaceful family life in a wealthy suburban neighbourhood, surrounded by designer furniture and tasteful art. In the first instance, Jonas appears as the incarnation of the modern Swedish man who advocates gender equality, is a model father, and as representative of the Swedish legal system defends vulnerable, abused women in court. The narrative is framed by his appearance on national TV in the first chapter where he comments on the new prostitution law and its implications: 'The entire Swedish rule of law rests on the fact that our principles are so transparent' (p. 11).

Transparency, however, does not apply to Jonas himself. From the beginning, it becomes clear that the lawyer leads a secret existence in which he, driven by an uncontrollable sexual need, visits prostitutes provided by the criminal underground milieu of the capital. His double life and the exposure of it constitute one part of the novel's plot. A court case, in which three Estonian brothel owners involved in trafficking are on trial, makes up the other part. The two plots, however, are intrinsically linked, as Jonas works as a professional TV commentator on the court case, while at the same time fearing exposure as one of the brothel's customers.

Despite the fact that Jonas Wahl is portrayed as the criminal wrongdoer, it can be argued that the double-sided nature of his personality serves as a hyperbolic magnification of a known configuration of male characters in Swedish crime fiction. The iconic originator of this recurrent archetype is Henning Mankell's Wallander figure who, as an advocate for vulnerable individuals and groups in society, will, at the same time, when removed from his usual professional context (and from Sweden), engage in activities contradicting his ethical standpoints.[8] Wallander's character trait of what Nestingen characterises as 'ambivalence and double vision' is in Wennstam's novel expanded to become the main thematic focus: under the polished surface of well-meaning moral principles for the common good lies an abyss of unsettling and destructive personal desires.[9] Whereas Wallander's contradictory behaviour in Mankell's novels is considered in terms of momentary lapses in his personality during periods of distress, the oscillation between public advocacy of a moral high ground and private engagement in conflicting shadowy activities is an immanent and constant part of Jonas's existence. Wennstam's novel furthermore establishes parallels between Jonas Wahl, his circle of male colleagues and Swedish masculinity more generally.

The Madonna and the whore

An essential part of Jonas's view of women is the categorisation of the female gender according to a traditional stereotyped dichotomy between the Madonna and the whore, defined in his own words via the omniscient narrator as 'the ones you fuck, and the ones you marry' (p. 61). His wife Rebecca on the one hand, and the prostitutes he visits clandestinely on the other, represent the two types of women that he cannot reconcile.

In her non-fictional text, *Flickan och skulden*, Wennstam has already contested this binary opposition, which she regards as an integrated part of Western thought. After having considered it in a historical perspective, she argues that '[t]he view of women as either Madonna or whore ... is so commonly accepted that most of us do not react against the two roles that a woman can choose between. That is just the way it is.'[10] In *Smuts*, the binary view of women is not merely an attribute of the male imagination; female sexuality is also acted out within this paradigm. The Madonna and the whore are juxtaposed in two scenes, which comment on the ways in which women are limited to either of these two socially constructed female roles. In the first passage, Rebecca remembers the imaginary world of her childhood in a flashback: 'So small, so short, she had been there in front of the mirror in her room playing bride ... The little girl had looked so excited. Dressed in a thin Lucia wedding gown and with an old, lacy tablecloth covering her long hair' (p. 212). In a parallel passage, Emma, Jonas and Rebecca's teenage daughter, discovers and plays around with her emerging sexuality, acting out another (or indeed, *the* other) female role:

> Emma tries to strike a pose in front of the mirror. She leans up against the wardrobe and drags one leg along the door. [She] puts her head back and sticks out her breasts. [She] imagines that she is in some kind of bar where different men are staring at her and feels their gazes, their desire. (p. 281)

The mother and daughter's self-reflection and imagined sexuality on the threshold between childhood and adulthood are both (per)formed in anticipation of a male gaze, which can confirm them as either housewife or sexual object. This dichotomy sets the scene for the discussion of Jonas's 'crime' of choosing the objectified (and commodified) over the sanctified woman.

The nameless prostitutes from whom Jonas buys sex are described merely by their (erotic) body parts fragmented into separated entities: 'He fixes his eyes on what he is there for: breasts, legs, arse' (p. 159); 'the one with the arse, the legs and the breasts' (p. 200). Defined by bodily attributes, the prostitutes are further objectified by Jonas's use of the impersonal pronoun 'den' (it) when referring to a woman he has paid for: 'He never looks them in the eyes. Not in its [this one's] either' (p. 159). The fragmentation and objectification are joined by a further degradation at the level of the narrative. Significantly, the criminal act (the buying of sex) is investigated from the perspectives of the perpetrator/husband/father, the wife, the children, the colleagues, the public prosecutor, the grassroots organisation and the journalist, who all – through the omniscient narrator – are able to express their opinion and emotional reactions. However, the prostitutes are not granted the narrative point of view and are thus left voiceless (pointless?). The representation of the prostitute in *Smuts* is therefore firmly inscribed within what Shannon Bell, in her Derridian reading of the prostitute's body, has described as 'a process which has produced "the prostitute" as the other of the other: the other within the categorical other, "woman"'.[11]

The marginalisation of the prostitutes within the female sphere intersects with the figure's inferior position in other hierarchical structures. First, and most evidently, the prostitutes are defined within a class system: while the perpetrator is a wealthy lawyer, the victims are low-paid girls at the bottom of the food chain. The masculine–feminine power relationship is therefore bound to the physical (sexual) authority of the man over the woman, and it is also related to an economic superiority. Secondly, the fact that the prostitutes in all cases are also foreigners adds a further process of othering to their position. This intersectionality of various identities (gender, class and ethnicity), however, remains unexplored in the novel because of the lack of narrative focus on any other aspects of their personality than their body (parts). This has the effect of reinforcing the socially constructed norms of marginalised femininity associated with prostitution. The exclusion of the perspective of the prostitutes means that they remain stigmatised outsiders instead of being made subjects in a productive counter-narrative. Wennstam's text thus undermines some aspects of its own polemic.

'I am a sadistic pig, a pervert and a rapist'

Despite the absence of the prostitute's voice, the novel gives the impression of providing a nuanced and in-depth discussion of prostitution and gender roles (for example, by including opinions from different professions and from both men and women via the omniscient narrator). Nevertheless, within this discussion the novel does produce a rather one-sided representation of male identity. In addition to Jonas's hypersexuality and the way he acts it out, there is no lack of other incidences of male sexism and perversion in the novel. The novel's men globally seem guided solely by their sexual libido, regardless of their income, social position, ethnicity or profession. Minor male extras equally convey the same set of attributes, as is the case, for instance, with the bus driver whom we meet briefly when Emma boards her school bus: 'The driver didn't look at the card she held out. His gaze was fixed on her breasts' (p. 20). In fact, the novel leaves no room for relativism when it comes to men's social engagement with the opposite sex. Even the young and seemingly righteous Melker, a prominent member of the grassroots organisation combating prostitution and described as 'more feminist than all [the] others' (p. 333), does not evade the novel's reductive male categorisation: 'Maria sometimes feels that she is the only one who can see through Melker's façade, and who believes that his engagement and combative spirit are superficial. He plays feminist to get hold of girls' (p. 333).

As is the case with Jonas (whose 'crime' is exposed at the end of the novel), male libido often leads to a fall. The other chief example of this is Göran Torheim, who – as the ultimate symbol of patriarchal power in his position of judge in the prostitution case – dies of a stroke in his car while an Eastern European prostitute performs fellatio on him (pp. 323–4). While his surname ('Thor's home') evokes associations of protection and phallic strength rooted in its connection with the mythological character (further consolidated by correspondence between the old Norse god's hammer and the judge's gavel), the finding of Torheim dead in his car, trousers down and penis limp, contradicts, and perhaps also ridicules, this evocation.

On the face of her novel's general attack on masculinity, Wennstam can be said to be part of a current in Swedish crime fiction, occupied in the wake of Stieg Larsson's Millennium trilogy with themes of male (sexual) violence against women and of female retribution. This thematic focus has received attention in international critical literature on the Scandinavian variant of the genre, for example in the collective volume *Rape in Stieg Larsson's Millennium Trilogy and Beyond*, which investigates the relationship between sexualised violence in Larsson's series and other Scandinavian and Anglophone crime novels.[12] A much-quoted scene from Larsson's *Män som hatar kvinnor* (2005; *The Girl with the Dragon Tattoo*, 2008), which has become emblematic of this tendency, has the female character Lisbeth Salander engage in a retributive act of violence in which she rapes her rapist and subsequently tattoos his abdomen with the words 'I am a sadistic pig, a pervert and a rapist.'[13] While no such act of violent revenge to right misogynistic wrongs takes place in *Smuts*, an underlying premise for the narrative seems to be that 'all men are potential rapists' and that this statement is metaphorically engraved on the Swedish societal body.[14]

There are moreover some points of commonality placing Wennstam in the same category as Larsson. Both novels display a paradigm of misogynistic violence corresponding to that set out by Barbara Fister in her discussion of Larsson: 'violence against women is a choice made by men who have achieved social and economic power and who act out that power by committing violent acts against women'.[15] It is also notable that this power relationship is played out within a state apparatus, as highlighted by Marla Harris:'[w]hat begins as a family matter in Larsson's novels ... reveals a systemic misogyny implicat[ing] almost every social institution in Sweden, including the national government'.[16]

The menace of Europe and the fear of penetration

The relationship between female inferiority and masculine hegemony in social, economic and institutional terms is in Wennstam's novel furthermore played out within the framework of Swedish national identity and its relationship with the wider international community. Wennstam peruses questions of male identity – and not least male sexuality – within the context of a breakdown of a national self-understanding, in the same way that, as Harris puts it, 'Larsson treats the sexual abuse of women as an (inter)national crisis'.[17] Consistently throughout *Smuts* an association between 'prostitution' and the 'foreign' is established via an emphasis on the international mercantile aspect of the sex industry. Besides the illegal immigrant prostitutes and brothel owners, the foreign 'intrusion' is also marked at the level of language. When Emma takes on her 'prostitute' identity (alone in front of her mirror or in online chatrooms), she switches from Swedish to English, which she speaks in broken sentences to her (imagined) male interlocutor: 'Looking at me?'; 'you like what you see?' (p. 281). Emma's unwitting mimicking of sentences uttered by the Eastern European prostitutes whom her father visits – 'you been here before?' (p. 159) – places the young adolescent's sexual construction of herself within a symbolic transnational perspective. When the young virginal teenager 'comes to her senses', rejects the role of the prostitute and begins exploring her sexuality from an 'appropriate' hand-holding approach, she is redeemed within the text's logic. Prostitution and foreignness are conceived as dangerous forces intruding the core of Sweden and threatening to destroy family and childhood experiences.

It is worth noting, moreover, that Jonas contracts his addiction to extra-marital 'dirty sex' in a foreign context. This happens when he is working in a United Nations peace-building team of lawyers in Sarajevo after the Yugoslav wars. In the first instance, Jonas is attempting to impose a Swedish superiority on the moral dilapidation of the other members of the European team: 'It was a given that their view on women was not directly sanitized measured in Swedish terms, but at the same time one could hardly expect that all countries had come as far with their work on gender equality' (p. 265). However, Jonas, who at the time of the incident is newly-wed and a new father, is soon to leave his moral high ground to descend into the world of sin occupied by the rest of the men in the European team. This happens on the way to the whorehouse:

> It was as if it was a different Jonas Wahl who left the restaurant with the other men. As if it was not the tired family father, who stumbled into the taxi laughing and sank down on the back seat. As if he had left a man behind him, and that there was another type of man, another type of masculinity, which was taking shape, as he sat there looking at the neon lights and bombed fronts of the buildings ... He probably felt continental. He felt un-Swedish in the proper and positive meaning of the term. Free and unleashed. So damned wonderful to be with other men, amongst peers who paid homage to their intellect and obeyed their inner voice. (p. 266)

Jonas's inability to stand up for his Swedish heritage has already been foreshadowed by the association of his name with the biblical Jonah, who finds himself incapable of preaching the word of God to the wicked people of Nineveh (Jonah 1: 2–3).[18] The beginning of Jonas's 'un-Swedish' sexual escapades is situated in contrast to the 'Swedishness' of a husband who is normally bound by 'gender equality' (p. 266). The lexical field of 'family/reproductive sexual activity/gender equality/Swedish identity' is thus opposed to 'male-herd behaviour/prostitution/misogyny/European identity'. Masculine sexuality relying on prostitution is firmly placed within a European multicultural context, but additionally within the symbolic setting of the ruins of Sarajevo as the ultimate example of incompatibility of cultures. Just as his biblical namesake, who tries to flee the presence of God, has to answer questions about his cultural belonging ('Tell us, on whose account this evil has come upon us? What is your occupation? And whence do you come? What is your country? And of what people are you?' (Jonah 1:8)), Jonas Wahl's cultural identity is questioned when he begins to engage in un-Swedish sexual activities. Sexual identity is thus inherently linked to a national and cultural identity.

Looking beyond the text, it is not difficult to stretch the characteristics of the relationship between Sweden and Europe further. Frequently, the Scandinavian welfare state is represented in terms of a focus on its female attributes as 'a benign institution protecting and nurturing the nation'.[19] The mythical notion of 'Moder Svea' (Mother Sweden), the national female personification of Sweden, also contributes to creating the sense of femininity associated with the Swedish state. In line with this, Risto Saarinen reads a masculine–feminine divide into the Scandinavian welfare state's encounters with international economic agendas: 'The social democratic ideology of *folkehemmet* can be seen as a womanist or small-scale communitarian ideal. The raw capitalism and globalization connected with criminals are in some sense masculine forces, aiming at destroying the weak members of society.'[20] Anthropologist Don Kulick takes things further and gives the discussion a concrete example directly applicable to the reading of *Smuts* when he analyses the wider cultural context for the *kvinnofrid* law of 1999. This law, he argues, 'is about much more than its overt referent "prostitution"' but rather a 'response to Sweden's entry into the EU' (on 1 January 1995).[21] Analysing the political rhetoric employed in the arguments for the introduction of the law, Kulick argues that 'prostitution may provide Swedish politicians, policy makers and journalists with a metaphor for Sweden's relationship to the EU'.[22] He continues: 'As a small, weak, innocent victim threatened with exploitation by a dirty masculinized foreigner like the EU, Sweden suddenly begins to look very much like a prostitute.'[23] This underlying discursive agenda of the law – and one which the novel unquestionably replicates – juxtaposes prostitution with foreignness and perceives them as an inseparable unity. The foreign prostitution networks in *Smuts* impose themselves on a Swedishness seemingly there to be violated. The pro-family, pro-gender-equality Jonas thus loses his national (and sexual) innocence in the encounter with the foreign. His daughter Emma, on the other hand, is almost captured by her own performance in the role of the foreign prostitute, but she does in the end not fall into the pitfall of European depravity. The textual 'protection' of Emma's virginity can here be accorded metaphorical equivalence to what Kulick designates 'the Swedish fear of penetration', expressed by the introduction of the anti-prostitution law as 'a way [for the country] of symbolically distancing itself from an EU that offers it rewards but threatens to exploit it'.[24]

This subtext of 'dirty' Europe's invasion of puritanical Sweden shines through in the novel's representation of the foreigner. On multiple occasions, misunderstandings or inability to communicate transculturally are emphasised, as here in a conversation Jonas is having with a lawyer colleague about 'a Mohammed' being accused of having attempted to murder his sister: 'Fundamentally, we do not speak the same language, you know. The guy has grown up here, so he speaks excellent Swedish. However, he is from a different planet. I cannot talk with him' (p. 33). Later in a conversation with a TV journalist, Jonas emphasises Swedish cultural supremacy when it comes to gender equality in his comment on the prostitution network case: 'Those men have a completely different view on women. They have a different set of values from you and me. I have often wondered if there exists a word for equality in Estonian or Russian' (p. 78). He continues: 'It's probably not coincidental that it's often men from such countries, and women for that matter, who function as pimps. Have you ever heard of Swedish pimps?' (p. 78)

This underlying discursive context of anxiety of Europeanisation and sexual otherness pervades the novel and its discussion of violence against women. The novel's account of a foreign infiltration in the form of Eastern-European prostitutes is part of a narrative about mercantile forces, which do not correspond with a Swedish sense of an egalitarian society. Ultimately, the effects of globalisation (in demographic, financial or sexual terms) threaten to destroy the family unit or – at a societal level – a Swedish sense of community. The ultimate breakdown of the relationship between Jonas and Rebecca thus symbolically happens because of foreign interference as well. When Rebecca's sister visits the Wahl family with her new hot-blooded Slavic boyfriend, Rebecca, too, experiences an awakening of a different type of sexual desire. Being drunk and having witnessed the boyfriend's erotic behaviour towards her sister, Rebecca, sexually charged at the end of the evening, assumes the role of the prostitute and invites Jonas to have anal sex with her. His wife's abandoning the mother/Madonna character for that of the whore, symbolised through the non-reproductive sexual act, is for Jonas a devastating intrusion into the domestic domain of something filthy and foreign: 'Last night the worlds met each other. Last night she became one of them. He has made her dirty' (p. 232).

Sexual and national identity

Wennstam's critique asserts that under the official Swedish discourse of gender equality, there exists a problematic and contradictory misogynistic attitude pervading society. The revelation of this misconception is significantly and symbolically directed at the judiciary, represented by Jonas, as the supposed uppermost guarantor for the upkeep of the country's moral codex. However, despite the text's attempts to create some balance in the discussion, Wennstam's novel falls into the trap of reproducing some of the dichotomies that it sets out to critique. While it gives the impression of nuanced and multifocal discussion – especially through the shared, and thus presumedly democratic and unbiased, narrative perspective of the text – it does not remove the ethical fixity of a victim–perpetrator opposition predicated on the female–male dichotomy. Furthermore, the suggestion that Jonas's (individual and psychological) Madonna–whore complex may be representative of the sexual identity of the entire male population of Sweden is a questionable generalisation. The text's immanent critique of male hegemony ultimately relies on gender stereotypes and further gender essentialising, which paradoxically places its feminist claims firmly within a structure consisting of multiple binary structures (self/other, man/woman, good/bad, Swedish/foreign, etc.).

Like Anne Holt's novels discussed in the previous chapter, Wennstam's *Smuts* concentrates on the (dis)comfort of the domestic environment into which it transfers a political and social matter. This combination is a selling point, in as much as the blurb on the novel's back cover emphasises the connection between the private and the public: '*Smuts* is a thriller and a strong family drama which lands right in the centre of the debate about sex purchase and trafficking.' The façade of the perfect family unit becomes identifiable with the self-promoted notion of Sweden as a model country for gender equality and anti-prostitution measures, while there are contradictory currents threatening to destroy the idyll. Treating sexual identity as an integral element of national identity, Wennstam's novel allies notions of feminine and masculine erotic desires to questions of Sweden's position within a European setting. Approaching prostitution as something utterly 'foreign' to the national self, the novel subsequently exposes the ideal-type Swedish man supportive of gender equality as 'contaminated' because of his contact with an un-Swedish sexuality imposed from the outside. The feminist critique promoted by the text is thus problematically linked with an idealised feminised image of the Swedish welfare state, unable to protect itself from intrusion in the form of commercialisation and Europeanism, conceived of as deviant forces corrupting the national self-understanding.

Virginie Despentes: gender and generic transgressions in Baise-moi

If Wennstam's novel makes the pair of the Madonna–whore the pivotal idea in its description of the female condition and assumes an inferiority of the prostitute in comparison to the position of the wife, Virginie Despentes (1969–) engages with alternative notions of gender and sexuality in a much more radical way by letting the prostitute take the subject position.

Despentes has, among other fictional and non-fictional texts, written three novels – *Baise-moi* (*Baise-moi*, 1994), *Les Chiennes savantes* (The Knowing Bitches, 1996) and *Apocalypse Bébé* (*Apocalypse Baby*, 2010), and a collection of short stories, *Mordre au travers* (Biting Through, 1999) – which to varying degrees employ characteristic features of crime fiction. These texts are generally inhabited and narrated by female protagonists and experiment with unconventional expressions of gender and violence, and Despentes's crime writing can thus be regarded, in Jordan's terms, as 'an outright rejection of the typical gender balance in crime fiction since it plunges the reader into a uniquely female environment'.[25] The following reading focuses on the representation of female protagonists in the first of the novels, *Baise-moi*, which is contemporaneous with Anne Holt's *Salige er de som tørster* (*Blessed Are Those Who Thirst*, 1994), discussed in the previous chapter.

Despentes's fictional work has frequently been characterised as 'radical' and can be viewed moreover as a literary exemplar of the crime fiction genre. While her novels might not be representative of a more mainstream French *polar au féminin*, there is justification for reading *Baise-moi* within the framework of crime fiction. First, *Baise-moi* does contain the *polar*'s universal elements – murder, victim, criminal and investigator – though the distribution of these is disproportionate in comparison with the more typical arrangement of roles. Secondly, when *Baise-moi* was initially published by the newly established (1989) alternative publishing house Florent Massot, it appeared under the imprint 'Poche revolver', dedicated to crime fiction, with a front cover connoting the hard-boiled genre. Thirdly, in France, Despentes's novels are repeatedly categorised as *polars* and often by literary journalists who also comment on more typical crime fiction.[26] It is therefore not surprising either that Despentes's texts – other than being read within the parameters of 'women's writing' – appear in the only extant book-length Anglophone academic studies of the *polar au féminin*.[27]

In the conclusion to her analysis of French reviews of Despentes's second crime novel, *Les Chiennes savantes*, Barfoot determines that 'woman writers are associated only reluctantly with the *roman noir*, and are not presented as capable of conscious innovation, nor of using the crime novel for political aims'.[28] By contrast, Barfoot's own reading of the novel characterises it as precisely 'a feminist rewriting of the hard-boiled novel'.[29] Barfoot's survey of reviews of *Les Chiennes savantes* further confirms the general tendency in the press of blurring the line between the author and the protagonist, as discussed in the previous chapter. The analysis of the material also reveals a lack of French media interest in Despentes's fictional articulation of her feminist project. Barfoot interprets this more broadly as the general attitude in the French press towards young female writers according to which 'we find a surprisingly uniform linguistic and critical stance ... a superficial and ironic treatment of their texts ... and an attitude towards the writers themselves which mixes prurience and condescension'.[30]

The extension of the notion of the *polar au féminin* to include a controversial and radical writer as Despentes demonstrates the power of labels and raises questions about categorisation more widely. From a journalistic and marketing standpoint it is a simplification corresponding with a clearly recognisable category. From a critical perspective the reading of Despentes is however more problematic. Despentes herself rejects obvious categories: 'I was astounded at always being compared to women writers, rather than to a Vincent Ravalec that I feel much closer to. There's an example of the construction imposed from outside that defines the feminine, and which frequently disfigures it.'[31] Importantly, however, the texts defy categorisation and themselves critique the various categories in which they are situated.

Female agency

Baise-moi follows the experiences of two young women, Manu and Nadine, whom we meet in their respective parts of the *banlieue*, where they are both exposed to male violence – and, in Manu's case, also rape. A coincidental encounter between the two young women at a point-of-no-return in both of their lives develops into a close friendship as they set off on a murderous and highly sexed journey through France in the novel's second part. From being passive female victims in the first part they become active perpetrators, sexually abusing their victims and cold-bloodedly killing passers-by. As well as employing characteristic features of the *roman noir*, the novel makes allusions to a multiplicity of generic templates: the road movie, pornography and novels that have acquired cult status through their depiction of 'ultra-violence' (for example, Bret Easton Ellis's *American Psycho* (1991) or Anthony Burgess's *A Clockwork Orange* (1962) and Stanley Kubrick's 1971 film version of the latter). Set in an urban – or more properly suburban – landscape, the novel explores themes of prostitution and rape, as well as its key concerns of female solidarity and female identity, particularly that of the female character as victim and as perpetrator.

This problematic status – that of dual identity – will be the focus of the present analysis.

Baise-moi's first description of Manu compares her character with that of her male friend, who has just informed her that the police have caused the suicide of one of their friends:

> Showing how moved he is, he starts painting pictures of the riots the accident ought to give rise to ... He's really getting into it. He is lofty and heroic. Manu is no heroine. She's used to a drab life, the short end of the stick and keeping her trap shut.[32]

The perspective of the chapter switches between Manu and her friend, while they engage in a conversation about 'police brutality ... injustice, racism, how young people have to react and get organised' (p. 13). The narrative consequently sets up a juxtaposition of virile, heroic masculine agency and tacit female passivity in the face of social injustice. This is the predominant idea in the first thirteen-chapter-long part of *Baise-moi*, where furthermore there prevails a gendered violence, which includes murder, brutal beatings, sexualised and racialised abuse and rape. Manu's strategy for survival in the *banlieue* is pretending that she is not aware of what is going on: 'See no evil, hear no evil, so people will leave them [her] alone' (p. 27). Likewise, Nadine is a character who has learned to endure life by making a barrier between herself and the outside world. She drinks heavily, smokes joints and physically blocks off the exterior by covering her ears with the headphones of her Walkman: 'She tries to imagine anything more frustrating than being in the city without a Walkman. Cut the tunes out of her ears – no way' (p. 31). As well as constituting an associated prop for the Nadine character, the Walkman has a playlist of songs with lyrics intersecting the narrative throughout the novel, which also function as a supra-narrative voice echoing Nadine's emotional register. Like the chorus in classical Greek theatre, Nadine's private music comments on and gives an alternative interpretation of the dramatic action. Where her Walkman allows her to escape the world, it simultaneously gives the reader textual access to her interior 'poetry'. The novel's second part, where the two girls set out on their journey together, symbolically begins with Nadine taking the cassette out of her Walkman and inserting it into the car stereo: '*Lean on me or at least rely.*'[33]

The turning point of the novel's first part is the chapter in which Manu and her acquaintance, Karla, are brutally raped. Manu's strategy for survival in this scene is the same as what has been the guiding principle for female endurance generally: 'She does as he says. Turns over when she is told to' (p. 48). Manu, covered in blood, dirt and shame after the rape, explains the violent sexual attack to Karla as something unavoidable and in the nature of being a woman: 'These are just things that happen ... we're never anything but girls [*filles*]' (p. 57). The double meaning of *filles* as both prostitute and the female gender more generally is implicitly a critical focus for the novel.

La femme publique

The prostitute is a central figure in Despentes's writing as the archetype of womanhood, or rather of a femininity constructed by patriarchal society in which women exist as exchangeable commodities to be bought and sold. When Nadine gets ready to go to work on the street, she dresses up and is ready to perform an act within this predetermined paradigm: 'When she's going to work, she always wears the same outfit, the same perfume, the same lipstick. It's as if she figured out what to wear and isn't interested in discussing it anymore' (p. 43).

In her critical autobiographical essay *King Kong théorie* (*King Kong Theory*, 2006), Despentes's account of her first real-life experience as a prostitute merges with her first appearance on TV in her role as famous writer after the controversy following her own film adaptation of *Baise-moi* in 2000: 'For the first time ever I went out in a short skirt and high heels. A revolution hanging on a few accessories. My only similar experience since has been my first TV appearance on a prime-time show for *Baise-moi*.'[34] In both situations, the change instigated by make-up and high heels immediately brings her into being – a transformation from a life in anonymity to 'being incredibly noticed' (p. 59) – and gives her in the first instance a sense of control over her surroundings. However, this control is limited and has a paradoxically addictive element that causes her precisely to lose control: 'There was an immediate change as soon as I put on the ultra-feminine uniform: sudden confidence, as with a line of coke. Afterwards – again, just as with coke – the whole thing became much harder to manage.'[35] The prevailing societal model for a woman is that she is judged on a scale of beauty, and that her success in life is dependent on her outer appearance and performance as a sexual object for the male gaze. Despentes's advocacy for the prostitute lies in the fact that she is acting precisely according to the same paradigm as everyone else:

Prostitutes are entertainment girls *par excellence*, who have pushed the logic of exhibition to the limit. Of course they are 'play-acting', everyone 'play-acts' in films and on TV! Why should there have to be a purity of truth in sex more than elsewhere?[36]

Femininity, according to Despentes, is part of the marketisation process happening in the public sphere, not only as it is expressed in the figure of the prostitute advertising and selling her body, but also as it appears in popular culture and the media and marketing industries: 'What women do with their bodies as long as they're around men with power and money actually seems to me very near to prostitution. I still don't catch the subtle difference between the sort of femininity sold in magazines and that of the whore.'[37] Moreover, the same conditions are present within the private sphere: 'it is not so different from what goes on in certain marriages'.[38] An easy conclusion in the reading of *Baise-moi* would be that Despentes exploits the role of the prostitute as the ultimate suppressed female by merely inverting the male–female power relationship as a subversive act. But it is not as simple as that.

Performing identity

The eye-opening encounter between Manu and Nadine gradually evolves into a process of self-realisation and mutual understanding. Experiences and thoughts previously silenced and suppressed now find a channel through which they can be expressed: 'Nadine smiles. She searches for words, hesitates at every new sentence. Realizes that she's not used to making an effort to explain herself. It's never bothered her before' (p. 98). This linguistic liberation is connected to the emancipation of the violated female body ('the body taken prisoner, forced to endure it'(p. 99)), which the two girls set free during the road trip in sexual encounters with multiple men over whom they exert an aggressive sexual power, sometimes with fatal consequences (for their sexual partners). The casting of Manu and Nadine as avenging females who take control of themselves and their surroundings inverts the roles within the power relationship between male and female actants from the first to the second part of the novel.

This shift in the two young women's status from dominated objects to domineering subjects is described by Manu – when they are celebrating their escape in a bar – as an existential awakening: 'This is our arrival into real life; we can celebrate that properly' (p. 103). The notion of their entrance into a true 'reality' is however destabilised by multiple allusions to a theatrical *mise-en-scène* where the girls find themselves having to invent their new identities. Manu thus describes their first joint killing as 'just like going onstage' (p. 117). With this realisation subsequently comes the need for a new language: as actors on the stage they must employ an adequate template for the dialogue. Manu comes to this conclusion after their shooting of a sales assistant (who has just furnished Nadine with a selection of new Walkmans): 'Fuck, we haven't got the formula right, haven't got the right line for the right moment ... we've got the crucial part down pat, the dialogue's got to be on the same level. You see, I don't believe in meaning without form' (p. 119). The script in which they are acting is that of the *roman noir*, and they are (de)constructing an identity as cold-blooded murderers according to an already existing formula, which, moreover, they are reformulating through their transgressive actions. The girls as active, powerful subjects are engaged in a creative process in which they constantly challenge received notions of identity at various levels (as characters in a genre, as women) and create new non-stereotypical, non-normative personages. The focus is on the substance of their actions; the form follows. This substantialisation is clearly linked with external bodily expressions and opposes itself to the view of the female body which Manu describes to Karla immediately after they have been raped in the novel's first part: 'It's like a car that you park in the projects, you don't leave anything valuable in it 'cause you can't keep it from being broken into. I can't keep assholes from getting into my pussy, so I haven't left anything valuable there' (p. 52). The body described as an empty, dehumanised shell deprived of its substance is symptomatic of the existential void felt by the girls before they meet each other and begin their sexual and murderous adventure.

What lies between Manu's first symbolic death (the rape) and her eventual actual death is the two girls' experiments with what substance can be put into the form – the shell – of the live female body. The form itself can also be altered and modified according to their liking, and different disguises are hence part of the role play in which they engage: Manu bleaches her hair (p. 112) while Nadine dyes hers black and buys 'a navy-blue suit and a leather briefcase' (p. 141). Later, Nadine cuts her hair short (p. 146), Manu dyes hers black (p. 188) and, after their final murder of an architect, Nadine dresses up in his 'black summer suit ... white shirt and a tie' (p. 227). Excess make-up and nail-polishing likewise form part of their daily rituals during the week they spend together. The multiple body transformations that the two girls perform represent a concerted attack on any sense of fixity of gender and sexual identity. Indeed, they are performances in the sense understood by Judith Butler, for whom 'what we take to be an internal essence of gender is manufactured through a sustained set of acts, posited through the gendered stylization of the body'.[39] By analogy with the construction of their performed gender identity, their equally performative criminal identity is similarly predicated on relations within society sustained by the credibility of the performance. Nor is their performance a case of art for art's sake. These are performances occurring within a commercial context.

The novel's title, *Baise-moi*, can be interpreted from the perspective of the narrative's first part as an erotic advertising tag displayed on the prostitute (Nadine) and the rape victim (Manu). In the second part, however, the sexual invitation is made on the basis of the girls' own sexual desire, and of their desire to be in control of their own bodies, if not indeed as a response to dominant masculinity with the alternative meaning of the imperative: 'fuck off'. With reference to the film adaptation *Baise-moi*, Bourcier characterises the title – as well as the film itself – as a *queering* of its pornographic content:

> [Virginie Despentes and Coralie Trinh-Thi, co-directors of the film] subject the expression 'Baise-moi' to the same treatment that lesbians, gays and trans people have inflicted on originally insulting terms like 'poofters', 'dykes' or 'queer'. By re-appropriating the language of porn, by bringing it down, they destabilise the very identity of the woman it denotes and the privileges of a dominant masculinity.[40]

The last sexual victim whom Manu and Nadine approach in a bar before taking him to a hotel room is made uncomfortable by their directness which, perhaps, does not conform with his received notion of male/female roles: 'He's disappointed, too, it would have been better if he'd had to chat them up, had the feeling of having to force them a little ... Girls never get excited like that just at the idea of screwing' (pp. 197–8). The girls' attitude towards the man also finds expression in Manu's transgressive recitation – or indeed rather repurposing – of the insult uttered by the man as he is about to leave the hotel room: 'You got it just right, found the right word, we are degenerate little sluts, asshole, but it isn't for you to say' (p. 201). There are clear resonances with queer critical concerns in the novel's confrontational re-appropriation of oppressive gender discourse.

Whereas *Baise-moi* is repeatedly categorised by the journalistic press as part of a homogenous *polar au féminin*, the novel itself explicitly defies and contests any easy categorisation. Its multi-generic, hybrid structure transcends and deconstructs all the genres into which it is easily situated and thus creates something else. Not only does the deconstruction of the *noir* script allow for an anti-hegemonic subversion of gender roles, but the novel's general generic hotchpotch also gives room for an epistemological playing with preconceived intrinsic and stable meanings of identity. Despentes's characters might be said to be acting within what Shannon Bell refers to as 'the contemporary postmodern', defined as 'a unique historical moment in which prostitutes, like other others of modernity, have assumed their own subject position and begun to produce their own political identity'.[41] In the novel's second part, which has its own – and controversial – system of domination, Nadine and Manu, in Butlerian terms, intervene in society's production of the female performative identity. By constantly changing shape and by constructing new identities, they are seemingly oblivious to any societal or generic norms. At the same time, the novel also offers reflections on the theatricality of self-representation, and its final return to a recognisable closing resolution within the logic of the *roman noir* (Manu's death and Nadine's arrest) emphasises the novel's own self-awareness of its status as fiction.

Conclusion: submission or subversion

In Wennstam's *Smuts*, the prostitute is a submissive object for male desires while being marginalised, if not entirely excluded (as a voiceless entity) from the narrative point of view. In Despentes's *Baise-moi*, however, the prostitute takes centre stage and becomes an active character revolting against her status as a doubly unprivileged figure. The two novels' employment of the figure of the prostitute thus signals not only different narrative methodologies, but also different critical concerns. Wennstam's novel may contain an attack on male dominance, but its women are constructed and continue to construct themselves within pre-established and immutable masculine paradigms. Despentes's novel, on the other hand, articulates its critique by exploring female sexuality and demonstratively recasting its female characters outside the male-defined feminine. The lack of female agency by marginalised identities in *Smuts* can thus seem symptomatic in contrast with the overt and strong assertion of subjectivity in Despentes's textual universe. Performativity plays a large part in both novels' construction of female identity. However, Wennstam's characters perform within a pre-existing dominant script, whereas Despentes's Manu and Nadine in their 'role play' improvise their performance and dissolve any overarching dichotomies as they go along. Ultimately, the two novels construct the prostitute as a 'site of politicized resistance' in Despentes's case or a 'site of oppression' in Wennstam's to use Shannon Bell's oppositional notions.[42] It might be possible then to argue that while Wennstam's novel is still coming to terms and engaging with binary structures prevalent to modernity, Despentes's novel – despite being published thirteen years earlier – consciously destabilises, if not breaks down, general binary divisions.

It will also be relevant here to make some more general conclusions combining the findings of the last two chapters. First, the protagonists – whether in their position as investigators or victims – in fact play a key role, but they also illustrate stark differences between Scandinavian and French crime fictions. Whereas the Scandinavian female protagonist (to some extent in Wennstam's novel, but definitely in Anne Holt's works) is able to function on an equal footing with men within a society in which gender and sexual difference have become unremarkable (at least on the surface), the French protagonists engage in transgressive behaviour as a revolt against a patriarchal society masquerading as one operating on universalist republican principles. At the same time, the French fictions revolt against the generic conventions of crime fiction. If the novels of Wennstam and Holt – whose protagonists, living in suburban Stockholm and Oslo, are far from marginal – appeal to the mainstream, the *polar au féminin* permits inclusion of novels that are far more radical in their critique of male dominance. While Despentes's and Tabachnik's texts might not represent the *polar au féminin* in its entirety, it is still noteworthy that these contributions exist, and also that 'radicalism' in the Scandinavian context is defined within parameters that are considerably less elastic. The *polar au féminin* can, particularly through its marginalised and subversive protagonists, adopt a confrontational stance that is overtly critical and political, whether within feminist or proto-queer parameters (Tabachnik and Despentes) or in a critical engagement with republican discourse (Manotti).

Moreover, the texts move beyond merely critiquing the masculine detective narrative by inserting active female agents into roles previously occupied by men. While they all explore themes of female victimisation (violence against women, sexual abuse, incest, trafficking, rape, murder and mutilation), their methods in dealing with these themes vary, as do the ideological frameworks in which they might be situated. Again, significant differences emerge in terms of themes treated. Scandinavian texts frequently stress the relevance of the intimate environment of the home, everyday life, relationships and especially the female protagonists' management of the balance between private and professional roles. If Holt's and Wennstam's novels bring the crime narrative into the private sphere, the female characters in the French texts, by contrast, are depicted in their confrontation with a gendered public space. Rather than being in the comfort of their homes, the French female protagonists are metaphorically but also quite literally 'on the streets' – if not entirely dislocated from a French setting (Tabachnik). Furthermore, in the case of Despentes's novel (and also Manotti's), the streets are significantly those of the peripheral *banlieue* with its symbolic outsider position in relation to a normative centre. The spatial stigma associated with the topographical extremity of the *banlieue* is analogous with the exclusion of the marginalised woman, considered in her relationship to the society that marginalises her. And whereas Scandinavian novels like Holt's might engage, despite a preoccupation with marginalised identities, in somewhat of a 'straightening of the queer', to paraphrase Rees, Despentes's work resolutely queers its subject-matter, contexts and medium, but above all queers the model of the hard-boiled male detective, writing against the *noir* script using marginalised female existences in order to validate non-normative identities.[43] Where the Scandinavian novels presume social consensus, in both Tabachnik's and Despentes's fictional worlds violence is an acting out of desires and wishes that do not comply with society's rules. This violence is reflected in the hyperbolic nature of the text, which is in a sense emblematic of the close relationship between genre and gender, in that the radical disturbance of the generic form is intertwined with radical disturbance of perceived notions of gendered roles.

Having examined various facets of gender-based marginalisation in the present section, the book turns in the next part to consider marginalisation through other aspects of identity, in particular in terms of ethnic otherness. Despite the differences and the clearly unique standpoints of the individual French and Scandinavian texts, the main general conclusion drawn in the current section is that the discussion of issues related to gender and sexuality in the Scandinavian examples is addressed from a central and non-controversial position, the perspective symbolically placed within a domestic milieu. The French crime novels, on the other hand, articulate their critique from a peripheral position with a subjectification of the marginalised as an essential feature. This orientation, as the next chapters will investigate, also plays an important role in the ways in which discussions of ethnic identity and cohabitation of different cultures take form.

Part III

Cultures in Migration

5

Bled *and* Banlieue *in French Crime Fiction*

Introduction

The previous part of the book demonstrated that the creation of categories such as the *femikrimi* and the *polar au féminin* clearly identifies a counter-reaction to the hard-boiled subgenre's earlier stereotypical depiction of female characters, and that the categories themselves hold a key position in gender debates finding expression in contemporary popular fiction. Investigating identity issues relating to ethnicity and immigration in the crime novel demands a different approach, mainly because there is no single clearly defined subcategory encompassing novels that deal with the designation of the foreigner as outsider. The critical position that the *femikrimi* and the *polar au féminin* are produced *by*, *about* and *for* women as an identified and particular part of society finds no equivalent stance when it comes to the identity of the writer, the protagonist or the reader as foreigner from a non-mainstream ethnic grouping. However, there are – in both the Scandinavian and the French contexts – a large number of crime novels that engage in various ways with problematics concerning cohabitation of different ethnic and cultural groupings. More nation-centred representations of the foreigner as the racial Other are now being joined by the voices of those designated as marginalised: these contributions are acquiring such new subcategorical nominations as the postcolonial crime novel, the *polar francophone*, the *polar urbain* and the immigrant crime novel.

Questioning identity issues relating to nationality, immigration, ethnicity, race and cultures, these crime novels might broadly be considered within a category which Behschnitt and Nilsson designate *multicultural literatures*. They define this as 'literatures written, read, and discussed in the context of migration, multiculturalism and multilingualism'.[1] While migration and multilingualism relate to the de facto effects and reality of globalisation in Scandinavia and France, multiculturalism is, however, not an easily definable concept and it certainly takes on different meanings and connotations in the two respective geographical-national contexts. A distinction must be made here between 'multiculturalism' as a term used to describe the reality of ethnically heterogeneous and culturally diverse societies, and the ideological notion of 'multiculturalism' as a means of relating to this reality. To discuss crime novels from the perspective of multiculturalism then necessarily implies an investigation of the socio-historical backgrounds and the particular national political and critical discourses that precondition them. This contextualisation is the starting point for the discussion and the focus of the first section, which will go on to present Scandinavian and French crime fiction contributions to debates on migration and the cohabitation of different cultures. In the second section, engaging with close readings of four novels, the analysis centres on similarities and key differences in the cultural representations of immigration and integration issues in Scandinavia and France.

Immigration in Scandinavia

Immigration into Scandinavia mostly happened from the second part of the twentieth century. Following rapid economic growth from the late 1950s onward, Scandinavian governments introduced intense labour recruitment campaigns beginning in the late 1960s, which resulted in immigration of workers mainly from Turkey, Pakistan and Yugoslavia. The oil crisis in 1973 led to restrictions in the labour immigration laws in all three Scandinavian countries. The mid-1980s saw the beginning of an increase in the influx of non-European refugees, leading to new demographic changes in Scandinavia. Accordingly, the immigration debate has, over the last three decades, as Ferruh Yilmaz explains, 'been transformed from being a labor issue to a cultural one, and immigrants who were originally characterized as workers (a class category) are turned into Muslims (a cultural category)'.[2]

While there is a high degree of similarity between the Scandinavian countries in numerous respects, the political approach towards the integration of immigrants has taken on different forms. Sweden has taken a liberal position and been deemed the 'flagship of multiculturalism', in opposition to Denmark, where a far more restrictive and assimilationist approach to integration has been put in place. Norway positions itself in between the two.[3]

An intensification of increasingly polarised attitudes in public debates in relation to immigration and integration has become a key political issue from the 1990s onwards. On the political scene, anti-immigration, right-wing populist political parties – arguing that the welfare state is being undermined through extensive immigration – have increased in popularity since the 1990s. The respective parties Dansk Folkeparti (the Danish People's Party) in Denmark, Sverigedemokraterna (Sweden Democrats) in Sweden and Fremskrittspartiet (Progress Party) in Norway all currently (2021) have representatives in the national assemblies and have had political influence on the countries' restrictive immigration laws introduced during the 2000s.[4] A further consequence of the rise of such parties is in the cultural domain: controversies surrounding the role of Islam in Scandinavia have provided a context where 'immigrants turned Muslims have increasingly become the Other against which national identities are narrated'.[5] This is not least true within the realm of the crime fiction genre where the foreign Other – especially in the figure of the Muslim immigrant – frequently appears.

In her chapter on Henning Mankell's novels and their depiction of a multicultural Sweden, Kerstin Bergman concludes that '[s]ince the 1990s, Swedish crime fiction has devoted much attention to the clash between traditional national identities and the processes of Europeanization and globalization'.[6] Immigration and conflicts caused by clashes between different ethnic population groups are topics that appear regularly not only in Swedish crime novels but in contemporary Scandinavian crime fiction generally. Chapter 6 will examine in greater depth how the representation of the 'foreigner' manifests itself in the Scandinavian context through a reading of two novels: Roy Jacobsen's *Marions slør* (Marion's Veil, 2008) and Paul Smith's *Mordet på imamen* (The Murder of the Imam, 2008).

Immigration in France

As distinct from the Scandinavian context, the background to the French representation of the foreigner is one of a longstanding colonial encounter and engagement that may well affect all forms of cultural representation of these issues, and certainly affects the crime fiction genre. Questions arise as to whether the colonial legacy has a particular effect upon the crime fiction genre, and thus offers a valid critical context.

The history of immigration in France – the encounter first with the colonial Other and later with the postcolonial Other – has been shaped by the country's colonial legacy and its various aftermaths, making the situation much more complex than in Scandinavia. The most significant aspect of this encounter has been in connection in particular with the Orient – as famously identified in Edward Said's account – and the importance of France's historical colonial engagement with North Africa is substantial, particularly in terms of current controversies surrounding the relationship of Islam to the secular French state.[7]

The story of immigration to France, with its origins partly in the colonisation of Algeria beginning in 1830, therefore goes back much further historically than that of immigration to many other countries, and is much more problematic and troublesome, not least in terms of the relationship between immigrants and the state – a state with very distinctive and specific features. It has much more far-reaching social, political and cultural consequences, above all in relation to France's secularist policy of *laïcité* affecting all state institutions. The assimilation policies of France in the nineteenth and twentieth centuries meant that in much of the French empire, French cultural knowledge was inculcated in the inhabitants of France's colonial territories. Assimilation also led to influxes of immigrants from the French colonies and of their cultures into the metropolitan centre, as well as to a degree of ethno-cultural diversification considerable in comparison with other European countries.

The republican universalism ostensibly underpinning assimilation policies has been at the heart of controversies surrounding the relationship of Islam – and by implication, of France's Muslim immigrant population – with French society. The most contentious aspect of this universalism is *laïcité*, perceived by many as a stick used to beat the Muslim Other within a selectively universalist framework intolerant of difference. The crisis arising from the 'affaire du voile' (the Islamic veil affair) in the late 1980s, and culminating in the 2004 legislation banning the wearing of the veil in schools and other state institutions, is in fact a continuation of debates that have been happening within French intellectual culture for some time, going back at least as far as Frantz Fanon's works on the identity of colonial subjects in the 1950s and 1960s.

Indeed, French intellectuals are all too aware of the problematics of the universalism that purports to define social life in France. Jacques Rancière, in an interview in *Le Nouvel Observateur*, asserts that 'universalism has been appropriated and manipulated'.[8] Michel Wieviorka, in his response to the question posed in his introduction to *Une société fragmentée* – 'what can the project of living together with our differences mean?' – concludes that this discussion in France is as good as 'impossible':

> The question relates in fact to a postulate which appears to have the status of the obvious: it appears tantamount to subjecting the national community and democracy to an immense danger to envisage acknowledgment of cultural particularisms in political life or in institutions, in which they can only have ravaging effects; these particularisms are not to express themselves beyond the private sphere, and any identity-based or community-focused demand which were to chance its arm in the public space must be rejected, suppressed, condemned.[9]

The opposition between the universalism of French republicanism and particularism – or *communautarisme* as it is pejoratively referred to – has been a constant in debates on immigration and integration in France.[10] The French assimilation model developed during the nineteenth and twentieth centuries for integrating the peoples of the colonies – a model that contrasts with the differentialist, multicultural Anglophone approach – finds renewed grounds in French integration laws passed in the 2000s.

The official French narrative of national identity as a homogenous collective under the concept of *le citoyen* (the citizen) finds echoes in much contemporary legislation. Indeed, the creation of the Ministry of Immigration, Integration, National Identity and Codevelopment in 2007 under Nicolas Sarkozy's government explicitly established that the integration of newcomers should happen within the parameters of universalist republicanism by having to, as one of the ministry's key assignments, '[participate] in the politics of remembrance and in the promotion of citizenship and of the principles and values of the Republic'.[11] In relation to this, Laura Reeck points out:

> Through the lens of French republican integration, two identifications have historically determined social identities in France: French or foreign. Ethnicity and race have never been operative social categories as there is no census reporting on them and consequently no standardised vocabulary for them. New ethnic and racial categories would stand to undermine the very foundation of the French republican model by fashioning minority groups with the majority.[12]

There is therefore a binary opposition between sameness and otherness, in which sameness is privileged as desirable, and attainable through assimilation and suppression of otherness. This state of affairs is arguably unique to, or at least more pronounced in, France, since it is so bound up with the founding ideals of the Republic. By contrast, whereas Scandinavian countries shared the social-democratic emphasis of French consensus politics in the post-war period, their approach to cultural difference and foreignness is somewhat different, as the following outline of the problematics of integration in the respective contexts suggests.

Politics of integration

Politically, the Scandinavian countries have generally been in favour of multiculturalist approaches to integration, and have been 'considered models for tolerance and openness towards cultural diversity'.[13] The Norwegian government, for example, defined the integration project in an early document as successful when '[a] foreign group becomes a well-functioning part of the host society, without losing its cultural or ethnic identity by assimilation'.[14] The French integration model has contrastingly cultivated an assimilationist approach to the integration of immigrants in which the notion of a universal citizenship has relegated ethnic, cultural and religious particularities to the private sphere. In France the debate surrounding a multicultural reality has continuously in critical commentary been characterised in terms of a dichotomy between a republican universalism promoting a notion of citizenship blind to any ethnic, cultural or religious identity, and a particularist, communitarian *dérive* – a deviation threatening to undermine the Republic. The French model has met with serious objections (from, for example, Wieviorka, Bourcier and Rancière) and has been accused of cultivating an 'ethnocentric universalism' resting upon 'assimilation in the fields of language, culture and, if possible, mentality and character itself'.[15] This model relies, says Wieviorka, on a strong notion of the state and its citizens:

> France, as a strong expression of the Nation-State, as a very well-integrated national society, is attached to republican values and to the principle of *laïcité*; it resists any recognition of cultural particularism in political life, in which it can only acknowledge citizen individuals. It cannot treat cultural differences in the same manner as other countries with more open political traditions.[16]

Meanwhile other countries – including, notably, the Scandinavian countries – have since the 1990s experienced serious objections to a perceived official state ideology of multiculturalism. While multiculturalism – as opposed to the French ideology of the One and Indivisible Republic – seemingly allows for 'hyphenated identities', it has been accused of undermining social cohesion and leading to a strengthening of differences rather than the promotion of integrated and peaceful cohabitation. This condition – diagnosed by the sociologists Aleksandra Ålund and Carl-Ulrik Schierup as 'ethnisation' – is one which Norwegian anthropologist Thomas Hylland Eriksen goes so far as to call *kulturterrorisme* (culture terrorism).[17] *Kulturterrorisme* involves the tendency of 'culturising' and reducing complex social processes to simple and static preconceptions about culture. This is particularly the case when a majority culture participates in discourses about 'immigrant cultures'.[18]

That the Scandinavian version of multiculturalism is undergoing a crisis at the same time as republican universalism is being called into question makes the issue of managing cultural diversity a suggestive and productive theme for the present investigation. One of the key points in the French context is whether crime fiction as a popular genre opens up a discussion of multiculturalism in a country where it is seemingly inadmissible. Another related question is whether crime fiction in fact offers a forum for discussion of a topic that in conventional political discourse is, as Wieviorka shows, beyond discussion. In the Scandinavian context the main points of interest concern the extent to and manner in which state discourse based on multiculturalist ideology is reflected in the crime fiction genre, and the ways in which the genre in this context deals with the reality of ethnic hybridity and cultural cohabitation. Ultimately, this part of the book investigates how the different politically defined social realities in Scandinavia and France find expression in a popular genre.

French crime fiction as littérature-monde

Whereas a considerable amount of Anglophone scholarly attention has been given to the topics of postcolonial and transcultural detective fiction in the twenty-first century, there has been minimal French academic engagement with crime fiction from a postcolonial perspective.[19] An explanation for this void in the critical discussion may be seen in relation to the late development of postcolonial studies in France. Critics, especially from outside France, have commented extensively on this.[20] One of the early advocates of the introduction of postcolonial studies in France, Jean-Marc Moura, reads the relative absence of postcolonial studies in French literary critical discussion as 'in keeping with the fact that French national identity is constructed on the abstract and universal notion of citizenship, which is supposed to transcend issues of race, gender and class, in order to create a society where all citizens are equal'.[21] The lack, or late arrival, of postcolonial studies in France has however not prevented fiction – not least crime fiction – from engaging with postcolonial issues. Writers from former French colonies have utilised the genre since the mid-1980s as a means of, in Pim Higginson's words, 'systematically turning away from a complex dialectical relationship to a French aesthetic model inherited from the colonial experience'.[22] However, the nature of the literary – and the political – association between France and its former colonies remains problematic in that the *métropole* (Metropolitan France) continues to exert a hegemonic sphere of cultural influence:

> According to the dominant French perspective, the division separating French and Francophone literatures is clear, and it is often taken to mean that the symbolic currency of the Francophone periphery is of lesser value than that of France though this does not of course prevent institutionalized Francophonie from using Francophone literature to justify its existence.[23]

The categorisation *polar francophone*, framed by the publishing industry to designate French-language crime novels written by non-metropolitan authors, brings with it the weight of what Pierre Halen has labeled the 'francophone literary system'. In this system, Halen argues, literary production is defined by a Franco-Parisian centre: 'Every "francophone" zone is subordinate, to a variable degree of course, to dependence on the French sphere, whose own products and value judgements (indexations) continue to be exported to the peripheral areas.'[24]

When forty-four writers in 2007 signed the World Literature manifesto – 'Pour une littérature-monde en français' – published in *Le Monde*, their action tapped into discussions of both the centripetal power of the institutionalised 'francophone literary system' exerted by the metropolitan publishing business, and the lack of intellectual engagement with postcolonial issues.[25] This polemical manifesto deprecates the relegation of 'literature from the "periphery"' and challenges the neo-colonial cultural hegemony that the central heartland exerts over 'francophone literature', denouncing the vision according to which 'a France seen as mother of arts, arms and laws continued to dispense its enlightenment, as a universal benefactress, concerned about bringing culture and civilisation to benighted peoples'. The *francophonie* thus constitutes, according to the signatories of the manifesto, 'the last avatar of colonialism'. The other main argument of the manifesto deals with the status of French literature, which the signatories deem 'a literature without any other object than itself' with no relationship with the world as it is.

Interestingly, the *roman noir* plays a significant role in the manifesto's argumentation. Not only is the programmatic declaration signed by a number of engaged crime writers (Didier Daeninckx, Patrick Raynal, Jean Vautrin), but it also explicitly mentions the *noir* genre in its listing of previous literary initiatives announcing 'the capacities of the novel to resist anything claiming to deny or subjugate it'. The manifesto stresses the *roman noir*'s capability to contest established French literary ideology and the genre's aptitude for moving beyond the official narrative and telling the world as it is: 'Others, concerned with speaking about the world they lived in, as before them Raymond Chandler and Dashiell Hammett had spoken about the American city, turned, following Jean-Patrick Manchette, to the *roman noir*.'

The fact that the publication of the manifesto was followed by abundant and often agitated reactions in the media, on the internet and in academic debates highlights demonstrably, as Christiane Albert states, 'how much relations existing between notions of language, literature and nation still today remain complex, conflictual and current'.[26] For Moura, the manifesto's message furthermore accentuates the immanent problematic of French research culture's engagement with French-language literature from outside the *Hexagone*. He argues that what he calls the manifesto's 'desire for a "'post-Francophonie"' ... questions the very methodological basis on which specialists of Francophone literature operate'.[27] The manifesto thus offers a method for reading *le polar francophone* within the paradigmatic context of World Literature, which also implies reading it as a *polar post-francophone*, a method of reading that this chapter will attempt to put into practice.

The immigrant in French crime fiction

French scholarship examining crime fictions dealing with the problematics of immigration and integration is fairly scant. One of the few academic studies investigating the figure of the immigrant in French crime fiction is Nadège Compard's *Immigrés et romans noir 1950–2000* (2010). The representation of the foreigner in the genre falls according to Compard's analysis into four temporally defined categories. The first of these describes the immigrant as a foreigner, stranger or outsider (1950–60), the second period deals with 'the immigrant' (the 1970s), in the third period (the 1980s), Compard finds a 'victimisation of the immigrant', and in the last period (the 1990s) the common theme is 'the culpability of France'. Her analysis leads to the conclusion that there is an overrepresentation of stereotypes in the *roman noir*'s depiction of immigrant figures reflecting contemporary discourses in French society:

> Yes, there are overriding figurations of the immigrant in the representation of immigrants, in particular because there are overriding figurations of the immigrant in our society, in political discussion or in the media context and in this sense the *roman noir* is indeed a reflection of reality. More than a distorted reflection of reality, the *roman noir* is a reflection of distortions of reality.[28]

Her inference is that a nominally left-wing universalism governs the representation, and that this ideological vision becomes increasingly more discernible during the period she describes. From the 1980s onwards, anti-racism expressed in the novels studied is linked with the 'omnipresence of universalism in the *roman noir*':

> Universalist anti-racism dominates the cultural representation of immigrants, whose original culture is often reduced to a mere expression of folklore. Accents and difficulties in use of French, the predilection for native languages, are treated less and less over the years and the indicators of integration are relatively many.[29]

Compard's period of interest ends in the year 2000 and does not include any references to the immigrant as observer and participant in the creation of imagery; neither does it include any immigrant or francophone crime writers. Compard's analysis briefly mentions that there is 'an evolution of differentialism' and that – with the example of Didier Daeninckx – 'differences in identity and culture are seen as a source of richness for France'.[30] However, the study rather unambiguously inscribes itself into a universalist discourse: cohabitation of different ethnic groups and cultures are observed from a hexagonal viewpoint from which (linguistic and cultural) assimilation is a sign of integration.

The following readings of two crime novels from the French context examine how voices from the periphery go beyond a mere contestation of the genre's received notions of the 'figure of the immigrant' by engaging in a discussion of national identity and challenging the nation's dealing with a multicultural reality. The first novel, Roger Fodjo's *Les Poubelles du palais* (The Bins of the Palace, 2011), deals with France's colonial legacy by highlighting the necessity of rewriting history to include hidden stories suppressed by the official political rhetoric. The second novel, Rachid Santaki's *Les Anges s'habillent en caillera* (Angels Dress in Riff-Raff, 2011), approaches the issues from another peripheral position, namely that of the *banlieue*, but at the same time rejects the peripherality and the binarism on which conceptions of the *banlieue* are premised. Both novels are set in and around Paris and use the symbolic power position of the capital as the starting point for a discussion of these issues.

Roger Fodjo's Les Poubelles du palais

Cameroonian writer Roger Fodjo's first novel, *Les Poubelles du palais* investigates links between France's colonial past and the present shape of the Fifth Republic in a story that accentuates hidden places and lost memories. The novel is published in L'Harmattan's series 'Ecrire l'Afrique' (Writing Africa), explicitly placing it within the paradigm of a francophone depiction of the African continent. However, the object of the novel's investigation is more accurately a representation of the dialectical relationship between imperial France and its former colonies, a relationship which is not solely defined by a white French hegemony but is complex by nature. Questioning the grand narrative of the French Republic, the novel accentuates and brings to light the *non-dits*, the things unsaid, of the nation's collective memory in relation to the slave trade, imperial power and exploitation of its African colonies. This questioning places the novel in ongoing controversies about the 'condition noire' – the status of black citizens – following the law initiated by French politician Christiane Taubira making 10 May a national commemoration day in France for the abolition of slavery and resulting in numerous publications challenging French identity policies.[31]

While working on an archaeological dig in the cellars of the Château de Versailles in order to finance his studies in France, the Beninian biology student Cyprien Guézo discovers a hidden inscription on the wall, hinting at the unfortunate fate of a slave and his daughter: 'In memory of Nabo and his daughter Louise-Marie, born of the

Queen, both of whom were condemned by the French royal court and transported.'[32] The story from the *ancien régime* about the disappearance of Nabo – a Dahomeyan prince abducted from his home country to serve as a slave at the court of Louis XIV – and his newborn 'half-caste' daughter with the Queen is intricately linked with Cyprien's personal family history. Cyprien, himself a descendant of the royal family of Dahomey, becomes determined to uncover the truth about what happened to his family in the past ('It's a question of the disappearance of a relative' (p. 20)) and to make this knowledge public ('what counts is eking out the truth and making it public' (p. 20)).

When Cyprien – with the aid of his friend Jules and of the latter's girlfriend, Yasmina – steals some classified documents from the French National Archives, he becomes the centre of a different investigation. A massive police operation led by police inspector Laurent Fournier has the purpose of preventing public exposure of the 'state secret'. The novel thus consists of two crime narratives, juxtaposed by the text's constant change of point of view from Cyprien and his friends to Fournier. The two parallel investigations are simultaneously also two criminal acts in an interdependent exchange where one investigator (the police, representing the state) is trying to expose the criminal (Cyprien) who himself is investigating the criminal acts of the state. By continuously contrasting and exposing the discrepancy between Cyprien's personal experiences and the official French narrative, the novel oscillates between treating the events of the past as either 'state secret' (Fournier's expression) or 'state crime' (Cyprien's expression). The figure of the detective in the incarnation of Fournier thus loses its immanent classic characteristics through his active participation in the erasure of traces, the destruction of clues and the silencing of the past. Antithetically, his criminal adversary, Cyprien, works towards resolving the mystery, discovering and, indeed, exposing the truth about a hidden and repressed past.

Cyprien and his friends are trying to reveal the truth about what happened to 'la métisse' (the half-caste), but their investigation is equally concerned with the cultural and ethnic 'métissage' ('mixing') of France. This is reflected in the fact that the three investigating protagonists represent a trio of minority identities in the French demographic landscape. Their Beninian, Corsican and Algerian backgrounds furthermore stress the postcolonial complexity and multifaceted relationship that France has with its former colonies, a relationship that cannot be reduced to a simplistic umbrella perception of France's relationship with the singular Other, but one insisting on plural 'Others' who have had different experiences in their respective encounters with colonial France. In the character of Yasmina, whose father was killed during the Algerian demonstration in Paris on 17 October 1961, the text links the injustices committed towards the 'princesse Noire' and her father (and by extension the African peoples) with other wrongs in the history of France that need rewriting: 'The name of the Black Princess and the reappearance of the Sun King are two paving stones thrown into the Seine. They'll make waves' (p. 250). Through this subtle reference to the corpses of the Algerian demonstrators thrown in the river after the 1961 massacre, the novel's fictional enquiry into the discriminatory crimes of the *ancien régime* converges with investigations into other more recent events subject to similar cover-up by official discourse.[33] The novel's focus on the *ancien régime*, moreover, is highly charged with symbolism in terms of the opposition between the periods preceding and following 1789 and the advent of the enshrinement of *liberté, égalité, fraternité*.

The novel displays from the outset a strong consciousness of the importance of history, articulated here by the narrator: 'Secrets are the real guiding lines of history. It's a mistake to think they create gaps; rather, they are mountains turned upside down towards the interior of the Earth. Thus buried, they become abscesses expanding under a fragile dressing' (p. 10). This vision of history, evocative of Foucault's conception of archaeology, characterised by Lisa Downing as 'the tracing of histories (archaeologies/genealogies) of silenced voices, the writing of the small narratives that have gone unheard in the traditional "grand narrative" of modern history', is profoundly archival and at the same time bodily, suggesting that evidence metamorphosed as pathological matter corroding the body (of society, of the state, of history) cannot disappear or be conveniently disposed of: items, bodies, of evidence remain 'buried deep' in archives.[34] And indeed, the search for the truth, specifically the truth about what happened to Louise-Marie, is an archival one: the three young people visit a vast number of locations in Paris, all major centres of cultural and historical knowledge (the National Archives, the National Library in Rue de Richelieu and at the site François Mitterrand, the Louvre, the Basilique de Saint-Denis, Sainte-Geneviève, the Panthéon). While libraries and archives contain important sources of information for Cyprien's investigation, the institutions of the Republic appear inherently non-accommodating, seemingly impenetrable and unwilling to provide the necessary documentation. 'No result' is the repeated message that Cyprien receives, when he searches for the story of

Nabo and Louise-Marie at the Sorbonne (p. 31). His experience at the local university library that 'the library is empty' (p. 31) expands into a universal – and anthropomorphic – silence residing in all Parisian libraries: 'the libraries are mute' (p. 35). The novel argues that this silence stems from an imperial discourse, which has existed uninterruptedly from the colonial past into the postcolonial present. At the novel's beginning, this continuum is merely noted as an obstacle to the investigation ('it is the political class which has censored publications from the Ancien Régime to the present day' (p.35)), whereas the rhetoric towards its end becomes more confrontational, criminalising the state's censuring of compromising material: 'it's the same document thieves and source-destroyers who have been operating from century to century and stalking researchers' (pp. 258–9).

Representing physical and symbolic benchmarks organising the trajectory of Cyprien's investigation, the Parisian institutions also constitute important 'lieux de mémoire' (memory scenes), as pointed out in a review of the novel by C(h)ris Reyns-Chikuma.[35] But as well as being sites holding the collective elements of memorial heritage, these places are also 'lieux de crime' (crime scenes), where documentation is hidden by time (the inscription on the wall in Versailles), misplaced (the important book at the National Library) or where staff are obstructive. Thus, Fodjo's novel critically engages with the vision represented in Pierre Nora's landmark work, *Les Lieux de mémoire* (*Rethinking France: Les lieux de mémoire*, 1984– 92), which, though authoritative, has been critiqued for omitting the 'lieux de mémoire' relating to France's colonial history and the role these have played in the construction of the nation.[36] *Les Poubelles du palais* becomes a fictional expression of the critique Nora's project has received in the academic sphere for being reductive and hexagonal in its perception.

The novel's concluding scene, gathering all the major characters ('culprits' and 'investigators' on both sides), takes place at the Panthéon, where Cyprien's investigation has led him to find the urn containing Louise-Marie's heart. The urn is buried in a concrete monument under the inscription 'TO THE UNKNOWN MARTYRS' (p. 272). The physical metropolitan monument depicted in the story contains the keys both to the crime narrative's resolution and to an unlocking of the obstacles that these 'lieux de mémoire' present to present-day relations between France and its former colonies. There is, moreover, a generic dimension to this scene, borrowing from classic detective fiction the trope of the gathering in the library as conclusion to the process of detection. The novel in fact offers a metacommentary on the utopian quality of detective fiction by self-referentially characterising the writing process within a rather idealistic reflection on the place of everything within the universe: 'Everything has a meaning. Every word finds its place in the sentence, just as every idea finds its place in human philosophy' (pp. 11–12). As in the detective novel, everything finds its proper place; all questions are resolved; order is restored.

The conclusion is preceded by another event involving resolution – this time, resolution, and assertion, of identity – when Cyprien finally finds the grave of his ancestor (who did escape from the royal castle and lived undercover as a nun in Moret). His reaction is a powerful, supernatural cry which penetrates the country, emphatically contrasting with the silence and filling the emptiness that has been the dominating factor in the story about his ancestor:

> 'Ancestor!!! Here I am!!!' he shouts with all the strength in his lungs. His piercing voice has produced an echo that can be heard in every street in the town. The buildings have shaken. This voice's echo has been heard spreading through the distant mountains surrounding the town of Moret. The voice has lashed out like an invisible flash of lightning. Not like a bottle thrown into the sea that haphazardly accosts just anyone, but rather like a note entrusted to a messenger that follows a precise destiny. From Paris to Abomey, the royal palaces have trembled. (p. 236)

The reclaimed existence and identity of Nabo and his daughter in Cyprien's contemporary presence is a fundamentally disturbing force, which, to use Homi Bhabha's term, can be identified as a 'disruptive temporality', a belated intervention by a colonial past that challenges our perception of contemporary practices for an understanding of time and therefore of cultural heritage.[37] In the same way as Cyprien's cry subsequently in the novel is accompanied by an article in *Le Canard* revealing the true story about 'the black princess', Fodjo regards his *polar* as a means of making the silenced 'audible' and reaching an audience with his message. The crime-fiction-reading audience is not the final destination for the communication, as Fodjo has announced in a lecture:

> I am conscious of the fact that the world cannot be changed all of a sudden by writing; however, I live in hope that the message of this novel will reach its intended recipient, for after the immense task accomplished by journalists in acknowledging the existence of the book and of its

content, it's now up to academics to distil this message as best they can in articles which stand a chance of reaching decision makers.[38]

Fodjo is explicit about the didactic policy-informing agenda of his work. Moreover, there is a related academic agenda; and indeed, again, Fodjo is quite clear about the strongly implied presence of key concepts in postcolonial theory in his work, having explicitly stated of *Les Poubelles du palais* that 'the novel is the refusal of Eurocentrism, a doctrine that places the West geographically and culturally at the centre of the world'.[39]

What the novel involves, then, is a restoration of order that takes the form of a retelling of the failed official narrative of the nation. It consists of a rewriting or reconstruction of history, not just of Africa and of its relationship with France, but of a particular course of events relating the fate of individuals to that of the collective. An important point made by the novel is that the history of France and that of its former colonies are symbiotically linked. This can be seen in terms of the authoritative notion in postcolonial theory of the 'empire writing back to the centre', operating at both a spatial and temporal level in the novel.[40] The act of writing back from the postcolonial periphery to the ex-colonial centre also requires a writing-back in time with the implication of having to rewrite history. The novel, moreover, is a case of the Other communicating to the centre through the centre's own institutional apparatus, engendering a critique both of the racial order and of the police and legal system maintaining a discriminatory power discourse, as exemplified by Fournier in his racist, neo-imperial stigmatisation of Cyprien in his initial reaction to him: 'Don't tell me that some little Sambo in sandals is going to derail our national Police Service' (p. 12). The racially discriminatory remark uttered by Fournier, a representative of the state, indicates a failure to realise that the hegemonic order can indeed be turned upside down. This is flagged at the beginning of the novel, which is also the outset of a process of self-realising change whereby Fournier – in his change of attitude at the end of the novel – comes to a personal realisation. In keeping with Cyprien's similar self-realisation, he finds his true identity. The crime narrative's restoration of order is in the novel's conclusion, linked with the individual's acquisition of knowledge or enlightenment as Fournier shakes hands with Cyprien and concludes: 'a wise man is one who has lost his prejudices' (p. 278).

In light of the above, it can be seen that even narratives set in France lend themselves to analyses borrowing their theoretical terminology from postcolonial criticism. In the case of *Les Poubelles du palais*, this is straightforward as there is a clear engagement with key concepts in postcolonial criticism (made fully explicit on numerous occasions by the novel's author): the narrative is expressly about the history of colonialism and its implications in modern-day France, and in modern-day relations between France and its former colonies. However, it is also possible, as the further examples will illustrate, to investigate traces of colonial ideology in metropolitan cultural representations that do not explicitly engage with colonialism and its history, which are firmly set within the *métropole*, but in which nevertheless the legacy of colonialism is never far from the narrative surface. That is, as Huggan has advocated, to 'reintroduc[e] Europe into the domain of postcolonial literary and cultural studies'.[41]

Rachid Santaki's Les Anges s'habillent en caillera

Les Anges s'habillent en caillera (Angels Dress in Riff-Raff, 2011), the second of three novels in Rachid Santaki's trilogy about life and death in Seine-Saint-Denis, follows the first-person narrator, Ilyès, alias Le Marseillais, through three periods of his late teenage years and early adulthood. The novel has a distinctive documentary style, announced by its black and white front cover depicting high-rise blocks in a manner reminiscent of Mathieu Kassovitz's film *La Haine* (1995). The novel's narrative is rhythmically intersected by multiple newspaper articles situating it in the textual space between documentary and fiction.

The novel's features correspond closely with those of the *polar urbain* identified by Jean-Noël Blanc in *Polarville* (1990). For Blanc, the *polar urbain* is a variant of the genre that denounces the *roman noir*'s mythological description of urban space. According to Blanc, what occurs in the *polar* in the 1980s is the emergence of a realist representation of the city: 'If the *polar*, for the first time in its history, is now looking in the city for what makes the city, it can no longer be content with seductive, devastating and fantasmatic imagery. Rather, it must penetrate into the concrete complexity of urban phenomena.'[42] Christina Horvath makes a similar distinction in *Le roman urbain contemporain en France* (2008), between 'narratives in which the city is a referent on the one hand, and on the other the urban novel'.[43] The *roman noir* belongs, for Horvath, to the first category. While situating the narration 'preferably in an urban setting', the *noir* genre does not, like the *roman urbain*, make the city its 'true focal point, indeed the narrative's protagonist'.[44]

In the case of Rachid Santaki's novels there is, however, an insistence on a merging of the *roman noir* and the *roman urbain*. On the one hand, the novel insists on the depiction of Seine-Saint-Denis as *ville-personnage*, an urban organism with its own bodily rhythms and emotional registers. On the other hand, the affiliation with the *roman noir* is confirmed in the name of Santaki's publishing house, Moisson Rouge, responsible for the publication and distribution of *Les Anges s'habillent en caillera*. Evoking the French title of one of the classic *noir* novels – Dashiell Hammett's *Red Harvest* (1929) – Moisson Rouge claims its attachment to the American *noir* tradition. Moisson Rouge's imprint, Le Syndikat, which published – as its very first publication – *Les Anges s'habillent en caillera*, however, defines its agenda on the back cover of Santaki's novel as being 'devoted to contemporary urban literature'.

Making the outer suburban environment the central point of the narration also allows for the transgression of another literary category, previously used to classify writers from the Parisian *banlieue*:

> Those writers pigeonholed as either 'banlieue' or 'urban' writers can be perceived as symbols of a new literary movement transcending the ethnic belonging of authors (the talk previously was of 'beur' literature, for example) in favour of placing the accent on their geographical belonging (to the Parisian *banlieue*).[45]

The first generation of *beur* writers are, as Hargreaves points out in his early study of *banlieue* literature, concerned with the description of an identity crisis (in relation to an identity that moreover is presumably male by default): 'Finding a way of being himself in France is the problematic which conditions most Beur fiction.'[46] Michel Laronde identifies the same problematic in his study of *beur* literature: 'the discourse of *beur* identity is a discourse of difference'.[47] The labelling of works by so-called second-generation immigrants as 'littérature beure' has received much commentary and critique from – amongst others – sociologist and novelist Azouz Begag, who accuses the term of creating a 'literary ghetto'.[48] Because of this 'literary ghettoisation', the term was abandoned for the lexical replacement of '*banlieue* literature' around 1995.[49] 'Urbain', however, is increasingly the term used to refer to the generation of young writers from the *banlieue* who started publishing after the widespread disturbances in November

2005. Santaki – whose novels are marketed precisely as *polars urbains* – may unproblematically be counted among these writers.

Classifying *Les Anges s'habillent en caillera* as a *polar urbain* taps into two discussions. Where the first of these concerns a development within the crime fiction genre taking place in the outer suburban rather than more literally urban *intra muros* landscape, the second identifies it as crime fiction in which this zone is the key subject and indeed protagonist. Santaki comments on his employment of the *banlieue* as protagonist in an interview in *Le Parisien*: 'Usually, in this genre, it's always the point of view of the police that's taken. I take the point of view of the *cité* [the peripheral housing estate].'[50] The novel's vision is however not that 'la cité' takes the perspective of a criminalised protagonist as opposed to that of the law-enforcing order; rather, the focus is the particular space in which both police and *banlieusards* must operate under the same conditions. This confluence is noted in the novel by Stéphane, a corrupt police officer, who explains to his colleague Michael: 'You know the borderline between us and the villains – there isn't one, and you have to accept that. These raids, these crimes, all that shit, that's not the law. You know this very well. So at a given moment, you go above, or you go below.'[51] 'La cité' – as a space outside the law where protection by a legal system does not exist – is defined by a general feeling of malaise transgressing into every societal grouping and erases differences between them. But it is also a cultural space where there is a shared understanding of urban art forms and activities: Stéphane, for instance, is both a practitioner and spectator of boxing and makes references to hip hop music in his conversations with his colleagues.

The text's insistence on the self-contained, autonomous status of the *banlieue* is reinforced by the anthropomorphism of this urban space as a living organism that breathes and functions in accordance with its inhabitants: the novel's second and third parts open with the scene-setting narrative observations that 'the northern *banlieue* is sleeping uneasily and will not be long to wake' (p. 59), and that 'the *banlieue* is irritated; its movements are under surveillance' (p. 117).

The *banlieue* is presented also as the site of living, organic communities where everyone knows one another, and in particular, where everyone knows one another's stories. This is made clear through the experience of the narrator, Ilyès, who at the beginning of the novel has just emerged from an eighteen-month prison sentence. Other people's knowledge of his story and his family is an essential part of his identity. His friend Yazid uses this to encourage him to settle scores with an enemy, stressing that 'I know your old ma and I've seen you grow up' in order to convince him that the community solidarity that their long association reflects is a reason for seeking out and punishing this enemy: 'in the neighbourhood, we're not united and it's destroying us' (p. 17). Long-term acquaintance and observation become an essential feature of life in the quartier. Of Hamed, the local barber, the narrator comments: 'He's been set up there for years; he's seen us grow up and hears all our conversations' (p. 15). Indeed, 'has seen me grow up' (and variations of the phrase) becomes a refrain for the first part of the novel in the presentation of the important characters surrounding Le Marseillais, as Ilyès is also known. Most significantly of all in this regard, the *banlieue* itself is declared as being among Le Marseillais's network of close protective relations, by playing the role similar to that of an older family or community member who has followed his development from child to criminal: 'Saint-Denis, my town, the one that saw me grow up, that saw me scale the heights of delinquency, the one that got me addicted to dosh' (p. 14). Like the *banlieue*, like the *ville*, the *quartier* also is not merely a tacit observer, but plays an active role in the formation of the boy's development. Even when Yazid turns out to be an informer and betrays Le Marseillais to the police, who subject him to a violent interrogation, community ties rooted in shared upbringing in the *quartier* remain hard to disentangle. Objecting to the violence of the interrogating officers, Yazid comments: 'He's a little lad from my neighbourhood ... His mother grew up with mine' (p. 236).

This sense of belonging within a self-contained local community of interconnected individuals with shared experience as their primary identity is reiterated throughout the novel. Indeed, the notion of identity as a fixed, and specifically national, quantity is contested in the text on various levels. For Le Marseillais, it is not simply a matter of having a dual national identity and having been exposed to both French and Moroccan cultures. The complexity and implications of the French assimilation project are symbolically exhibited in the fact that Le Marseillais picks up and develops a love for 'French *chanson*'. It is not in France that he learns about Aznavour, Brel, Brassens and Renaud, but from a girl he meets in Morocco during his annual 'holidays in the *bled* [home village]' (p. 36). In Saint-Denis – where the only accepted music among Le Marseillais's peers is rap – this displacement and ensuing reintroduction of French culture back to France from the former colonies plausibly amounts to a commentary on the absurdities and the shortcomings of a cultural 'civilising mission' only concerned with canonical French contributions. The underlying critique of the official discourse that dictates that 'being French' means to demonstrate an appreciation for appropriate French culture becomes apparent when Le Marseillais – on the day when he, in legal terms, acquires the status of a French citizen – is stopped by the police: 'the day I turned eighteen, I was driving around in my first car and the pigs subjected me to an identity check' (p. 36). The police's examination of his boot reveals a pile of 'easy-listening CDs' of French *chansons*, which makes him pass the identity 'assessment'.

Ilyès's complicated and non-fixed identity in fact arguably reflects the social reality in the Parisian *banlieue*. In his sociological study of Saint-Denis, Bernard Dinh describes the inhabitants' sense of identity as based on the local rather than national:

> Identification with the nation and the territory seems of marginal relevance in comparison with an identification with community, ethnicity or faith, which allows a connection to be made with the group to which one belongs, one's land of origin, and sense to be made of staying and envisaging the future here in conditions of existence deemed acceptable.[52]

The notion of 'home' is accordingly for Le Marseillais not connected with a feeling of national affiliation either with France or Morocco; rather his sense of identity is linked with a strong connection to the local: 'le bled' in his country of origin and the close-knit community in Saint-Denis.

Language is also an important signifier of identity, or rather, in particular, of the lack of fixity of identity. Making much use of an intermixing of languages, with frequent recourse to *verlan* and slang, the novel describes a hybrid community identity that is as linguistic as it is cultural. This can be seen in the novel's title, which, while evoking the titular conventions of *noir*, also contains the word 'caillera', the *verlan* transformation of 'racaille', a term habitually associated in the popular imagination with the *banlieue*; elsewhere in the novel, *verlan* and *argot* are intersected by loan words from the native languages of the inhabitants' families, especially Arabic. The vocabulary of the 'téci', *verlan* for 'cité', represents in turn an expression of the confluences of immigration and globalisation.

There is perhaps a further symbolic allusion to hybridity in the surreal presence within the novel of a zebra, or at least a zebra that is perceived by Yazid, who issues an urgent entreaty to Le Marseillais: 'Look at the zebra, it's coming over, clock that!' ('Regarde le zébre, il s'approche, téma, téma'). Le Marseillais's response – 'Shut your fucking gob, screw your mother with your zebras' ('Ta gueule putain, nique ta mère avec tes zébres', p. 243) – is uttered in the language of the *banlieue*, but contains an allusion to another representation of the *banlieue*, Mathieu Kassovitz's *La Haine* (1995), in which the Jewish *banlieusard*, Vinz, sees a Friesian cow strolling through the graffiti-painted desert of concrete apartment blocks, and utters the words 'clock that, holy cow' ('téma, la vache').[53] The intrusion of the cow into the environment is mirrored in the soundtrack to the scene in question, where Edith Piaf's 'Je ne regrette rien' is sampled with NTM's 'Nique ta mère' by a DJ in a top-floor apartment. *La Haine* presents the intrusion of an unfamiliar image and a clash between two superficially incompatible spheres of reference, along with an individual experience – only Vinz (and the viewers of the film) can see the cow. Santaki's novel performs a similar operation, but it does so more allusively. It arguably exploits the symbolism of Kassovitz's film – in particular, that of the intrusion of an unfamiliar image perceived from a uniquely personal perspective – to make a more general point precisely about spheres of reference that appear superficially incompatible but ultimately are potentially highly productive when perceived or represented via a particular subjectivity.

By exhibiting the hybrid nature of the language of the *banlieue*, along with Le Marseillais's shuttle between Saint Denis and his home village in Morocco and the ethnic diversity of the people populating 'le 93' (as the Seine-Saint-Denis *département* is referred to by postcode), *Les Anges s'habillent en caillera* constitutes, according to Timo Obergöker, 'a type of literature calling into question the national narrative conceived as the reflection of the unity of one language, one land and one people'.[54] But there are further indicators of cultural hybridity, such as food and (as seen earlier) music. After Le Marseillais returns home from prison in the novel's incipit, his mother's meal evokes his *other* home in North Africa, problematising the notion of home: 'My mother's tagine is so good. Its secret formula of spices on vegetables whips up the colours of Morocco and the savours of the *bled*' (p. 18). The 'bled' – the home village – is notably distinct from the national homeland of origin in the same way that the quartier is distinct from the French territory. In another area of sensory experience, 'French music carries me away [m'emporte]; I like the writing and the melodies' (p. 36). The verb *emporter* has a double meaning, denoting both an immediate emotional carrying-away and a symbolic cultural displacement. Stimulating sensory inputs, then, whether they are gastronomical or musical, are vehicles to emotional and cultural transportation and serve as linking devices in Le Marseillais's self-understanding and self-realisation.

Whereas Saint-Denis is described, in classic realist style, with a mimetic focus on detailed spatial markers – le 129 (a kebab bar on Rue Gabriel Péri), the Basilique Saint-Denis, Place du 8 mai 1945, Place du Caquet – and on the infrastructure that links them to each other, there are very few references to a France outside Seine-Saint-Denis. When Le Marseillais spends the first part of his sentence in Nanterre – barely 20 kilometres away from Saint-Denis – he feels alienated and alone, not least because of his strong feelings towards the place where he has grown up. When he is transferred from the prison in Nanterre to that of Villepinte, he affirms that 'I'm back in the house, in my ninety-three' (p. 111). If the protagonist is grounded in his habitual locale, the diegesis more generally is grounded firmly in reality, and the novel offers an implicit commentary on the relationship between reality and the fictions that sometimes represent it. When Yazid expresses concern over the violence of Ilyès's interrogation, Stéphane retorts: 'Shut it ... We're not in *Raï*, you're not Nordine! Life isn't a movie. Do you think we're going to kill him? ... We're going to make him talk, you'll get your money, and he'll go to prison' (p. 237).[55] Criminality and law enforcement are banalised rather than glamorised. At the same time, the claims to mimetic exactitude of the *polar urbain* are bolstered.

It remains, however, that French crime fiction in the twenty-first century could indeed be said to follow the patterns of representation in the mainstream literary tradition, undergoing the shift in perspective outlined by Michel Laronde in his conclusion to his study of immigration and identity in the *beur* novel:

> If History in its circularity (between the beginning and the end of the 20th century) has shifted Exoticism from the discourse of the Westerner to the discourse of the Oriental positioned internally in the West (thus as a Foreigner), I expect this discourse in its resurgence to be refashioned by the new perspective that the Oriental has on it.[56]

What Laronde sets up as a hypothesis for the future in 1993 is confirmed in Santaki's novel where the 'Western' or 'colonial' gaze is entirely omitted and the narration centres on the self-contained multicultural world of the *banlieue*. The notion of a centre–periphery dichotomy between Paris and its suburban edges is in the text inverted, or perhaps indeed subverted, by the absence of a normative focalising perspective or representational filter. The centre of the capital thus lies at the fringe of the *banlieue*'s reality and is represented as a mythical, unapproachable site observable from a distance and only in the form of an outline of a Parisian cliché: the Eiffel Tower. Arguably, the novel subverts not only perceived notions of the Parisian high-rise suburbs, but also the social premises of *beur* fiction frequently accentuating the question of the *banlieue* as the periphery.

Conclusion: the view from the fringe

Santaki's and Fodjo's crime novels are contrapuntal writings from the fringes of society (the periphery of Paris and Benin as a former French colony), both contesting received notions of the places and characters that they describe. The notion of place and of its construction through history – individual or collective – is significant in both texts, which exhibit not only an immigrant perspective, but also an emigrant perspective. The position of the abandoned country of origin, or – in the case of Santaki's text – the local community, thus plays a significant role in the development of the protagonists' self-understanding.

Inversion as principle is in both cases a dominant feature. This manifests itself at a narrative level where the traditional agents of crime fiction are abandoned for more fluid categories or overturned roles, and at an ideological level where the notions of majority/ minority, centre/periphery and normativity/deviancy are put into play and demonstratively inverted. Santaki's and Fodjo's novels insist in their analysis of French republicanism on a change of perspective not unlike the inversion that Laronde employs to characterise the *beur* novel: 'it is the discourse (or Gaze) of the Other that dictates how things are seen: in an inversion of perspective, the (Oriental) Other becomes the speaking Self in the face of the (Western) Self who becomes the Other, recipient of discourse'.[57]

Both novels are written after what Charles Forsdick and David Murphy have described as the 'postcolonial turn' taking place in France after 2005.[58] The texts' approach is inherently postcolonial in the sense that they explicitly and conflictingly deal with issues of colonialism and its aftermaths. The novels can therefore be seen as fictional contributions to a debate in an academic climate in which 'many French scholars remain largely suspicious of (when not completely hostile towards) postcolonial approaches to literature'.[59] Contributing to an inclusive understanding of France as a complex postcolonial construction, the two novels emphasise that issues relating to the centre/periphery dichotomy are far from having been solved. Refraining from mere description, they engage with societal injustice within the Republic transformatively.

In the following chapter, the focus will be on how Scandinavian crime fictions – in quite different ways from the French – deal with issues emerging from the cohabitation of multiple cultures in Scandinavian novels contemporary to those of Santaki and Fodjo.

6

Self and Other in Scandinavian Crime Fiction

The widespread enthusiasm for Nordic crime fiction resulting from what is habitually termed the 'Scandinavian invasion' can arguably be said to have been initiated by Danish author Peter Høeg's novel *Frøken Smillas fornemmelse for sne* (*Miss Smilla's Feeling for Snow*, 1992), responsible, according to Barry Forshaw, for 'the geographical relocation of the crime genre northward'.[1] What is distinctive about Høeg's novel – falling within the remit of both literary and genre fiction – is that it deals with issues of ethnic and cultural identity in an emphatically postcolonial context. The novel's prevalent theme is the negotiation of identity for Smilla, who tries to navigate between Greenlandic and Danish cultures. While Høeg in *Frøken Smillas fornemmelse for sne* explicitly addresses complex issues relating to the negotiation of cultural identities, it is a novel that is quite distinct, if not indeed unique, in its approach to multi-ethnicity and mixed cultures and in its postcolonial critique of Danish society. Smilla is a loner, both in the novel where she struggles to find her place literally and emotionally, but also in terms of the novel's place on the literary crime fiction scene in its way of critically engaging with postcolonial questions of cultural and ethnic identity.

The representation of Self and Other in Scandinavian crime fiction, riding on the wave initiated by Høeg in the early 1990s, has been somewhat understated. This understatement is not so much in a thematic sense, since a multitude of Scandinavian crime fictions deal precisely with issues of globalisation and multiculturalism, but more in terms of the ways in which such works approach these topics. While Høeg approaches Otherness through the postmodern and highly ambivalent Smilla character, the representation of the foreign Other finds more stereotypically constructed expressions in other bestselling Scandinavian crime novels. Stieg Larsson's *Millennium* trilogy (2005–7) is an example that – rather than rendering the complex and ambivalent relationship of cultural cohabitation – for Nestingen and Arvas 'exoticize[s] and heighten[s] Otherness, making it impossible to fit into an everyday framework in any plausible way'.[2]

Whereas France has experienced an emergence during the last three decades of crime fiction written in French by writers from the former French colonies and ethnic minority writers within the *Hexagone*, Scandinavian crime fiction still remains a field occupied almost exclusively by white, ethnic Scandinavian writers. Accordingly – while novels have a clear focus on issues relating to immigration and cohabitation of different cultures – the discussion of these issues appears to a certain extent mono-directional and self-contained. In other words, these novels are involved in processes of 'writing the Other' and of representing the Other that are part of the dominant culture's response to minority cultures.

Crime fiction in the context of 'literature of migration'

Scandinavia's lack of crime fiction writers of non-Scandinavian ethnic background seems unusual in comparison with the prevalent presence of writers with immigrant-status in France. Considering the massive interest the publishing business and the public have shown in the Scandinavian variants of the crime fiction genre during the last decades, and the fact that these countries have percentages of immigrants in their populations equivalent to that of France, the question arises as to why the absence exists and why so prominently in the Scandinavian context.[3] This is a question that surprisingly remains unexplored in crime fiction studies, whereas if the perspective is broadened to Scandinavian literature generally, there exists a sizable amount of academic engagement with the Danish notion of 'indvandrerliteratur' (immigrant literature) and critical commentary – especially in Denmark – on the dearth in Scandinavia of writers with a 'foreign' background.

In Denmark, Hans Hauge noticed in 2010 that 'considering how much the immigration debate has occupied the political and public agenda over the past 15–20 years, it is peculiar how little this is reflected in literature'.[4] Critical commentary is occupied with the rudimentary and often reductive representation of 'foreigners' by ethnic-Danish authors, and the fact that they infrequently take centre stage, and almost always appear as minor fictional characters.[5] The lack of writers with other ethnic backgrounds, who would be able to counter this simplified literary image of the 'foreigner', is read as a sign of the Danish cultural establishment's self-reliant 'national' attitude:

One could question whether the tradition for 'foreign' voices in Danish literature and film has been slight, not so much because there have been few writers and directors with foreign backgrounds and few literary works and films concerned with immigration and cultural encounters, but rather because these artists and their works have lived a shadow existence in Denmark – a country which historically has placed considerable weight on the national coherence, the idyllic self-image and the homogenous and homogenising narrative.[6]

In line with this observation about the strong national narrative, Hauge compares the position of 'immigrant literature' to the lack of interest in literature from the former Danish colonies: '[w]e [have] also got an immigrant literature, but it plays no main role. Its status is often as the Danish "colonial literature" – Icelandic, Faroese and Greenlandic. The subaltern can talk, but is seldom heard.'[7]

While the Danish term 'indvandrerlitteratur' (and the equivalent Norwegian and Swedish terms) has been extensively employed by Scandinavian media, it has been met with critique from (especially Swedish) academia as a concept that 'implies categorisation and dichotomisation, ethnification and racialisation'.[8] With reference to Fredric Jameson, Magnus Nilsson discusses 'immigrant literature' as a tool for a hegemonic cultural discourse, arguing that 'ethnicity has come to function as ... a "master code or interpretive key" for understanding Swedish society'.[9] The frenzy for 'immigrant literature' is creating a myth about ethnicity rather than reflecting it. This, according to Nilsson's perspective, is inevitable within the discursive context of multiculturalism. Søren Frank argues for the use of the term 'migration literature' instead of 'migrant literature', reasoning that '"migrant literature" (like *indvandrerlitteratur*) refers directly to the biography of the writer and thus connotes a compulsory (and therefore very problematic) link between authorial background and literary theme'.[10] In crime fiction studies, a similarly problematic connection between thematic literary content and authorial biography is also frequently made. A signal example is Gosselin's definition of 'multicultural detective fiction', which bears some resemblance to the critiqued notion of 'immigrant literature' in Scandinavian literary criticism insofar as its interpretative approach to texts rests on similarly autobiographical premises:

Multicultural detective fiction is the detective story in the hands of authors whose cultural communities are not those of the traditional Euro-American male hero, whose cultural experiences have been excluded from the traditional detective formula, and whose cultural aesthetic alters the formula itself.[11]

Reading Scandinavian crime fiction within the parameters of the (problematic) discursive cultural context of 'indvandrerlitteratur' allows first for a questioning of the absence within the genre of writers with 'foreign' backgrounds. Secondly, it draws attention to the fact that crime fiction – far from being a self-contained entity – operates within a broader frame of cultural discourse and that it is dependent on and in constant dialogue with this broader field. Finally, it highlights the fact that Scandinavian crime fiction in its monocultural representation of immigrants has followed a pattern that resembles that of literary fiction.

How, then, is it possible to identify and characterise a cultural discursive context in which a productive discussion of Scandinavian crime novels thematising migration and textualising personal or collective experiences of a multicultural society can take place? A large number of contemporary Scandinavian crime novels might be considered as being what Behschnitt and Nilsson define as 'multicultural literatures' ('literatures written, read, and discussed in the context of migration, multiculturalism and multilingualism'), or what Frank terms 'migration literature' ('all literary works that are written in an age of migration – or at least ... those works that can be said to reflect upon migration').[12] Both these categories refer to literary works not necessarily written by authors with a multicultural or immigrant/ emigrant background, but which at the same time in some form or another engage with questions of multiculturalism or migration. As such, these approaches allow a shift away from a biographical focus on the origins of authors to an arguably more objective and productive emphasis on discourse, as Nilsson's argument suggests:

> The key to understanding the relationship between ethnicity and literature is the insight that ethnicities are *culturally constructed identities*. And this insight implies in turn that literary texts can never be considered as an *expression* of any ethnic culture or identity. The fact that ethnicities are cultural constructions implies that they are *constituted* in cultural practices. And given that fiction is one of these practices it must be regarded as a phenomenon contributing to the *construction* of ethnic identities.[13]

The readings that follow will thus consider crime fiction first and foremost as cultural practice, and pay particular attention to questions of cultural constructions of identity.

Representations of the 'foreigner'

Examining the representation of 'the immigrant' in Danish literature from a historical perspective, Hans Hauge characterises a development having moved from centring on the immigrant as 'worker', via a focus on cultural and ethnic Otherness, to the present-day perspective in which, he argues, '[immigrants] are almost solely considered as a religious group'.[14] Scandinavian crime fiction demonstrates a similar shift in the perception of the immigrant from *class* via *culture/ethnicity* to an identity of which *religion* – specifically Islam – is presented as the defining feature.

Accordingly, in *Den skrattande polisen* (*The Laughing Policeman*, 1968), the fourth novel in *Roman om ett brott*, Sjöwall and Wahlöö depict and comment on the poor living conditions and the exploitation of the first wave of immigrant workers to Sweden in the 1960s.[15] The foreigner in the novel appears as a very minor, subordinate character who speaks rudimentary broken Swedish, lives in dormitory-style accommodation and remains unnamed during the interview that investigator Beck and his colleague carry out: he is simply referred to as 'the Turk' or 'the Arab'. The reductive representation of 'the Turk' is however firmly inscribed within a subversive discourse about economic injustices related to the foreigner's status as worker, the conversation focusing on his low weekly pay as a lorry driver, the high rent he must pay and the Swedish landlady 'raking in money'. The novel's ideological subtext in relation to the immigrant is thus, in Nancy Fraser's terms, associated with 'the paradigm of redistribution'.[16] In the 1990s and 2000s, the representation of the 'foreigner' becomes firmly inscribed in the 'paradigm of recognition' instead, with novels having a strong focus on injustices based on the ethnic individual's status in Scandinavian societies.

One of the most prominent examples of the contemplation of the 'foreigner' from an inside perspective and of this figure's influence on Scandinavian societies and cultures is to be found in Henning Mankell's Wallander series (comprising ten novels published between 1991 and 2009). The first novel in the series, *Mödare utan ansikte* (*Faceless Killers*, 1991), accentuates this thematic focus with its opening chapter in which an elderly farmer couple are brutally attacked and tortured by unknown intruders in a bucolic Scanian setting. The woman survives and manages before she dies a couple of days afterwards to utter the word 'foreigner'.[17] The subsequent investigation focuses on various interpretations of this word, not least on how the word can be misinterpreted by the press and public opinion, and reinforce already existing xenophobic attitudes. Indeed, the rest of the Wallander cycle could be said to continue this investigation into the notion of the foreigner and indigenous Swedes' relationship with newcomers. Central to a discussion of these issues in Mankell's work is the character of Kurt Wallander, as it is through his perspective (focalised via an omniscient third-person narrator) that the world and the 'foreigner' – whether victimised or villainised – are observed and told. The authoritative status of Wallander as someone speaking on behalf of a silenced Other is therefore an enduring feature of the series. Most important, however, is perhaps Wallander's self-reflexivity and his continuous interpretation of his own position and identity. This is, as highlighted by Nestingen, intricately connected with a Swedish state struggling with transformation in the post-1989 era.[18] The link between Wallander's physical and emotional unease – his unhealthy lifestyle, depression, alcoholism and diabetes – and a (regional) Swedish identity is reinforced through imagery, evoking melancholy in both environmental and personal human contexts. The novels' setting in Ystad in the southern Swedish district of Skåne is counterposed with intimidating intrusions from the outside world. Slavoj Žižek reads this relationship between the global and the local in Mankell's work as an expression of how popular fiction adapts to and reflects global capitalism, where the 'main effect ... is discernible in its dialectical counterpart: the powerful re-emergence of a specific *locale* as the story's setting – a particular provincial environment'.[19] In this provincial setting, a constant over the course of the Wallander cycle, is the intrusive presence of the globalised world in the form of the foreigner, as Nestingen argues:

> The Other is always present in Mankell's crime novels, and Wallander is transformatively entangled with Others. Solidarity is Mankell's response to these entanglements, yet that solidarity must always grapple with the ambivalence of confronting oneself amid heterogeneity that challenges one's own worldview and rational categories.[20]

The ambivalence that Nestingen ascribes to Wallander also extends into notions of physical space and nationality, which Mrozewicz captures in the concepts of *border* and *boundaries* in her discussion of Mankell's novels: 'the first one is rooted in the old world with pronounced national divisions, while the other anticipates a globalised world with the question of borders at stake'.[21] There are indeed 'porous borders', both in terms of geography and social identity – the ambiguities of a changing Sweden are seemingly in parallel with those of what can be seen as an 'in-between' character. Wallander's nostalgia for the old times and the idea of a transition into something new and anxiety-provoking is not – as is the case in Sjöwall and Wahlöö's work – solely linked to the rise and fall of the social-democratic welfare state, but is also associated with a transition from homogeneity to heterogeneity in cultural and ethnic terms.

To sum up the characteristics highlighted by academic commentary on the Wallander series, Mankell's novels establish a detective type deeply conflicted at a personal level; they expose a certain nostalgia for the disappearing foundation of the welfare state; they have a strong focus on the provincial *locale*, functioning as a nexus of anxieties about intrusions from the outside world. Mankell's texts and academic engagement with them establish the considerable shift in the perception of the 'foreigner' from a low-ranked member of the working class to a cultural/ethnic immigrant approachable by the ethnic-Swede in a spirit of solidarity, but who can also induce sentiments of unease and anxiety:

> Wallander's struggles invoke a diversity of questions and demands about the emergent transnational system's ethical and cultural failings, articulating a struggle for their redress. Wallander becomes a particular name that speaks for the dispossessed of the global era. Yet Mankell recognizes the stupendous narcissism and ethnocentrism of such a position, its incapacity to include the subaltern.[22]

Nestingen's characterisation of the Wallander figure as a struggling Swedish Self, speaking on behalf of the Other and having the awareness of the power constellation this perspective entails, also implies that if there is a struggle within what Nancy Fraser defines as the 'paradigm of recognition' in the case of Wallander, it is solely from the perspective of the observer who has to come to terms with how the world is affecting him.[23]

Characteristic of most critical engagement with Mankell's work is affirmation of its deep involvement in a humanitarian project frequently linked to the author's real-life activism around third world issues. Nestingen thus highlights both Mankell and his Wallander character for their sense of 'solidarity'.[24] Bergman reads a similar authorial intentionality into the texts: 'Mankell enables the reader to identify with Wallander and his biases, while simultaneously realizing that the biases are nothing but just prejudices that ought to be fought and suppressed.'[25] Correspondingly, McCorristine argues that 'Mankell is a good example of a committed writer taking aim at injustice in his society'.[26] This stands in contrast with the fact that Mankell's Wallander texts themselves can be viewed as locked in a bipolar constellation of Self and Other, an us–them dichotomy easily describable in the terminology of postcolonial studies. The use of possessive pronouns in McCorristine's conclusion to his article about Wallander accentuates this feature of criticism: 'Wallander's investigations ... reflect the increasing sense of disorientation and insecurity among contemporary Swedes about *their* place in the world, and about the place of the Other in *their* world'.[27] In the context of the Wallander character's self-centred outlook, this is an insight that is monophonic in scope by not including voices of the subaltern.

One possible way of differentiating between critical interrogation and symptomatic reflection, between *orientalism* being played out or depicted in Mankell's novels, is that proposed by Magnus Nilsson in his engagement with the notion of 'immigrant' literature, which he reads using Fraser's distinction between two different political approaches to identity: *affirmation* versus *transformation*.[28] Fraser herself defines these as follows:

> By affirmative remedies for injustice I mean remedies aimed at correcting inequitable outcomes of social arrangements without disturbing the underlying framework that generates them. By transformative remedies, in contrast, I mean remedies aimed at correcting inequitable outcomes precisely by restructuring the underlying generative framework.[29]

When Stenport argues that the Swedish consensus ideology, of which she asserts that Mankell's Wallander novels are a part, 'raises pressing questions of the moment, yet refrains from answering any of them', she inscribes Mankell's work firmly within the affirmative politics characteristic according to Nilsson of mainstream multiculturalism, defining the multicultural society 'primarily in ethnic terms'.[30] The same can be said about most critical engagement with Mankell's crime novels, illustrating emblematically how critical issues can be elided by a simplistically affirmative approach. The absence of engagement incorporating and exposing what Nilsson characterises as 'the hegemonic Swedish discourse about the so-called multicultural society' signals the usefulness and applicability to contemporary crime fiction of the transformative and deconstructive approach outlined by Fraser. Such an approach, as applied by Nilsson to 'immigrant literature', is arguably applicable to the study of literature more widely in its engagement with cultural diversity.[31] Accordingly, the following discussion of two fictional representations of the most emblematically controversial symbol of contemporary cultural difference – the Muslim Other – will attempt to go beyond affirmative tropes present in works such as Mankell's and in criticism of them.

The Muslim Other

As the investigations of numerous scholars indicate, relationships between the Baltic states/Russia and Scandinavia occupy a particularly significant place in Scandinavian crime fiction: authors frequently cited include Henning Mankell, Stieg Larsson, Leif Davidsen and Kim Småge, all of whom investigate crime within a post-1989 perspective.[32] The representation of the Russian or Eastern European foreigner, however, seems to have been superseded in the post-2001 era by a new type of foreigner: the Muslim Other. This will be the focus of the following readings of Norwegian author Roy Jacobsen's novel *Marions slør* (Marion's Veil, 2008) and Danish author Paul Smith's *Mordet på imamen* (The Murder of the Imam, 2008). These two novels by 'non-migrant' writers can both be characterised as migration literature inasmuch as they deal thematically with questions of migration. What is significant, however, is that neither novel in its approach to the topic of migration possesses any 'nostalgia' for the old homogenous Scandinavian nation states found in the Wallander figure. Rather, both novels engage with the globalised, multicultural conditions present in contemporary society – albeit in different ways – by introducing a representation of the (Muslim) Other in the role of the investigator.

Roy Jacobsen: Marions slør

Julie H. Kim asks in her introduction to *Race and Religion in the Postcolonial British Detective Story*: 'what is more "othering" than to be murdered, no longer being part of the living community – or perhaps not really having been, even in life, part of that community?'[33] In Roy Jacobsen's *Marions slør*, the central victim – a young woman and second-generation immigrant with a Pakistani background – is quite precisely 'othered' by death at the beginning of the novel.

Found in a skip containing shattered glass from discarded windows and doors, the young female body is missing a hand and covered in a hijab. The lack of transparency, symbolically emphasised by the broken glass and the veil, ties in with the crime narrative, which the third-person narrator comments on in the novel's first sentence: 'It was a story without a *clear* beginning.'[34] An essential part of the ensuing investigation consists of reconstructing Nasreen's identity from the shattered pieces that remain. The fragmentation of Nasreen's body – physically dumped as rubbish on the outskirts of the city as a social space – is also symbolic within the narrative of the social and cultural segregation within Norwegian society on which the novel centres, and indeed of what Graham Huggan refers to as an 'age of fragmentation' in Western societies.[35]

The overarching textual imagery of disintegration, fragmentation and shattering – alongside the amputated limb as a metaphor for the separation of the ethnic individual from the social body – is further visually reinforced by the original Norwegian front cover, which foregrounds precisely these aspects of the novel. The illustration depicts nine differently coloured individual hands separated from their bodies in a three-by-three grid on a dark-red background, the cut-off hands decorated with stamp-like 'tattoos' representing, for example, an elephant, a lotus flower or other iconic symbols referring to different cultures and religions from around the world. The victim, moreover, has been reduced to the role of the Silent Other, excluded from knowledge and power, and is presented in terms of ready-made associations existing in the public sphere and of predetermined notions about her cultural identity.

At the immediate narrative level, Nasreen's missing hand plays an important role in the investigation. The corpse itself becomes a (bodily) jigsaw puzzle of missing pieces and of wrong pieces when another woman's cut-off hand is discovered wearing Nasreen's ring. The subsequent investigation takes the form of the (re)assembly of all the pieces to enable the reconstruction of Nasreen's identity by giving her dead body a name, a distinctive personality, a soul and a social life. Emphasised by the covering-up of Nasreen's face with a veil, the murder is an act of concealment. The hijab covers over a young woman, who never wore a head scarf when she was alive, having left a traditional life with her Pakistani family to live with her ethnic-Norwegian boyfriend and pursue her university studies.

The process of reassembling the dismembered body and identity of Nasreen also parallels the reconstruction – in Todorov's term – of the crime narrative's primary story. Marion is employed as an investigator for a special unit designed to 'work with ethnic-related crimes [that] for political reasons [is] named "The Contact Group for Intercultural Conflict Resolution"' (p. 19). The team in fact constitutes its own microcosm of a multicultural Norwegian society: besides Marion, there is the team's leader, the Scot McNaughton, Reza – a 'second-generation immigrant of Pakistani origin' (p. 19) – and William, an intellectual brought as a child to Norway by his bourgeois Iraqi parents, who fled their country because their democratic ideals conflicted with Saddam Hussein's regime. The cultural and ethnic diversity of the team, of which Marion is the only member of ethnic-Norwegian background, is within the narrative regarded as an asset, reinforced by the fact that the team members have all had a personal encounter with 'ethnic criminality' in some form or another in the past and therefore 'have all been hand-picked because [they] know the "enemy as [themselves]"' (p. 100).

In juxtaposition with the media's subdued treatment of the murdered Muslim girls, described by the narrator as 'a line of tragedies treated with pity, murders of guests from far-away, partly un-wanted, yes even illegal, and women' (p. 173), there is a pronounced difference – rendered by an ironic narrator – in the public's reaction to the murder of a rather miserable white man. The new murder is described as 'an attack on the innermost soul of the nation, on the white man's masculine skin in the city of Trondheim, the solar plexus of the saga of the king' (p. 173). At the individual level, however, all of the victims share two common characteristics. First, none of them are missed: their family and acquaintances do not report them missing, a social invisibility that McNaughton comments on, noting 'All this damned absence of the feeling of loss' (p. 104). Secondly, 'they had a strong dream of living in harmony with people from other cultures' (p. 168). The crimes moreover have a resonance that goes far beyond Norway, provoking '[f]ive death screams that had all been overheard, in line with an injustice which has escalated and become habitual, like the world's poverty, Africa's illnesses and the Middle-East's wars' (pp. 268–9).

This new and extended contemporary context also has its effect on characters' immediate surroundings, and indeed provokes through a changed environment a new kind of nostalgia in the protagonist, who is:

> at all sides surrounded by immigrants and ethnic Norwegians, a bustling busy afternoon at the end of September, in the cosy little corner of

the community suddenly in the middle of having its richness of colours replaced by hard, old-fashioned black and white contrasts in the neighbourhood where Marion buys her food and eats kebabs and sandwiches with bacon and fried eggs of which the immigrants have taken over the production. The original Norwegian kitchen and the miserable lentil soup from the Helmand province side by side in all its usual everyday friendly tolerance, the new and the old. (pp. 50–1)

The nostalgia that Marion exhibits here is not Wallander's nostalgia for a homogenous country of the past, but a vision of a society having gone through a process of seemingly peaceful and harmonious integration of immigrants to then finish in a segregated community where the ethnical and cultural lines are drawn up. This vision is later in the novel reiterated in the description of Oslo as a 'smiling, everyday-like, normal, modern city, a slowly pulverizing ethnic grinder which it had taken decades to set in motion, and which was now threatened by the past and about to come to a stop' (p. 262).

The novel deploys a range of immigrant stereotypes: Russian villains involved in trafficking; illegal immigrant workers employed by Norwegian farmers and living under horrible living and pay conditions; Hassan at Tariq's kebab shop where Marion buys her dinner; Eastern European prostitutes. The novel exploits clichés and stereotypes while at the same time leaving some room for a critique of them in the name of an encompassing 'friendliness' mixed with suspicions. McNaughton states that this is a characteristic Norwegian attitude towards foreigners: 'the ordinary Norwegian can really be emphatically prejudiced ... but he does not like being mean, certainly not for long, then he begins to feel uneasy. The Norwegian likes to feel friendly, if you understand what I mean' (p. 170).

The representation of foreigners in the novel exposes the idea of the 'ethnic grinder', which in the novel's optic seems to imply perfect assimilation. Besides Nasreen who has turned her back on her Muslim family, we also meet the well-integrated Pakistani who runs a chain of fast-food restaurants and has even bought a 'hytte' (a Norwegian cabin). Perhaps most accentuated is William, as a member of the police team the personification of a model immigrant, described by Marion as 'the final and illustrative example of the nation's glorious passion for integration. The Norwegian William. The art of the possible' (p. 343). Reza, the team's other Muslim, ends up being involved in a retributive killing of the original murderer: the explanation for his 'fatal weakness' (p. 336) lies precisely in the fact that he is not assimilated but struggles between two irreconcilable cultures, according to Marion's interpretation: 'he didn't know where he wanted to be, he wanted to be both places, both in his family and in Norwegian society, the bitter and the sweet which cannot be mixed, which will produce nausea, which undermines your self-respect' (p. 337).

For the police team there are only two probable murderer profiles compatible with the brutal nature of the murders and the personal background of the victims: either the murders are committed by an extreme racist organisation or individual, or by an extreme Islamist organisation or individual. Blinded by a reductive vision of the world and by their own unnavigable prejudices, the team continuously find themselves at dead ends in the investigation. The investigation is conducted in accordance with discursive practices fostering a dichotomising black-and-white world view, summed up by Marion in an early stage of the investigation: 'Close your eyes and focus on "white hand" and "black hand". Both of them are atrocious. But they belong to each their own atrocity. Each their own world' (p. 58). This Manichaean concept runs through the novel's imagery and is repeated in harsher terms further into the novel when McNaughton claims in relation to the three murdered Muslim women and two ethnic-Norwegian men: 'It looked in other words like war. Between two genders. And two cultures' (p. 246).

When the murderer is finally revealed as Fennevold – an ordinary 'hypnotically anonymous' Norwegian man (p. 351) – it breaks down the black-and-white pattern by which both the investigation and the public have been seduced. Near the end of the novel, Marion retrospectively reflects on the team's incapability to find this murderer sooner:

> We didn't find Fennevold in time, because we weren't looking for Fennevold. The team is not created to find Fennevold. It is created to find Nasreen's brothers. A racist organisation. A fanatical Islamist. It is created to find the signs of the times. And *that* is always something completely different from the truth. (pp. 337–8)

Marion reasons that this is also an attitude prevalent in Norwegian society, seen in its reaction to the exposure of Fennevold as the murderer: 'Both the immigrant milieu and the ethnic-Norwegian parts of the population want a murderer they can understand. They cannot stand the sight of Fennevold. Because Fennevold resembles the people. The Norwegian people' (p. 336).

The novel is far less a narrative about an investigator's trajectory through serial murders, than a case of investigating the associations and preconceived perceptions attached to images of the (Muslim) Other. This thematic concern is built into the novel's narrative structure. While the team is investigating the murders, another investigation begins: the team itself is investigated by an examination committee. This examination – taking place chronologically after the case is closed – intersects with more plot-driven chapters in the novel's second half. McNaughton finds himself before a tribunal of unnamed members interrogating him on the investigation team's failure to discover Reza's involvement in Fennevold's murder. The narrative purpose of this embedded meta-investigation however remains unclear until the novel's final pages. The committee's prolonged and at times harsh interrogation of McNaughton, which insinuates ethnicity as being the key to understanding the conflictual disagreement of the team, is at the novel's conclusion irrevocably refuted by McNaughton. During the final session before the tribunal, the power relationship in the interrogation is reversed: McNaughton now asks the questions to an ever more confused and vocally weak chairman:

> McNaughton, alert:
> 'It was our individual competencies which didn't suffice. Irrespectively of our cultural background, do we agree on that?'
> 'Ehm … yes.'
> 'Yes, I just wanted to hear you say it, because I totally agree.'
> The chairman, now completely ruined:
> 'What are you trying to insinuate?'
> 'That our problems were not at all linked to ethnicity?'
> 'Ehm … no. What?' (pp. 370–1)

The novel's *mise en abyme* of the investigation plausibly indicates an attempt at challenging prevalent public discourse on society's disintegration as a symptom of ethnic diversity. However, within the textual universe, this attempt remains superficial when it becomes obvious that McNaughton will be forced to step down as the leader of the team as a consequence of the case.

Fennevold's motives for committing the murders remain unclear, bringing the novel's conclusion back to where it started, with questions unanswered: 'a story without a beginning, and without an ending either' (pp. 352–3). Toft Hansen argues that *Marions slør* gives 'neither an affirmative nor a subversive answer … but a reflexive investigation of the topic … arising from the fact that the novel refuses to leave the reader with a resolution and clarity'.[36] Rather, I would argue, that the text applies a consensus-seeking agenda in which its sense of a narrative continuum of uncertainty relates to its notion of historicity as circular motion, always finding its way back to the known, and reinforcing a sense of the inertia of tradition. Despite the undoubted success of the 'ethnic grinder' in turning out model assimilated citizens, a return to the starting point is inevitable not only in a narrative sense, but also when it comes to societal organisation and discourses surrounding it. This becomes apparent in Marion's final conclusion after the closure of the case:

> the ethnic dividers had appeared again, yes, actually they were fully in place ... the old positions had been occupied and reinforced by all of those who had been right all the time and who were now right again, the way it had always been in this country. (p. 375)

The hint of irony in Marion's closing comments subtly makes an attempt at approaching Norwegian segregational attitudes, but it ends with an acceptance of the status quo.

The reception of Marions slør

Magnus Nilsson places his discussion of 'immigrant literature' as 'part of a more general discourse about the so-called multicultural society, having become hegemonic in the public sphere during recent decades'.[37] This dominating discourse, which he terms the 'ethnic lens', is revealed in the press interest in *Marions slør*, confirming this strong focus on ethnicity in the Norwegian public sphere, in that the reviews foreground aspects of multiculturalism and identity politics.[38]

One feature of the reviews is that *Marions slør*'s status as crime fiction is put aside and focus is given to the novel's sociological study of contemporary Norway. Terje Stemland, in his review for the Norwegian newspaper *Aftenposten*, thus describes Roy Jacobsen's novel as a 'very topical criminal study of multicultural Norway'.[39] Another feature further accentuating the novel's reception within the realm of identity politics can be found in the Norwegian newspaper *Dagbladet*'s controversial categorisation of *Marions slør* as a 'norsk innvandrerroman' (Norwegian immigrant novel). This nomination caused Noman Mubashir, a journalist for NRK (the Norwegian state broadcaster), immediately to reciprocate with a critique of the absence in the Norwegian literary landscape of writers of foreign descent, highlighting his disappointment that the 'new novel from the immigrant milieu comes from a middle-aged white man'.[40] Unni Malmø, interviewed in the same article as Mubashir, completely denounces the use of the term 'innvandrerroman', in line with Nilsson, because its application 'is about satisfying Norwegians' imagination about immigration'.[41] *Marions slør* as a novel advocating ethnic identity is also found in NRK's review of the novel:

> It is ... about the Norway that we are in the midst of creating – or perhaps rather are in the midst of allowing to be created. A place where political correctness deprives us all of the sense of security that we can despite everything talk with each other, as long as it is a conversation based on mutual respect.[42]

An article in the Danish newspaper *Berlingske Tidende*, published after the launch of the novel's Danish translation, accentuates this sense of unease over identity politics by focusing on the differences between Norway and Denmark in their attitudes towards immigrants, both in political terms and in terms of public opinion. The article features an interview with Roy Jacobsen, in which he explains his own agenda: '[I] make an attempt at challenging the preconception in fiction that immigrants automatically equal criminality. I have as far as possible tried to break away from the clichés dominating crime novels so that readers' own preconceptions and prejudices are tested.'[43]

Returning to Fraser, the underlying discursive propositions of the reviews are palpably rehearsed within the 'paradigm of recognition'. While the reviews focus on the novel's thematic 'questioning' of discriminatory preconceptions about immigrants and cultural injustices, the press's engagement with the novel is firmly inscribed in what Fraser refers to as 'mainstream multiculturalism', proposing affirmative remedies to 'redress disrespect by revaluing unjustly devalued group identities, while leaving intact both the contents of those identities and the group differentiations that underlie them'.[44] The fact that Roy Jacobsen's novel is read primarily through the filter of 'immigration', and through use of the notion of the 'immigrant' as a collective term that needs to be explored, suggests applicability to the Norwegian context of Nilsson's view of 'ethnic othering [as characteristic of] contemporary Swedish debates about literature and the multicultural society'.[45]

The overarching premise for the advancement of the novel's crime, investigation and (absence of) resolution is the juxtaposition of ethnic prejudices and 'politically correct' attitudes. Prevalent in this is a highlighted conceptualisation of Norway as a fundamentally harmonious country disturbed only momentarily by murders committed with a motive presumed to be ethnicity-related. In an interview, Jacobsen emphasises what he refers to as the 'consensus mentality in Norwegian society' as the novel's underlying fabric.[46] The textual ambivalence is not unlike that of Mankell's Wallander novels: on the one hand *Marions slør* contains a descriptive account of societal prejudices and cultural divides, while on the other hand the text itself falls into the trap of reproducing well-rehearsed tropes about the so-called 'multicultural society'. The novel's insistence on a dichotomous view of the world, reproduced in much of the textual imagery, reinforces these tropes.

While the novel makes a point of challenging the crime fiction genre's stereotypes and clichéd images of the foreigner through use of counter-stereotypes, the novel's own interpretation of a 'consensus mentality' is wholly reliant on an image of the well-assimilated 'model immigrant' in the figure of William, who is beyond issues of cultural ambivalence and identity struggles. These are the same issues that lead Reza astray into his criminal actions and bring about his personal and professional downfall. Moreover, through William and Reza, the novel replicates a frequently employed, but problematic, popular distinction between the good, secularised, westernised Muslim and the bad, anti-Western, fundamentalist Muslim.[47] Disintegration here is the real danger for successful cultural cohabitation: the investigating body is, through Reza's involvement in the killing of Fennevold, damaged in the same way as the girls' hands are cut off and a well-functioning society dismembered when some of its members are murdered.

Paul Smith: Mordet på imamen

As highlighted by Toft Hansen in his analysis of the role of Islam in Scandinavian crime fiction, novels dealing with the Islamic experience within post-secular Scandinavian societies do not produce a uniform entity, but cover a spectrum reaching from 'more traditional critical approaches to Islam [to novels trying] to kick-start a nuanced debate about the Muslim faith'.[48] Danish author Paul Smith's novel *Mordet på imamen* (The Murder of the Imam, 2008) places itself in the latter category by directly addressing a number of questions relating not only to Islam, but to the West's encounter with the Muslim world.

At the novel's outset a Swedish man is found killed in his house, remotely situated in a forest in northern Halland, south of Gothenburg. The man is former alcoholic and village misfit Wahid Abu Svensson, newly converted to Islam and known locally as 'the Imam'. What for the local police appears to be an easily solvable case with the village's National Socialist as the obvious suspect soon becomes transnational in scope when two further imams are murdered, first in Aarhus and then in Oslo. The investigation's geographical movement from a local to an international setting is echoed by the composition of the investigating team, consisting of two couples based locally in Halland: police officers Ingvar Windén and Ayan Mohammed Gyrhan, alongside Jan Åkesson and his girlfriend Helena Maria Cirio.

This fictional plot is expressly situated in the midst of immediate current historical temporality with references to events that have intensified public and political debate on the 'immigrant question', such as the attack on the World Trade Center (2001), the murder of the Swedish Social Democrat Anna Lindh (2003) and the Danish Mohammed cartoon controversy (2005). Insisting on employing the names of real, contemporary persons involved in public debate (newspaper editors, politicians, cartoonists, etc.), *Mordet på imamen* inserts its narrative into a realist, recognisable setting, specifying the novel's temporal context as 2006. However, the novel also plays around with an emphasised fictional reality by employing characters from other contemporary crime novels in minor roles. The main investigator in Swedish Liza Marklund's crime novels, Annika Bengtzon, thus appears in *Mordet på imamen* as a journalist who, writing for a Swedish tabloid paper, presents unnuanced claims, jumps to easy conclusions and is the target for a critique that the novel launches against the sensational press and its treatment of Muslims.[49] This rather caricatured image of Annika Bengtzon perhaps also implies criticism towards certain aspects of Scandinavian crime fiction playing a role in shaping the popular imagination by uncritically contributing to the reproduction of stereotypes. Moreover, Paul Smith's novel also engages with stereotypes in the crime fiction genre – and in the popular imagination – by being more subtly and generically subversive in the creation of its own detective figures.

Detective figures

Windén embodies a recognisable Scandinavian male detective character: he is 'thoroughly Swedish' (p. 69), middle-aged, 'dressed as

[a] secondary school teacher' in 'a dark-brown and slightly wrinkled corduroy suit' (p. 70) and retreats to a workaholic existence to avoid increased domestic tensions with his wife and children. His unhealthy lifestyle with a tendency to eat pastries and drink too much coffee causes him to have a 'constant problem of 5–10 kilos of excess weight' (p. 117). Windén's resemblance to Mankell's Kurt Wallander – an association further reinforced by the novel's primary setting being Halland on the south-west coast of Sweden and the letter 'W' as initial of his surname – is striking, almost to the point of being a caricature. A further allusion to the 'classic' Swedish detective is established by Windén's troublesome relationship with Sapö, the Swedish secret service, a characteristic that he shares with both Wallander and Sjöwall and Wahlöö's main protagonist Martin Beck. Windén, as a representative of the typical Beck/Wallander figure, does not, however, get much narrative focus in the novel. Neither does Jan Åkesson, whom the Swedish police employ as a consultant in the first murder case. Instead, the novel openly rejects the standard by insisting on giving the point of view to two women: Windén's colleague, Ayan, and Åkesson's partner Helena, both immigrants. Although introduced as inferior female sidekicks to their male counterparts, these two women are both given more full-bodied characters than them. It is indeed through the interior point of view of these two women (mediated via the omniscient third-person narrator) that large parts of the novel are narrated. Also, it is their insights that lead to the case being solved.

Both Ayan and Helena can be said to personify the 'new specimen' in international crime fiction: 'the so-called "hybrid-detective" whose role acknowledges cultural multiplicity'.[50] Ayan ticks a number of boxes for identity categories: she is a young, black, Somali woman, and furthermore a Muslim; Helena is a Chilean national who came to Sweden as a refugee fleeing the turmoil after Pinochet's coup in 1973. Both women are well established in Swedish society and know how to navigate it both professionally and socially.

The character of Ayan oscillates between being in a binary relationship with Windén (young/old, culturally Muslim/culturally Christian, woman/man, black/white, African/European) and having a professional function in society that eliminates these schismatic structures: she is a policewoman as he is a policeman. However, it is not Ayan's professional status as investigator, but her branding as 'foreigner', that is repeatedly evoked in the novel. Ayan's character functions as a prism through which a multitude of different visions of the foreigner in the novel are refracted. It begins with the first obvious suspect in the Wahid Abu Svensson murder case, the neo-Nazi K.G., who agonises over the black female police officer interviewing him: 'The bitch had Mohammed as her middle name, that is a Muslim nigger in the Swedish police ... She probably had AIDS' (p. 63). When Ayan and Windén later interview Wahid's sister and her husband, who are devoted Pentecostal missionaries, Ayan 'senses the prejudices of the woman who probably equated Osama bin Laden with [her] religion' (p. 148). She is also commented on as someone who deviates from the common image, as noticed by the woman whose child has found the body of Wahid: 'the Somalians in Gothenburg dressed differently, in an exotic manner, from this woman [Ayan], who wore blue jeans, a long dark-green shirt and an even longer dark-grey jacket' (p. 69). The same woman also refers to her as 'the African', but she has to reconsider this categorisation when met with Ayan's articulate Gothenburg dialect (p. 70). These prejudices relating to Ayan's ethnicity and religion are joined by a quasi-orientalist sexist gaze making her an exotic and at times erotic Other. Alf Karlsson, member of Säpo, asks in a conversation with Windén: 'How is your new colleague? I mean, apart from the fact that she is extremely good-looking? Don't tell me that cultural diversity has no advantages' (p. 122). Ayan's erotic appeal is encapsulated as part of her exoticism. This racial othering and the othering of Ayan as a woman are suggested by a female witness earlier in the novel who focalises Ayan in an essentialising subjectivity by reducing her to the fact that she has 'large and sensual ... "bedroom eyes"' (p. 69).

Ayan rejects the various attitudes to her Otherness. She counters the explicit and negative preconceptions about her racial and religious identity with didactic responses, demonstrating her superiority in terms of knowledge and her aptitude for navigating the Swedish social landscape. The textual construction of Ayan's identity responds to the minor characters' epithetical preconceptions, and she becomes a counter-stereotype who can sweep away all judgemental clichés linguistically, intellectually and professionally. As a parallel to the character of William in *Marions slør*, Ayan is an impeccably well-cultured and seamlessly assimilated immigrant, to the extent that she surpasses ethnic Swedes in her 'Swedishness'. Before her police career, she studied history at university and knows more than enough about Karl XII to expose and correct the neo-Nazi suspect's manufactured image of the Swedish king, and on several occasions, her knowledge about Swedish history, place names and culture exceeds that of even the 'thoroughly Swedish' Windén.[51]

The excessive idealisation of Ayan overtly functions as a deconstruction of a negative, stereotypical image of Muslim women. It also contrasts with the novel's cover image, depicting the face of a hijab-covered woman whose clothing blends in with the black background. The question remains as to how effective this method is, and whether or not the use of the 'hybrid-detective' in this case actually promotes a recognition of cultural differences. The novel's 'construction of ethnicity', to employ Magnus Nilsson's term, through the use of counter-images, might allow for a rejection of stereotypes, but it leaves little room for cultural shadings or nuances.[52] Because Ayan antithetically responds to perceived notions of Muslim Otherness, she necessarily adapts to a normative Swedish worldview, becoming more Swedish than the Swedes themselves.

Reception and its context: the Mohammed cartoon controversy

The novel includes as one of the clues in the investigation the Danish cartoonist Kurt Westergaard's much-debated caricature of the prophet Mohammed wearing an ignited bomb in the shape of a turban, referred to as the 'exploding head' drawing, and originally printed in the Danish newspaper *Jyllandsposten* in September 2005. A print of this drawing is pinned to the wall in Wahid's house where his body is found. The following investigation centres on the symbolism of the placement of this controversial cartoon at the crime scene. Furthermore, the cartoon also becomes the starting point for the novel's interrogation of representations of Muslims in the public sphere. The novel from this point onwards thematically evolves around the increasingly xenophobic attitude exhibited in the Danish media in the wake of the Mohammed cartoon controversy, which Peter Hervik has characterised as the 'Scandinavian Nexus of exclusionary thinking that primarily seems to revolve around anti-Muslim racism'.[53]

Helena's investigation into media and political commentary on Kurt Westergaard's cartoon at the public library in Aarhus exposes the ideological narrative subtext. This subtext is expressed in the form of her ironic interior monologue. Reading *Jyllandsposten*, she contemplates her findings:

> If one were to believe the letters to the editor, Muslims in Denmark were incessantly churning out murdered Christians on a conveyor belt. Strange that they did not write where they got their sensational knowledge from.

190

There was in fact nothing about these daily serial killings in the news sections of the newspaper. (p. 216)

Her contemplations also query the purpose of *Jyllandsposten*'s printing of the cartoons in the first place, prompting the question, reported indirectly by the narrative: 'had freedom of speech become the new religion in a so-called secularised country?' (p. 216).

Ayan's and Helena's analytical interpretation of cultural conflicts and their origins – informed by their extensive reading – are further complicated by the novel's shifting between two Nordic countries, opening up a binary series: there are two murdered 'imams', one in Sweden, one in Denmark (the Norwegian imam does not get much attention); the investigation proceeds in parallel in two places; the action is witnessed from insider and outsider perspectives. The narrator moreover takes the voices of the two immigrant women and makes them spokeswomen for the novel's immanent ideology.

This ideological standpoint is difficult to disentangle from the contextual climate of the novel's publication. If the reception of *Marions slør* was characterised by a focus on the novel's analysis of Norwegian society and consensus-seeking identity politics, the media's reading of *Mordet på imamen* foregrounds its political immediacy as an asset with readings accentuating the novel's relevance because of its treatment of current affairs. The publication of *Mordet på imamen* in early March 2008 coincided with a renewed intensification of the Mohammed cartoon controversy. After the arrests of three people on 12 February 2008 accused of having planned to murder Kurt Westergaard, seventeen Danish newspapers made a collective editorial decision to re-publish the much-debated cartoons the following day. The re-publication led to renewed tensions between Denmark and the Muslim world, demonstrations in Pakistan and Gaza, and a new boycott of Danish products in several countries in the Middle East. Subsequently, press reviews of the novel link its thematic focus to the issues occupying the headlines of Danish newspapers at the time of its publication. Commenting on the novel's weaknesses as a crime narrative, the review on the Danish libraries' national website, *Litteratursiden*, highlights the novel as being 'highly topical' and justifies the recommendation precisely with reference to the novel's actuality: '[The novel] is recommended though and especially now with the renewed intensification of the Mohammed drawings controversy.'[54] The novel's aesthetic success is thus downplayed in comparison with its functionality – and relevance – as a novel providing political commentary on issues relating to the 'crisis' coinciding with its publication. Typical press reaction included that of Klaus Rothstein in *Weekendavisen*:

> Show me a recent Danish crime novel or thriller that is not in one way or another about Islamist terrorists. No, that branch of literature does the same as political debate, which, as we know, has been infested with Koran and caricature, and now we have Paul Smith who attempts to combine the thrill with political commentary.[55]

Likewise, Peter Nørskov, in his review in *Århus Stiftidende*, demonstratively reads the novel in the concurrent political context with the suggestive article title 'Imam-mord midt i en krisetid' (Imam murders during a time of crisis).[56] The article, rather than properly engaging with the novel itself, focuses insistently from its first sentence on the resemblance between the character of the second imam who is murdered in the novel, Ahmed Balasa, and the imam of the Grimshøj mosque in Aarhus, Ahmed Akkari.[57] The review thus takes as its starting point and dominant focus a section of the novel constituting only a minor preoccupation in the fictional text, and, moreover, goes beyond mere comparison to assert an identity between the fictional imam and a real-life counterpart:

> During the first Mohammed controversy, he [Akkari] joked in front of a French TV photographer about blowing up Nasar Khader and the [Danish] Ministry of Integration. At a time when hatred against Denmark and the Mohammed cartoonist Kurt Westergaard has been resurrected in some Muslim countries ... Ahmed Akkari, the former Aarhus imam, is himself murdered in cold blood on his way to work in the Grimshøj mosque in Brabrand.[58]

The review moreover omits any reference to *Mordet på imamen*'s thorough analysis of geopolitical concerns as the background understanding for the 'crisis'. Nor does it mention the novel's multifaceted and philosophical discussions of the relationship between Western and Muslim cultures or – perhaps most importantly – the unnuanced representation of Muslims within the Danish press that Helena characterises as a 'freakshow [in the name of] freedom of speech' (p. 215) defined by a rhetoric of 'mockery, insults and ridicule' towards Muslims (p. 218). By making Akkari the centre of the review and by employing (parts of) the novel's plot as a retributive reaction to real-life events, Nørskov manipulates the novel into a simplistic position highlighting precisely what the novel itself advocates against.

Schooling of the foreign Other

The novel's concern with detecting the individual source of the 'imam murders' intertwines with the philosophical reading of 'our time' and the exposure of pronounced and also more subtle Islamophobic tendencies within Swedish and Danish societies. Discussion in *Mordet på imamen* of encounters between Christian and Islamic cultures proceeds, as the novel's subtitle – *en filosofisk krimi* (a philosophical crime novel) – suggests, from a philosophical standpoint, and employs a vast apparatus of Western philosophers and thinkers to support its arguments. Longer passages of philosophical exposition, intersecting with the novel's more plot-driven parts, explicate Christianity and Greek philosophy's intertwinement with Islam, different directions within Islam, American and European involvement in the Middle East and its consequences for the development of the region, and the history of modern Sweden (including the aristocracy's and political and financial elites' alliances with Nazi Germany during the Second World War). Alongside this philosophical and socio-historical analysis of the Muslim world's relationship with the West, the novel features the formal characteristics of an academic essay (there is an extensive use of footnotes and in-text brackets with birth and death dates of philosophers and historical figures). In this two-component genre-hybrid, the 'murder of the imam' is thus examined through both an academic investigation and a criminal investigation. Well suited for the novel's overlap between essayistic and novelistic writing modes, the intellectual and knowledgeable characters of Ayan and Helena serve the purpose of enlightening the reader. The critical – and perhaps, for the popular genre, pretentious – philosophical reflections tie in with the novel's own didactic representation of the foreigner and in particular its discussion of the status of the Muslim immigrant in contemporary. Sweden and Denmark. Ayan and Helena are not there to explore themes of identity, belonging or exile – as was the case, for example, in Peter Høeg's *Frøken Smillas fornemmelse for sne*. Rather, the narrative insists on positioning these two women of foreign descent as the bearers of (Western) cultural, philosophical and historical knowledge and places the textual emphasis on their contribution to a profound and nuanced analysis of (Western) society. Their highlighted presence in the novel as investigators explicitly challenges the genre's stereotypes and counters the monopoly of a mono-directional point of view, most usually typified by a middle-aged white man commenting on and being anxious about a changing society defined by its diversity. Windén as the representative of the Wallander figure is categorically rejected, caricatured and pushed into the background to give prominence to the voice of his colleague, who represents various identities (young/ female/black/Muslim/Somali) that have previously been voiceless in the Scandinavian variant of the crime fiction genre. However, while the novel plays around with the notions of insider- and outsiderdom and contests the stereotypes of the genre, it is noteworthy that it does so within a (white/male) Western paradigm: both Ayan and Helena have been schooled in and employ Western concepts of knowledge and rationalism in their argumentation and analyses.

Conclusion: the view from the centre

In both Jacobsen's and Smith's novels there exists a sense of disintegration and breakdown relating to the condition of individuals and of society in the absence of social norms and values. At the forefront of both, however, is not nostalgic reflection on the social-democratic construction of the welfare state, which plays a role of reference in Wallander's imagination – albeit with the knowledge that it is a paradise lost. Rather, the two texts foreground the 'multicultural society', and their plots are played out within the ideological context of 'mainstream multiculturalism', in Nilsson's understanding of the terms.[59] Like Mankell's Wallander novels, these two narratives are concerned with writing the ethnically and culturally foreign Other, but in adding a further layer, *Mordet på imamen* and *Marions slør* also provide an explicit commentary on the discourse within which ethnic identities are created and displayed in public imagination and the media.

Perhaps the fundamental contradiction – or indeed dialectical premise – for the two novels is the following: on one hand they are part of a fictional corpus in contemporary Nordic popular culture 'inventing', as Nestingen rightly states, 'stories that call to mind and challenge background understandings', so that these 'texts ... use crime to engage with debates over individualism, collective claims, the status of national homogeneity, gender, and transnational relations';[60] on the other hand, however, the texts themselves are part of an affirmative discursive context in which they unwittingly propagate an ethnocentric vision and reproduce some of the tropes that they themselves oppose. In *Marions slør* the distinction between William as the 'good Muslim' and Reza as the 'bad Muslim' underpins the logic that runs through media representation of Muslims. *Mordet på imamen* explicitly engages with preconceptions and stereotypical representations, but by creating a counter-stereotype in the character of Ayan falls into a similarly reductive paradigm. 'The ethnic grinder' creates, to all intents and purposes, a normative ideal of the model immigrant, a figure also found in media debates and to which Hervik in that context refers to as 'the "apostate" or the "civilised other", a person of Muslim background who has embraced "Our" values and denounces Islam and "Islamism"'.[61] What can be seen in these novels' articulation of topical issues is an interdependence between popular culture and debates in the public sphere.

A further possible way of looking at the dialectical relationship between a critical position and symptomatic reproduction of common tropes is to examine the murder as the centre of the conflict. If we see murder as the ultimate violent 'resolution' to an individual or collective conflict, the murders of the imams and of the young Muslim women metaphorically expose what German philosopher Alex Honneth has in another context called the '"brutalization" of social conflict', arising from 'a state of society where struggles for social recognition escalate and become anomic because resolution can no longer be found in the existing systemic spheres of negotiation'.[62]

The analysis in chapter 5 and chapter 6 has indicated that there is a clear contrast between the respective treatment of issues of ethnic and cultural diversity in French and Scandinavian crime fictions. Crime writing in French tends to be positioned within the context of a universalism that it frequently critiques. In the case of both Santaki and Fodjo, there is an explicit concern with countering a non-inclusive ideology, a concern aligned with a more general apprehension of the problematics of the overarching ideology of universalism in France, as outlined by Wieviorka:

> Our starting point is in a concern with loosening the grip of the dominant mode of thinking which, in the name of a somewhat over-pervasive universalism, forbids any reflection on the space for cultural difference in society, and postulates, at its most extreme, that, in the absence of any place for it, its only acceptable future is in its pure and simple dissolution – that is, assimilation.[63]

Fodjo, for example, through promoting an anti-colonial and moreover anti-neo-colonial project in *Les poubelles du palais* is thereby contesting a generally uncontested universalism.

While French crime fiction narratives have included many voices from immigrant writers engaging either explicitly or more subtly with debates on relationships between minority and majority identities, the Scandinavian tradition remains culturally monophonic, and immigrants are generally represented as anonymous and voiceless (*Marions slør*) or adapting to the normativity of the majority culture (*Mordet på imamen*). In contrast to what we have seen in readings of French crime fiction, negotiation of identity in the crime fiction mainstream relates primarily to a Scandinavian Self in a society that is to all intents and purposes homogenous, where outsiders – in particular, ethnic outsiders – are not fully integrated, and therefore lack any effective voice or indeed identity. The villainised or victimised stereotypes of the 'foreigner' clearly find expression in *Marions slør* and *Mordet på imamen*; however, both make explicit attempts to turn around the pivot of the stereotype and engage critically with issues of stigmatisation and representational oppression. Contrastingly, in the French crime fiction tradition there is clearly an engagement with the problematics of colonialism and postcolonialism in a more polyphonic sense. Here, transcultural encounters are described both from an internal perspective by metropolitan writers (Manotti, for example) and from 'external', peripheral perspectives by writers from the *francophonie* (*le* (post-) *polar francophone*) or from an internal periphery symbolically and concretely situated in the *banlieue*. This latter (peripheral) category is practically unexplored in the Scandinavian context.

By contrast with fiction, Scandinavian scholarly discussion is far from lacking in such exploration. What is in fact striking is that critical, academic engagement with cultural diversity as literary topic takes very different forms in the Scandinavian and the French contexts, and, moreover, differs radically from the literature itself in its approach. In France, for example, where fiction clearly problematises the legacy of colonialism within the national territory, 'postcolonial studies' has, in the academic field, been a minority interest. The French crime fiction genre over at least three decades has been able to discuss the complexities of cultural diversity and its relationship with the country's colonial past, but academic engagement has remained – until recently – wary of the topic. In Scandinavia the situation is perhaps the opposite: the crime fiction genre is reliant on stereotypes in its representation of immigrants. Even novels directly critical of reductive public discourses about the foreign Other discuss cultural cohabitation and diversity at a rudimentary level. However, academic engagement (with other countries') postcolonial or minority writers has existed since the early 1990s.

It might be concluded that the representation of issues of cultural difference and identity in the respective crime fiction contexts discussed here should be seen within those contexts' overarching salient features: in the case of Scandinavian crime fiction, a tendency to reflect on the post-welfare state relatively superficially and affirmatively in terms of easily discernible symptoms and outcomes, and in the French version of the genre, systematic attempts to reflect on the condition of the Republic critically and transformatively.

Conclusion: Closing the Case

This project was aimed initially to investigate the reception of the Scandinavian crime novel in France in the wake of the considerable and unparalleled media attention it had been receiving after the French translations of Stieg Larsson's *Millennium* trilogy (2006–7). French media representations of the *polar scandinave* emphatically focused on the Scandinavian variant of the genre as one displaying a particular political and critical engagement with societal organisation. While mediatisation of this Scandinavian publishing phenomenon focusing on its interrogation of the welfare state is not unique to France, it has a particular resonance in a country with a well-established and genuinely critical crime fiction tradition, and one moreover proposing a critique that is – in Fraser's terms – transformative rather than merely affirmative. On closer examination, it becomes apparent that the French media accords greater complexity to the *polar scandinave* than it does to the *polar domestique* – which is in fact more subversive in nature. Therefore, one of the first conclusions to be drawn from this research is that the reception in France of the *polar scandinave* overstates the political engagement of the Scandinavian crime novel. Secondly, there is at least some obfuscation of the nature of this engagement, which is relatively superficial compared to that of its French counterpart.

At the centre of the analysis has been a comparison of the ways in which Scandinavian and French crime novels engage respectively with the Nordic social model and the French Republic, especially in terms of how these two social models accommodate difference. Both sociocultural contexts have faced challenges to their post-war settlements in the late twentieth and early twenty-first centuries (in the form of neo-liberalism, immigration, globalisation, Europeanisation, etc.). Both have, since the 1980s, and even more markedly in the 1990s, been witness to a similar sense of decline or breakdown of the social consensus. In France, this is expressed in terms of a 'crisis of universalism' and in Scandinavia in terms of a 'crisis of the welfare state'. In the crime fiction genre, however, already in the 1960s and

1970s, there are attempts to address issues viewed as constituting an initial corrosion of the social systems, as we have seen in the novels by Sjöwall/Wahlöö and Manchette, discussed in chapter 1.

Exploring the Scandinavian critical crime novel in juxtaposition with the French equivalent shines greater light on the specific and distinct kinds of engagement present in the two traditions. If the Scandinavian crime novel situates its social critique within the context of the welfare state's decline, the French crime novel, conversely, engages critically with the very premises of the modern French polity and the foundation on which the Republic is built. When the contemporary Scandinavian crime novel stages the 'trauma' of the dismantling of the social-democratic settlement, the causes of this trauma are generally attributed to an intrusion of external forces disturbing previously homogenous and harmonious nation states. In the case of Sjöwall and Wahlöö's *Story of a Crime*, the criminal act is that of capitalism's destruction of 'true' Swedish social democracy. In Mankell's novels from the 1990s, the focus is on the notion of a 'paradise lost' and 'anxiety' over the transformation of the welfare state caused by immigration and globalisation. In the case of Wennstam and Dahl, emphasis is given to the Europeanisation of the Swedish state, regarded either as an unsettling and intrusive threat (Wennstam) or in more constructive terms (Dahl). Smith's and Jacobsen's representations of the ethnic and cultural Other likewise engage with a heterogenisation of the Scandinavian region.

In France, crime fiction does not propose an account of a 'story of a crime' in terms of a decline caused by external agents from outside the system disrupting the social consensus. Rather, the French crime narratives examined in the present study offer a transformative account of the internal contradictions and weaknesses of the French republican model, which, conversely to that of the Scandinavian welfare state, is not presented in a nostalgic light. It is thus not coincidental that Manotti in *Bien connu des services de police* makes direct allusions to the 1789 'Declaration of the Rights of the Man and of the Citizen', or that the novels of Fodjo and Santaki directly or indirectly engage with the legacy of French colonialism. The difficulty that the French model has in terms of accommodating difference finds its explanation in the Republic's structure of selective universalism rooted in the country's ideological underpinning and history. The tenacity of this model, and its widespread acceptance within the French political establishment, makes it hard to contest within 'normal' channels. The *polar*, however, as has been demonstrated, is a privileged site for challenging its pervasive assumptions.

The study has further identified a more general development in the way that justice is imagined. This development is consistent with what Fraser refers to as the 'shift in the grammar of political claims-making' arising in the post-1989 era.[1] Characterised by a move away from justice being understood in terms of 'redistribution' to a preoccupation with 'recognition', this shift, as has been demonstrated, is discernible in the history of crime fiction as well. Whereas Manchette and Sjöwall/Wahlöö both offer similar critiques of crimes relating to advanced capitalism and class differences, crime fiction has, at least since the 1990s, turned away from questions of capitalism and class, and towards a paradigm of identity. This general shift in thematic and political preoccupation happens both in France and Scandinavia. However, when group identity displaces socio-economic interests as the critical focus, it becomes evident that the French examples offer a much more radical critique than their Scandinavian counterparts. Here it can be argued that because issues of identity are more difficult to discuss within the paradigm of the more rigid social model of French universalism, the critique that is possible within the flexible discursive space offered by fiction – outside the parameters of usual political conversation – becomes more innovative, far-reaching and provocative. This has implications for genre and style as well as content.

Generic differences

Traditionally, the detective was, in Gill Plain's words, 'the lynchpin of the [crime fiction] formula, providing certainty and stability at the centre of the narration'.[2] Whereas the position of the investigative figure in the French tradition has been considerably manipulated, Scandinavian crime fiction maintains the centrality of the detective, despite his or her frequently unstable and ambiguous role.

A suitable keyword to describe the mode of critique in the French *polar* is *déplacement*, understood as an insistent positioning of the perspective in a peripheral location in order to counter a normative or hegemonic centre. This dislocation can be observed as a shift both in concrete physical and in more allegorical terms. For example, the focus is shifted from the metropolitan city centre to the *banlieue*, from the *hexagone* to ex-colonies, from a male to a female perception, or from a hetero-normative to a homosexual perspective. Likewise, in French crime fiction of the period covered by the present study, narrative voice, and by implication the critical positioning of the text, is typically decentred. Despentes's political feminist enterprise, for example, is inscribed within a transgressive queering of the text during which templates of both genre and gender are significantly disturbed. The topographical point of departure for this transgression is the liminal space of the *banlieue*. This suburban space is similarly the setting for Manotti's and Santaki's novels, in which Frenchness and republican norms are read through the prism of marginalised identities – including those of immigrants and women. The *banlieue* is thus a symbolic space situated exactly on the outskirts of the locus of normative activity, not quite within but also not separated from the centre.

Applied to the crime fiction template, then, topographical *déplacement* is coupled with a shift in narrative perspective away from the investigator as the trustworthy and authoritative centre of focus. Instead, the point of view is almost systematically in the French *polar* that of a marginalised figure, usually in the role of either victim or perpetrator (or a combination of the two): the revolutionary kidnappers in Manchette's *Nada*, the abused women in Tabachnik's *Un été pourri*, the prostitute/queer figure in Despentes's *Baise-moi*, the post(/ex)-colonial immigrants in Fodjo's *Les Poubelles du palais* and the *banlieusards* in Santaki's *Les Anges s'habillent en caillera*. If point of view is not inscribed solely within a non-normative character, a polyvocal structure allows for voices from a diversity of backgrounds to be heard, as for example in Manotti's *Bien connu des services de police*. While identities are being constructed in the French variant of the genre, in the same vein as in its Scandinavian counterpart, these various identities are also being problematised – or, indeed, critiqued in terms of their construction – because the liminal position from which the construction emanates is ambiguous and troublesome. The French *polar* thus engages critically with the powerful overarching state discourse and opens space for debate on alternative social models.

By contrast, the critical aspect of Scandinavian crime fiction is to a great extent found in the main investigator's inquiry, analysis and judgement of the society that (s)he lives in. Through the perspective of the investigator – a character showing sympathy and solidarity with vulnerable and marginalised members of society – the Scandinavian crime narratives evoke a fundamental humanism, an ethical position of equality and an acknowledgement of difference. Importantly, this social conscience is in the Scandinavian crime novel emphatically articulated from a centralised position, predominantly within the structures of the police as a state institution. Diversity and difference are negotiated from within this structure as well. The police procedural, as the dominating Scandinavian subgenre, prominently showcases communal integrity through its inclusive investigating team. The team functions as a microscopic reflection of Scandinavian society, designed to display a notion of equality between various groups of the population. The collective protagonist thus promotes gender equality (Holt, Smith, Jacobsen, Wennstam); accommodates ethnic and cultural diversity (Dahl, Smith and Jacobsen); and welcomes non-mainstream sexualities (Holt). In other words, the integration of non-normative or minority identities into the societal body generally conveys an impression of an open-minded, tolerant and inclusive Scandinavian society.

However, this accommodation in the Scandinavian context is also one conditioned upon assimilation to the norms of the majority, and often, characters positioned outside this collective ensemble are not given much of a voice. While the incorporation of non-normative identities seems unproblematic in the discussion of gender and sexual identities, the inclusion of other ethnic characters is successful only when they perform according to mainstream prescriptions. When Scandinavian crime fiction mounts a critique of the exclusion of different vulnerable groups in society, it is articulated from the central perspective of social solidarity with a sense of having to 'rescue' or 'protect' subaltern members of society. Where injustice is highlighted, it is usually not voiced by the excluded, who within the crime narrative commonly assume the status of silenced victims (the prostitute and the old man in Holt's novels or the young murdered Muslim woman in Jacobsen's *Marion's slør*). Ultimately, given that the narrative voice in Scandinavian crime fiction is socially hegemonic and tends to endorse an ideological state discourse on identity issues, it can also come across as didactic and somewhat ethnocentric.

Open cases

The two distinct cultural settings of France and Scandinavia have two distinct crime fiction traditions, each with different concerns, and each informed by setting-specific discourses of citizenship. The different ways in which the Scandinavian police procedural and the French *polar* address these concerns are reflected in how these models deploy or – as is frequently the case – subvert generic conventions. The generic form is reflective of content – and of cultural or societal context. While the Scandinavian police procedural generally maintains a clear structure of crime (murder)–investigation–resolution, the disturbance of the generic template – as of the underlying ideology of the state – is more radical in the French *polar*. In the latter, there is frequently no single crime, the plot centres less on the investigation and the narrative usually ends on an open or ambiguous note, suggesting no resolution.

The specificity of the corpus is of course an important consideration here, in that the observations that have been made may appear somewhat sweeping if applied to all crime fictions from the two settings. A project of this kind necessarily requires a process of making various choices. In prioritising the close readings of a smaller selection of texts over a more general reading of a larger corpus, the study evidently cannot regard the texts as wholly representative of their respective crime fiction traditions in their entirety. Rather, the aim has been to discuss texts rendered *possible* by conditions obtaining within the discursive configurations of Scandinavia and France, and to read these texts on their own merits. The choice of texts from the (most) engaged end of the crime fiction spectrum in both cultural settings may well have validated the critical approach and preoccupations of the book. Conclusions drawn on the basis of these can subsequently be verified (or falsified) through readings of other – and perhaps less critically engaged – crime novels.

The culturally comparative approach constituting this book's methodological basis has sought to move the study of crime fiction beyond the arbitrary paradigm of the nation state, the matrix under which generic developments and themes have commonly been examined, in order to look at other issues pertaining to the status of the individual subject vis-à-vis the prevailing polity. By placing the French and Scandinavian crime narratives on an axis of commonalities (crime fiction, Western-European cultures, global conditions pertaining to advanced capitalism and late modernity, etc.) as well as on an axis of local particularities (*polar*/police procedural, crises relating to post-welfarism/republican universalism, specific historical conditions for immigration, etc.), the book's comparative analysis allows identification of nation-specific aspects within the two traditions which an analysis grounded in one setting alone may not have identified, particularly in relation to the differing articulation (in France and Scandinavia) of questions of ethnicity, gender, sexuality and other issues of belonging, citizenship and difference.

Again, the corpus of highly engaged works discussed in the present study – which performs thematic readings of citizenship, gender, sexuality and ethnicity – may well inevitably have prioritised these issues to the exclusion of others of equal interest and importance. It is doubtless the case that a wider corpus could have afforded possibilities for investigating the intersectionality of a wider variety of identities, as well as a wider variety of political and social perspectives.

Indeed, regarding the priorities for crime fiction critics, there are further studies to be done more generally on the role that crime fiction plays in reflecting contemporary society. One thing reconfirmed by the present study is that there are significant differences between national crime fiction traditions, as often as not rooted in the relationship between citizens and the polity to which they belong, or indeed feel as if they do not belong. Just as there is no monolithic European crime fiction template, nor is there an amorphous Nordic Noir; there is thus doubtless room for a comparative study of Scandinavian crime fictions specific to the variants of the Nordic model that have developed within national settings that are far from homogeneous.

What is also striking is that crime fictions' reflection of the societies from which they emerge has taken on particular urgency in the postmodern, post-industrial age, where the experience of the human subject is one of dislocation, whether in relation to society or technology. Undoubtedly, the crime fiction genre in view of its engagement with identity issues will continue to thrive in this multicultural global environment where it plays a vital role in discussing cultural cohabitation and the accommodation of differences. The refugee crisis in Europe, the rise of right-wing populist anti-immigrant parties in both France and Scandinavia, the uncertain future of the European Union, terrorist attacks in Western Europe and the political cataclysms that they produce represent new critical moments with which it seems likely that the crime fiction genre, as societal chronicler and debater, will continue to engage.

Notes

Introduction

1 Andrea Goulet and Susanna Lee, 'Editors' Preface: Crime Fictions', *Yale French Studies*, 108 (2005), 1.

2 See, for example, Naomi Schor, 'The Crisis of French Universalism', *Yale French Studies*, 100 (2001), 43–64; Joan Wallach Scott, 'French Universalism in the 1990s', *Differences*, 15, 2 (2004), 32–53.

3 Schor, 'Crisis', 43.

4 Schor, 'Crisis', 52–3.

5 Claire Gorrara, 'French Crime Fiction: from *genre mineur* to *patrimoine culturel*', *French Studies*, 61, 2 (2007), 213.

6 Christophe Evans, 'Secouer la cendre dans les olives: une lecture socio-politique de Manchette', in Alain Pessin and Marie-Caroline Vanbremeersch (eds), *Les œuvres noires de l'art et de la littérature* (vol. 1) (Paris: L'Harmattan, 2002), p. 88.

7 Gorrara, 'French Crime Fiction'.

8 Evans, 'Secouer la cendre', p. 87. All in-text translations are my own, unless otherwise stated.

9 Diana Holmes and David Platten, 'Introduction', in Diana Holmes et al. (eds), *Finding the Plot: Storytelling in Popular Fictions* (Newcastle-upon-Tyne: Cambridge Scholars, 2013), p. 2.

10 Marc Angenot, 'Qu'est-ce que la paralittérature?', *Études littéraires*, 7, 1 (1974), 9–22 (10–11).

11 Yves Reuter, 'Littératures/paralittératures: classements et déclassements', *Les Cahiers des paralittératures*, 3 (Liège: CLPCF, 1992), pp. 37–47 (42–3).

12 Patrick Raynal, 'Le roman noir est l'avenir de la fiction', in 'Roman noir: Pas d'orchidées pour les T.M.', special issue, *Les Temps Modernes*, 595 (1997), 88–99 (91).

13 Raynal, 'Le roman noir', 91.

14 As a comment on this binary construction of culture, Gallimard launched in 1992 'La Noire' under the editorship of Patrick Raynal. This imprint, discontinued in 2005, was presented with a front cover explicitly evoking Gallimard's iconic literary imprint 'La Blanche'. See, for example, Véronique Rohrbach, *Politique du polar: Jean-Bernard Pouy* (Lausanne: Archipel, 2007), pp. 22–3.

15 Holmes and Platten, 'Introduction', p. 1.
16 Jean-Marc Moura, 'The Evolving Context of Postcolonial Studies in France: New Horizons or New Limits?', *Journal of Postcolonial Writing*, 44, 3 (2008); Marie-Hélène Bourcier, 'Cultural Translation, Politics of Disempowerment and the Reinvention of Queer Power and Politics', *Sexualities*, 15, 1 (2011), 93–109.
17 Pekka Kosonen, 'Globalisation and the Nordic Welfare States', in Robert Sykes, Bruno Palier and Pauline M. Prior (eds), *Globalization and European Welfare States* (Basingstoke: Palgrave, 2001), pp. 153–72 (p. 171).
18 Kosonen, 'Globalisation', p. 171.
19 Francis Sejersted, *The Age of Social Democracy: Norway and Sweden in the Twentieth Century*, trans. Richard Daly (Princeton, NJ: Princeton University Press, 2011), p. 3.
20 Paula Arvas and Andrew Nestingen, 'Introduction: Contemporary Scandinavian Crime Fiction', in Andrew Nestingen and Paula Arvas (eds), *Scandinavian Crime Fiction* (Cardiff: University of Wales Press, 2011), pp. 1–18 (p. 8). See also Jakob Stougaard-Nielsen, *Scandinavian Crime Fiction* (London: Bloomsbury, 2017).
21 On the themes of nostalgia and melancholy in Scandinavian crime fiction, see Shane McCorristine, 'The Place of Pessimism in Henning Mankell's Kurt Wallander Series', in Nestingen and Arvas (eds), *Scandinavian Crime Fiction*, pp. 77–88; Stougaard-Nielsen, *Scandinavian Crime Fiction*, pp. 10–13.
22 Henning Mankell, *Pyramiden* (Stockholm: Leopard, 1999), p. 1.
23 Nestingen and Arvas include Iceland and Finland in their *Scandinavian Crime Fiction*. However, the current study does not include these Nordic countries because of their more peripheral association (geographically, linguistically, historically as well as culturally) with the Scandinavian countries. In the case of Finland, the country's geopolitical position as a country bordering Russia is a significant thematic concern in Finnish crime fiction. See Paula Arvas, 'Next to the Final Frontier: Russians in Contemporary Finnish and Scandinavian Crime Fiction', in Nestingen and Arvas (eds), *Scandinavian Crime Fiction*, pp. 115–28 (p. 115). Also, the country's literature is less accessible to speakers of Scandinavian languages, who cannot immediately understand Finnish (a Uralic language). Of much more recent date and much less dominant is Iceland's crime fiction tradition. See Katrin Jakobsdóttir, 'Meaningless Icelanders: Icelandic Crime Fiction and Nationality', in Nestingen and Arvas (eds), *Scandinavian Crime Fiction*, pp. 46–61 (p. 47).
24 In recent history, one can think of these countries' different situations during the Second World War (Norway and Denmark were occupied by Germany, and Sweden maintained its neutrality policy), or the fact that Denmark joined the EU (the then EEC) in 1973, Sweden did not join until 1995, and Norway remains a non-member.
25 Stougaard-Nielsen, *Scandinavian Crime Fiction*, p. 206.
26 For example, Thierry Maricourt, *Dictionnaire du roman policier nordique*

(Amiens: Encrage, 2010); Nestingen and Arvas (eds), *Scandinavian Crime Fiction*; Barry Forshaw, *Death in a Cold Climate: A Guide to Scandinavian Crime Fiction* (Basingstoke: Palgrave Macmillan, 2012).

27 Kerstin Bergman, *Swedish Crime Fiction: The Making of Nordic Noir* (Milan: Mimesis, 2014), p. 173.

28 See Anne Grydehøj, 'Nordic Noir', in Annika Lindskog and Jacob Stougaard-Nielsen (eds), *Introduction to Nordic Cultures* (London: UCL Press, 2020), pp. 117–29 (pp. 122–3).

29 Nina Kildal and Stein Kuhnle, 'Introduction', in Nanna Kildal and Stein Kuhnle (eds), *Normative Foundations of the Welfare State: The Nordic Experience* (London: Routledge, 2005), pp. 1–10 (p. 1).

30 Rasmus Bo Sørensen, 'Krimiens samfundskritiske kalkule', *Information*, 5 June 2008; Jakob Stougaard-Nielsen, 'Velfærdskrimien og dens kritik: Anders Bodelsens *Tænk på et tal* (1968) som eksempel', *Aktuel forskning, Litteratur, kultur og medier* (Odense: Institut for litteratur, kultur og medier, Syddansk Universitet, 2013), pp. 49–63.

31 Robert Geyer, Christine Ingebritsen and Jonathon W. Moses, *Globalization, Europeanization and the End of Scandinavian Social Democracy* (Basingstoke: Macmillan, 2000), p. 2.

32 Andrew Nestingen, *Crime and Fantasy in Scandinavia: Fiction, Film and Social Change* (Seattle: University of Washington Press, 2008), p. 10.

33 Nestingen, *Crime and Fantasy*, p. 10.

34 Claire Gorrara, *The Roman Noir in Post-War French Culture* (Oxford: Oxford University Press, 2003), p. 2.

35 Gill Plain, *Twentieth-Century Crime Fiction: Gender, Sexuality and the Body* (Edinburgh: Edinburgh University Press, 2001), p. 7.

36 Plain, *Twentieth-Century Crime Fiction*, p. 9.

37 Examples, in chronological order, include: Ed Christian (ed.), *The Post-Colonial Detective* (Basingstoke: Palgrave Macmillan, 2001); Maureen T. Reddy, *Traces, Codes and Clues: Reading Race in Crime Fiction* (New Brunswick, NJ: Rutgers University Press, 2003); Julie H. Kim (ed.), *Race and Religion in the Postcolonial British Detective Story* (Jefferson, NC: McFarland, 2005); Nels Pearson and Marc Singer (eds), *Detective Fiction in a Postcolonial and Transnational World* (Farnham: Ashgate, 2009); Nadège Compard, *Immigrés et romans noirs (1950–2000)* (Paris: L'Harmattan, 2010); Julie H. Kim (ed.), *Class and Culture in Crime Fiction* (Jefferson, NC: McFarland, 2014).

38 John Scaggs, *Crime Fiction* (London: Routledge, 2005), p. 104.

39 One example of the former is the series in which this study is published, dedicating volumes to French, Scandinavian, Italian, German and Iberian crime fiction. Besides collected volumes juxtaposing articles from different national traditions but without imposing contrastive analyses, comparative studies such as Nicola Barfoot, *Frauenkrimi/Polar féminin: Generic Expectations and the Reception of Recent French and German Crime Novels by Women* (Frankfurt: Peter Lang, 2007) are rare.

Chapter 1

1 Per Wahlöö, 'Grisen är ett gåtfullt djur', in *Tryckpunkter: 23 författare i egen sak* (Stockholm: Nordstedts, 1967), p. 176. All in-text translations are my own, unless otherwise stated.

2 Franck Frommer and Jean-Patrick Manchette, *Le récit d'un engagement manqué* (Paris: Kimé, 2003), p. 44.

3 Ernest Mandel, *Delightful Murder: A Social History of the Crime Story* (London: Pluto, 1984), p. 10.

4 Charles Baudelaire, *Le Peintre de la vie moderne*, in *Charles Baudelaire: Œuvres complètes*, ed. Claude Pichois (Paris: Gallimard, 1976), pp. 683–724 (p. 695).

5 Edgar Allan Poe, *Histoires extraordinaires*, trans. Charles Baudelaire (Paris: Gallimard, 1973).

6 See, for example, Mandel, *Delightful Murder*, p. 19; Jon Thompson, *Fiction, Crime, and Empire: Clues to Modernity and Postmodernism* (Chicago: University of Illinois Press, 1993), p. 43; John Scaggs, *Crime Fiction* (London: Routledge, 2005), p. 33.

7 Kim Toft Hansen, 'Knowing the Unknowable: Detecting Metaphysics and Religion in Crime Fiction', in Peter Baker and Deborah Shaller (eds), *Detecting Detection: International Perspectives on the Uses of a Plot* (London: Continuum, 2012), p. 150.

8 Toft Hansen, 'Knowing the Unknowable', p. 150.

9 Jacques Dubois, *Le roman policier ou la modernité* (Paris: Armand Colin, 2006), p. 7. See also David Platten, *The Pleasures of Crime* (Leiden, Rodopi, 2011), pp. 23–5.

10 Mandel, *Delightful Murder*, pp. 10, 120, 124.

11 Thomas Kuhn, *The Structure of Scientific Revolutions* (Chicago: University of Chicago Press, 1970), pp. 2–3.

12 Kuhn, *Scientific Revolutions*, p. 6.

13 Kerstin Bergman, 'From National Authority to Urban Underbelly: Negotiations of Power in Stockholm Crime Fiction', in Lucy Andrew and Catherine Phelps (eds), *Crime Fiction in the City: Capital Crimes* (Cardiff: University of Wales Press, 2013), pp. 65–84 (p. 68). See also David Geherin, *Scene of the Crime: The Importance of Place in Crime and Mystery Fiction* (Jefferson, NC: McFarland, 2008), pp. 161–7.

14 Maj Sjöwall and Per Wahlöö, *The Abominable Man*, trans. Thomas Teal (London: Harper Perennial, 2007), p. 45.

15 Maj Sjöwall and Per Wahlöö, *Murder at the Savoy*, trans. Joan Tate (London: Harper Perennial, 2007), p. 93.

16 Sjöwall and Wahlöö, *Abominable Man*, p. 14.

17 Fredric Jameson, 'Postmodernism, or, The Cultural Logic of Late Capitalism', *New Left Review*, 146 (1984), 59.

18 Jameson, 'Postmodernism', 59. In *La Condition postmoderne: rapport sur le savoir* (1979), Jean-François Lyotard similarly defines the period:

'the status of knowledge is altered as societies enter what is known as the postindustrial age and cultures enter what is known as the postmodern age ... [as having been] underway since at least the end of the 1950s, which for Europe marks the completion of reconstruction'. *The Postmodern Condition: A report on Knowledge*, trans. Geoff Bennington and Brian Massumi (Manchester: Manchester University Press, 1986), p. 3.

19 Fredric Jameson, 'The Aesthetics of Singularity', *New Left Review*, 92 (2015), 101–32 (104).

20 Thompson, *Fiction, Crime, and Empire*; Scaggs, *Crime Fiction*; Stephen Knight, *Crime Fiction since 1800: Detection, Death, Diversity* (Basingstoke: Palgrave Macmillan, 2004).

21 Fredric Jameson, *Postmodernism, or, The Cultural Logic of Late Capitalism* (Durham, NC: Duke University Press, 1991), p. 46.

22 Lyotard, *Postmodern Condition*, p. xxiv.

23 Charlotte Beyer, '"Death of the Author": Maj Sjöwall and Per Wahlöö's Police Procedurals', in Vivien Miller and Helen Oakley (eds), *Cross-Cultural Connections in Crime Fictions* (Basingstoke: Palgrave Macmillan, 2012), p. 146.

24 Lyotard, *Postmodern Condition*, p. xxiii; Jean-Patrick Manchette, *Chroniques* (Paris: Payot, 1996), p. 48.

25 Jean-Patrick Manchette, *Romans noirs* (Paris: Gallimard, 2005), p. 130. *L'Affaire N'Gustro* was published in April 1971. *Laissez bronzer les cadavres!*, co-written with Jean-Pierre Bastid, had been published in February earlier the same year.

26 Manchette, *Romans noirs*, p. 172.

27 In addition to their fictional writings, the authors are equally engaged in theoretical and critical production in which they comment on their use of the genre. Manchette writes articles on the crime fiction genre for various newspapers and journals and continues to develop his critical views in his diary, published as *Journal 1966–1974* (Paris: Gallimard, 2008). Sjöwall, and especially Wahlöö, write essays and newspaper articles explaining how they deploy the genre to form a critique of the Swedish welfare state.

28 Nels Pearson and Marc Singer, 'Introduction: Open Cases: Detection, (Post)Modernity, and the State', in Nels Pearson and Marc Singer (eds), *Detective Fiction in a Postcolonial and Transnational World* (Farnham: Ashgate, 2009), pp. 1–14 (p. 1).

29 Maj Sjöwall and Per Wahlöö, 'Kriminalromanens fornyelse', *Politiken*, 30 July 1971.

30 Sjöwall and Wahlöö, 'Kriminalromanens fornyelse'.

31 Sjöwall and Wahlöö, 'Kriminalromanens fornyelse'.

32 Manchette, *Chroniques*, p. 48.

33 Manchette, *Chroniques*, p. 21.

34 Richard Shephard, 'Interrogation of Maj Sjöwall: Q and A by Richard Shephard', preface to Maj Sjöwall and Per Wahlöö, *Roseanna*, trans. Lois Roth (London: Harper Perennial, 2006), pp. 7–13 (p. 10).

35 Christophe Evans, 'Secouer la cendre dans les olives: une lecture socio-politique de Manchette', in Alain Pessin and Marie-Caroline Vanbremeersch (eds), *Les œuvres noires de l'art et de la littérature* (vol. 1) (Paris: L'Harmattan, 2002), p. 112.

36 Sjöwall and Wahlöö, 'Kriminalromanens fornyelse'.

37 Stefan Eklund, 'Deckardam', *Svenska Dagbladet*, 18 June 2010, *www.svd.se/deckardam/av/stefan-eklund* (accessed 12 June 2019).

38 Manchette, *Chroniques*, pp. 80–1. For an analysis of May 1968 and its impact on French cultural life (including the renewal of the crime fiction genre), see Margaret Atack, *May 68 in French Fiction and Film: Rethinking Society, Rethinking Representation* (Oxford: Oxford University Press, 1999), p. 123.

39 Manchette, *Chroniques*, p. 200.

40 Manchette's articles, appearing between 1976 and 1995 in *Charlie Mensuel*, *Polar*, *Le Magazine littéraire*, *Le Matin* and *Les Nouvelles littéraires*, are collected in the Rivage publication *Chroniques* (1996).

41 Marcel Duhamel, 'Collection Série noire', *http://www.gallimard.fr/Divers/Plus-sur-la-collection/Serie-noire* (accessed 12 June 2019).

42 Manchette, *Chroniques*, p. 12.

43 Manchette, *Chroniques*, pp. 29–30.

44 Manchette, *Chroniques*, p. 16.

45 Manchette makes numerous references to Marcuse's writings and Debord's *La Société du spectacle* both in *Chroniques* and in *Journal*.

46 Manchette, *Chroniques*, pp. 77–8.

47 Robert Deleuse, 'Petite histoire du roman noir français', in 'Roman noir: Pas d'orchidées pour les T.M.', special issue, *Les Temps Modernes*, 595 (1997), 53–87 (61).

48 Benoît Mouchart, *Manchette: le nouveau roman noir* (Paris: Seguier Archimbaud, 2006), p. 109.

49 Serge Loupien, 'La lutte des casses', *Libération*, 15 March 1982.

50 See Anne Argouse and Hugues Peyret, *Mort pour la cause du peuple* (Rouen: Antoine Martin production, 2012), DVD. The documentary analyses the historical background for the Gauche Prolétarienne and the context for the assassination of Overney.

51 Manchette, *Journal*, pp. 442–56.

52 Manchette, *Journal*, p. 457.

53 Manchette, *Romans noirs*, p. 341. This edition is hereinafter referred to by page number in the text.

54 Atack, *May 68*, p. 132.

55 Jean-François Gérault, *Jean-Patrick Manchette* (Paris: Encrage, 2000), p. 69.

56 Manchette, *Chroniques*, p. 76.

57 Manchette, *Chroniques*, p. 76. Manchette's italics.

58 Guy Debord, *The Society of the Spectacle*, trans. Ken Knabb (Berkeley: Bureau of Public Secrets), p. 2.

59 Manchette, *Journal*, p. 470.

60 Manchette, *Romans noirs*, p. 133.

61 Manchette, *Chroniques*, p. 17.

62 Barry Forshaw, *Death in a Cold Climate: A Guide to Scandinavian Crime Fiction* (Basingstoke: Palgrave Macmillan, 2012), p. 17; Thierry Maricourt, *Dictionnaire du roman policier nordique* (Amiens: Encrage, 2010), p. 170.

63 *Mannen som gick upp i rök* (*The Man Who Went Up in Smoke*, 1966), *Mannen på balkongen* (*The Man on the Balcony*, 1967), *Den skrattande polisen* (*The Laughing Policeman*, 1968), *Brandbilen som försvann* (*The Fire Engine that Disappeared*, 1969), *Polis, polis, potatismos* (*Murder at the Savoy*, 1970), *Den vedervärdige mannen från Säffle* (*The Abominable Man*, 1971), *Det slutna rummet* (*The Locked Room*, 1972), *Polismördaren* (*Cop Killer*, 1974), *Terroristerna* (*The Terrorists*, 1975).

64 Sjöwall and Wahlöö, 'Kriminalromanens fornyelse'.

65 Sjöwall and Wahlöö, 'Kriminalromanens fornyelse'.

66 Sjöwall and Wahlöö, 'Kriminalromanens fornyelse'.

67 Sjöwall and Wahlöö, 'Kriminalromanens fornyelse'.

68 Sjöwall and Wahlöö, 'Kriminalromanens fornyelse'.

69 Evans, 'Secouer la cendre', p. 87; Bergman, *Swedish Crime Fiction*, p. 22.

70 See Jameson, 'Postmodernism', 54.

71 Sjöwall and Wahlöö, 'Kriminalromanens fornyelse'.

72 See Kalle Lind, 'Maj Sjöwall', *Faktum*, 24 May 2012, *www.faktum.se/maj-sjowall* (accessed 25 May 2019). In the interview, Sjöwall discusses the two social-democratic governments – of Tage Erlander (prime minister 1946–69) and Olof Palme (two-term prime minister 1969–76 and 1982–6) – in power when *Roman om ett brott* was written.

73 Sjöwall and Wahlöö, *Murder at the Savoy*, p. 93.

74 Sjöwall and Wahlöö, *Roseanna*, p. 2.

75 Lind, 'Maj Sjöwall'.

76 Dawn Keetley, 'Unruly Bodies: The Politics of Sex in Maj Sjöwall and Per Wahlöö's Martin Beck Series', *Clues*, 30, 1 (2012), 55.

77 Keetley, 'Unruly Bodies', 55.

78 Lisbeth Hertel and Eyvind Larsen, 'Sjöwall og Wahlöö interview', *Information*, 19 October 1973, 14.

79 Tzvetan Todorov, 'Typologie du roman policier', in *Poétique de la prose* (1971; Paris: Seuil, 1978), pp. 9–19 (p. 11).

80 Sjöwall and Wahlöö, *Roseanna*, pp. 1–2.

81 Sjöwall and Wahlöö, *Roseanna*, p. 7.

82 In the sentence introducing the dredging machine, both English and French translations omit the vessel's official name, adding further to the image: 'Det hette egentligen Gripen men kallades givetvis Grisen och råkade just då ligga i fiskehamnen i Gravarne.' ('It was in fact named "Gripen" but was naturally called the Pig and happened just then to be lying in the fishing harbour at Gravarne.'). Sjöwall and Wahlöö, *Roseanna* (Stockholm: Norstedts, 1965), p. 5. 'Gripen' is in Swedish both the definite form of

the gryphon and the past participle of the verb 'to catch'/'to arrest'. Metaphorically the quotation situates the police in a position between the symbol of the divine, powerful creature, in mythology protecting treasures and precious possessions, and the derogatory use of the term 'pig' to signify a police officer. In his essay 'Grisen är ett gåtfullt djur' (The Pig is a Mysterious Animal, 1967), Wahlöö's commentary on the police force is implicitly linked with the use of the term 'pig' in the essay title.

83 Sjöwall and Wahlöö, *Roseanna*, p. 72.

84 Shephard, 'Interrogation of Maj Sjöwall', p. 9.

85 Sjöwall and Wahlöö, *Roseanna*, p. 29.

86 Maj Sjöwall and Per Wahlöö, *Polismördaren* (Stockholm: Piratforlaget, 2012), p. 133, e-book.

87 See, for instance, chapter 10 of *Den vedervärdige mannen från Säffle*, mostly dedicated to analysis of the development of the police force in the wake of the reform. Sjöwall and Wahlöö, *Abominable Man*, pp. 50–7. In a long paragraph in *Polismördaren* some of the same points are repeated. Maj Sjöwall and Per Wahlöö, *Cop Killer*, trans. Thomas Teal (London: Harper Perennial, 2007), p. 118.

88 Sjöwall and Wahlöö, *Cop Killer*, p. 182.

89 The crossword is also used as an overarching framework for the series' Marxist critique of the condition of the Swedish welfare state: in the very last passage of *Terroristerna* (1975), Kollberg, Beck's colleague, picks up a letter tile providing the solution to a Scrabble-like crossword game and concludes *Roman om ett brott* with the utterance: 'X – X as in Marx'. Maj Sjöwall and Per Wahlöö, *The Terrorists*, trans. Joan Tate (London: Harper Perennial, 2007), p. 324.

90 Sjöwall and Wahlöö, *Abominable Man*, p. 71. This edition is hereinafter referred to by page number in the text.

91 Sjöwall and Wahlöö, *Roseanna*, p. 50.

92 Michael Tapper, 'Dirty Harry in the Swedish Welfare State' in Nestingen and Arvas, *Scandinavian Crime Fiction*, p. 23.

93 Nestingen, *Crime and Fantasy*, p. 217.

94 Kerstin Bergman, 'Beyond National Allegory: Europeanisation in Swedish Crime Writer Arne Dahl's *Viskleken*', *Clues*, 32, 2 (2014), 20–9 (20).

95 Bergman, *Swedish Crime Fiction*, p. 33.

96 Gérault, *Manchette*, p. 92.

97 See, for example, Dominique Manotti, 'Roman noir', *Le Mouvement Social*, 219–20, 2–3 (2007), 107.

98 Gorrara, *Roman noir*, p. 16.

99 Gérault, *Manchette*, pp. 12–13. See also Jean-Paul Schweighaeuser's detailed description of the *néo-polar* as publishing phenomenon within the context of what he refers to as 'l'explosion de 1979' and the subsequent establishment of new series by French publishing houses, considerable media attention, etc. This leads on the one hand, Schweighaeuser argues, to literary innovation and renewal of the *néo-polar* by already established

writers, but, on the other hand, it also brings about profit-seeking writers who contribute to a 'banalisation' and 'standardisation' of the genre. *Le roman noir français* (Paris: Presses Universitaires de France, 1984), pp. 71–90.

100 Jean Fourastié, in *Les Trente Glorieuses, ou la revolution invisible de 1946 à 1975* (Paris: Fayard, 1979), identifies the eponymous 30-year period of post-war prosperity as 1964–75; Sejersted temporally defines the 'golden age of Social Democracy' in Scandinavia as 1940–70. See Sejersted, *Age of Social Democracy*.

Chapter 2

1 Krishan Kumar, *From Post-Industrial to Post-Modern Society: New Theories of the Contemporary World* (Oxford: Blackwell, 2005).

2 Kumar, *From Post-Industrial to Post-Modern Society*, p. 143.

3 Stuart Hall, 'Introduction: Who needs Identity?', in Stuart Hall and Paul du Gay (eds), *Questions of Cultural Identity* (London: Sage, 1996), pp. 1–17 (p. 17).

4 Zygmunt Bauman, 'Identity in the Globalising World', *Social Anthropology*, 9, 2 (2001), 121.

5 Bauman, 'Identity in the Globalising World', 121.

6 Bauman, 'Identity in the Globalising World', 129.

7 Nancy Fraser, *Justice Interruptus: Critical Reflections on the 'Postsocialist' Condition* (London: Routledge, 1997), p. 2.

8 Fraser, *Justice Interruptus*, p. 2.

9 Joan Wallach Scott, *Parité: Sexual Equality and the Crisis of French Universalism* (Chicago: University of Chicago Press, 2005), p. 1.

10 Nathalie Debrauwere-Miller, 'Parcours historique des féminismes intellectuels en France depuis Beauvoir', *Contemporary French Civilization*, 38, 1 (2013), 23–46 (23). All in-text translations are my own, unless otherwise stated.

11 See article 8.1 of the French data protection law: 'Loi 78-17 du 6 janvier 1978 modifiée', *www.cnil.fr/fr/loi-78-17-du-6-janvier-1978-modifiee* (accessed 1 June 2019).

12 Naomi Schor, 'The Crisis of French Universalism', *Yale French Studies*, 100 (2001), 43–64 (48).

13 Schor, 'Crisis', 48.

14 Schor, 'Crisis', 48.

15 Eléonore Lépinard, 'The Contentious Subject of Feminism: Defining *Women* in France from the Second Wave to Parity', *Signs*, 32, 2 (2007), 375–403 (389–90).

16 Lépinard, 'Contentious Subject of Feminism', 376.

17 Pierre Bourdieu, 'Quelques questions sur le mouvement gay et lesbien', in Didier Eribon (ed.), *Études gay et lesbiennes* (Paris: Éditions du Centre Pompidou, 1998), pp. 45–50 (p. 47).

18 Bourcier, 'Cultural Translation', p. 99.
19 Bourcier, 'Cultural Translation', p. 96.
20 Bourcier, 'Cultural Translation', p. 97.
21 Anne Phillips and Sawitri Saharso, 'The Rights of Women and the Crisis of Multiculturalism', *Ethnicities*, 8 (2008), 291–301 (291). See also Schor, 'Crisis', 52–5.
22 Katharyne Mitchell, 'Geographies of Identity: Multiculturalism unplugged', *Progress in Human Geography*, 28, 5 (2004), 641–51 (642).
23 Jacques Rancière, 'Les idéaux républicains sont devenus des armes de discrimination et de mépris', L'Obs, 4 April 2015, *bibliobs.nouvelobs.com/ essais/ 20150403.OBS6427/jacques-ranciere-les-ideaux-republicains-sont-devenus-des-armes-de-discrimination-et-de-mepris.html* (accessed 14 May 2019).
24 Sune Sunesson et al., 'The Flight from Universalism', *European Journal of Social Work*, 1, 1 (1998), 19–29 (19).
25 Christopher S. Browning, 'Branding Nordicity: Models, Identity and the Decline of Exceptionalism', *Cooperation and Conflict*, 42, 1 (2007), 28.
26 Peter Baldwin, *The Politics of Social Solidarity: Class Bases of the European Welfare State 1875–1975* (Cambridge: Cambridge University Press, 1990), p. 43.
27 Gøsta Esping-Andersen, *The Three Worlds of Welfare Capitalism* (Oxford: Polity/Blackwell, 1990), p. 28; Browning, 'Branding Nordicity', 27; Mikko Kuisma, 'Social Democratic Internationalism and the Welfare State after the "Golden Age"', *Cooperation and Conflict*, 42, 1 (2007), 9–10; Jorma Sipilä (ed.), *Social Care Services: The Key to the Scandinavian Welfare Model* (Aldershot: Ashgate, 1997), p. 5; Lars Trägårdh, 'Sweden and the EU: Welfare State, Nationalism and the Spectre of "Europe"', in Lene Hansen and Ole Wæver (eds), *European Integration and National Identity: The Challenge of the Nordic States* (London: Routledge, 2002), pp. 130–81 (p. 131); Thomas Hylland Eriksen, *Immigration and National Identity in Norway* (Washington, DC: Migration Policy Institute, 2013), p. 3.
28 Ole Wæver, 'Identity, Communities and Foreign Policy: Discourse Analysis as Foreign Policy Theory', in Hansen and Wæver (eds), *European Integration*, pp. 20–49 (p. 25).
29 What follows is a summarising account of the characteristics of the Nordic model that are of importance for the present study. A more detailed account would seek the historical roots of contemporary Scandinavian national identities. This would necessarily include a historical contextualisation dating at least back to nineteenth-century nationalist movements, in addition to a comparison of internal differences between Sweden, Norway and Denmark (see, for example, Nanna Kildal and Stein Kuhnle (eds), *Normative Foundations of the Welfare State: The Nordic Experience* (London: Routledge, 2005)). A thorough analysis of the development of the Nordic welfare state in the twentieth century is proposed in Niels Finn Christiansen, Klaus Petersen, Nils Edling and Per Haave (eds), *The Nordic Model of*

Welfare: A Historical Reappraisal (Copenhagen: Museum Tusculanum Press, 2005). For a discussion of the historical basis for the Scandinavian social care model, see Sipilä (ed.), *Social Care Services.* A historical contextualisation of gender equality as a trademark of the Scandinavian welfare model can be found in Kari Melby, Anne-Birte Ravn and Christina Carlsson Wetterberg (eds), *Gender Equality and Welfare Politics in Scandinavia: The Limits of Political Ambition?* (Bristol: Policy, 2008).

30 Esping-Andersen, *Three Worlds*, p. 27.

31 See, for example, Kosonen, 'Globalisation', p. 160; Hansen and Wæver (eds), *European Integration.*

32 Bo Bengtsson, Per Strömblad and Ann-Helén Bay (eds), *Diversity, Inclusion and Citizenship in Scandinavia* (Newcastle-upon-Tyne: Cambridge Scholars, 2010), p. 1.

33 Christiansen and Markkola (eds), *Nordic Model*, p. 10.

34 Nanna Kildal and Stein Kuhnle, 'The Nordic Welfare Model and the Idea of Universalism', in Kildal and Kuhnle (eds), *Normative Foundations*, pp. 13–33 (p. 25).

35 Christiansen and Markkola (eds), *Nordic Model*, p. 10.

36 Melby, Ravn and Wetterberg (eds), *Gender Equality*, p. 4.

37 See, for example, Maarit Jänterä-Jareborg, 'Religion and the Secular State in Sweden', in Javier Martinez-Torrón and W. Cole Durham (eds), *Religion and the Secular State: Interim National Reports* (Provo, UT: Brigham Young University, 2010), pp. 669–86.

38 Melby, Ravn and Wetterberg (eds), *Gender Equality*, p. 2.

39 Helga Hernes, *Welfare State and Women Power: Essays in State Feminism* (Oslo: Universitetsforlaget, 1987), pp. 9–29.

40 Melby, Ravn and Wetterberg (eds), *Gender Equality*, p. 6.

41 Anette Borchorst and Birte Siim, 'Woman-friendly Policies and State Feminism: Theorizing Scandinavian Gender Equality', *Feminist Theory*, 9, 2 (2008), 207–24 (221).

42 Diana Mulinari, 'Women Friendly? Understanding Gendered Racism in Sweden', in Melby, Ravn and Wetterberg (eds), *Gender Equality*, pp. 167–83 (pp. 167, 179).

43 Anette Borchorst, 'Women-friendly Policy Paradoxes: Childcare Policies and Gender Equality Visions in Scandinavia', in Melby, Ravn and Wetterberg (eds), *Gender Equality*, pp. 27–42 (p. 40).

44 Browning, 'Branding Nordicity', 27.

45 Browning, 'Branding Nordicity', 32–5.

46 Browning, 'Branding Nordicity', 42.

47 Kosonen, 'Globalisation', p. 164.

48 See, for example, Kosonen, 'Globalisation'; Kuisma, 'Social Democratic Internationalism'.

49 Kuisma, 'Social Democratic Internationalism', 9, 17.

50 Thomas Hylland Eriksen, 'Diversity versus difference: neo-liberalism in the minority debate', in Richard Rottenburg, Burkhard Schnepel and

Shingo Shimada (eds), *The Making and Unmaking of Difference* (Bielefeld: Transaction, 2006), pp. 13–36 (p. 34).

51 Tobias Hübinette and Catrin Lundström, 'Sweden after the Recent Election: The Double-Binding Power of Swedish Whiteness through the Mourning of the Loss of 'Old Sweden' and the Passing of "Good Sweden"', *NORA: Nordic Journal of Feminist and Gender Research* 19, 1 (2011), 42–52.

52 Hübinette and Lundström, 'Sweden after the Recent Election', 44.

53 Hübinette and Lundström, 'Sweden after the Recent Election', 50.

54 Staffan Marklund, *Paradise Lost? The Nordic Welfare States in the Recession 1975–1985* (Lund: Arkiv, 1988).

55 Ole Wæver, 'Nordic Nostalgia: Northern Europe after the Cold War', *International Affairs* 68, 1 (1992), 77–102 (77).

56 Michael Tapper, *Snuten i skymningslandet: Svenska polisberättelser i roman och film 1965–2010* (Lund: Nordic Academic Press, 2011), p. 465.

57 Shane McCorristine, 'The Place of Pessimism in Henning Mankell's Kurt Wallander Series', in Andrew Nestingen and Paula Arvas (eds), *Scandinavian Crime Fiction* (Cardiff: University of Wales Press, 2011), pp. 77–88 (p. 77); Henning Mankell, *Pyramiden* (Stockholm: Leopard, 1999), p. 1.

58 Kildal and Kuhnle (eds), *Normative Foundations*, p. 6.

59 Andrew Nestingen, *Crime and Fantasy in Scandinavia: Fiction, Film and Social Change* (Seattle: University of Washington Press, 2008), pp. 5–8.

60 Fredric Jameson, 'Postmodernism, or, The Cultural Logic of Late Capitalism', *New Left Review*, 146 (1984), 59.

61 Browning, 'Branding Nordicity', 46.

62 Manchette's unfinished novel *La Princesse du sang* (*Ivory Pearl*) was published posthumously in 1996.

63 Franck Frommer and Marco Oberti, 'Dominique Manotti: Du militarisme à l'écriture tout en parlant de politique', *Mouvements*, 15–16 (2001), 41–7 (46).

64 Frommer and Oberti, 'Dominique Manotti', 45.

65 Frommer and Oberti, 'Dominique Manotti', 43.

66 Dominique Manotti, 'Roman noir', *Le Mouvement Social*, 219–20, 2–3 (2007), 107.

67 Véronique Desnain, '"L'Histoire du crime": The Crime Novels of Dominique Manotti', in Louise Hardwick (ed.), *New Approaches to Crime in French Literature, Culture and Film* (Bern: Peter Lang, 2009), pp. 151–70 (p. 164).

68 Manotti, 'Roman noir', 109.

69 *www.dominiquemanotti.com* (accessed 16 April 2019).

70 Desnain, 'L'histoire du crime', p. 164.

71 Desnain, 'L'histoire du crime', p. 164.

72 Dominique Manotti, 'Schreiben, um zu verstehen', *Das Argument*, 309 (2014), 476.

73 Manotti, 'Schreiben', 476.

74 Dominique Manotti, 'BAC de Marseille: l'omertà,' *Libération*, 16 October 2012, *https://www.liberation.fr/societe/2012/10/16/bac-de-marseille-l-omerta_853678* (accessed 17 April 2019).

75 Manotti, 'BAC de Marseille'.

76 Stéphanie Binet, 'Panteuil, faux bourg, vraies bavures,' *Libération*, 21 August 2010, *https://next.liberation.fr/livres/2010/08/21/panteuil-faux-bourg-vraies-bavures_673365* (accessed 29 April 2019).

77 Manotti, 'BAC de Marseille'.

78 Dominique Manotti, *Bien connu des services de police* (Paris: Gallimard, 2010), p. 31. This edition is hereinafter referred to by page number in the text.

79 Schor, 'Crisis', 48.

80 Sarkozy made the statement in the apartment of the parents of an 11-year-old boy shot dead in crossfire between rival gangs in 'la cité des 4000', a housing estate in Paris's northern *banlieue*. For an analysis of the event and of Sarkozy's rhetoric in general, see David Dufresne, *Maintien de l'ordre* (Paris: Hachette, 2007).

81 'Déclaration de M. Nicolas Sarkozy, Président de la République, sur les efforts en faveur de la sécurité intérieure, notamment le rapprochement de la police et de la gendarmerie, à Paris le 29 novembre 2007', *https://www.vie-publique.fr/discours/168718-declaration-de-m-nicolas-sarkozy-president-de-la-republique-sur-les-e* (accessed 23 October 2020).

82 *Bien connu des services de police* was published at a time when Nicolas Sarkozy's preoccupation with questions of national identity was at the centre of his political agenda. The creation of the ministry of immigration, integration, national identity and codevelopment after Sarkozy's election in 2007, and the ensuing launch by its minister, Eric Besson, of the official debate on national identity at the end of 2009 and the beginning of 2010, are testimony to the emphasis placed by Sarkozy's presidency on the theme of 'qu'est-ce qu'être Français aujourd'hui?'

83 Manotti, 'BAC de Marseille'.

84 Manotti, 'BAC de Marseille'.

85 Patricia Osganian, Anne-Sophie Perriaux and Julienne Flory, 'Nos fantastiques années fric: une affaire d'État?', *Mouvements*, 67 (2011), 34–43 (35).

86 Peter Kirkegaard, 'Arne Dahl: Le véritable héritier de Sjöwall et Wahlöö', *Études Germaniques*, 65, 4 (2010), 833–54.

87 Arne Dahl, 2007. 'Forord', in Maj Sjöwall and Per Wahlöö, *Strisser, strisser*, trans. Bjarne Nielsen (Aarhus: Modtryk, 2007), pp. 5–8 (p. 5).

88 Peter Kirkegaard, *Blues for folkhemmet: Næranalyse af Arne Dahls* Europa Blues (Aalborg: Aalborg Universitetsforlag, 2013), p. 179.

89 Kerstin Bergman, 'Beyond National Allegory: Europeanisation in Swedish Crime Writer Arne Dahl's *Viskleken*', *Clues*, 32, 2 (2014), 20–9 (21). Bergman has in an earlier article pointed to Europeanisation as a general tendency in Swedish crime fiction, in which 'new "European" crime novels

further explore the concept of European identity, and envision a common Europe beyond its division into nation states'. Kerstin Bergman, 'Initiating a European Turn in Swedish Crime Fiction: Negotiation of European and National Identities in Mankell's *The Troubled Man*', *Scandinavica*, 51, 1 (2012), 56–78 (71).

90 Karsten Wind Meyhoff, 'Digging into the Secrets of the Past: Rewriting History in the Modern Scandinavian Police Procedural', in Nestingen and Arvas (eds), *Scandinavian Crime Fiction*, pp. 62–3.

91 See, for example, Nestingen, *Crime and Fantasy*, pp. 223–54.

92 Michael Tapper, *Swedish Cops: From Sjöwall and Wahlöö to Stieg Larsson* (Bristol: Intellect, 2014), p. 3.

93 On the doppelgänger figure in detective fiction, see, for example, Ilana Shiloh, *The Double, the Labyrinth and the Locked Room: Metaphors of Paradox in Crime Fiction and Film* (New York: Peter Lang, 2011), pp. 25–86.

94 Arne Dahl, *Europa Blues*, trans. Alice Menzies (London: Vintage, 2015), p. 17. This edition is hereinafter referred to by page number in the text unless otherwise stated.

95 Wind Meyhoff, 'Digging into the Secrets of the Past', p. 62.

96 Dan Stone, *Goodbye to All That! The Story of Europe since 1945* (Oxford: Oxford University Press, 2014), p. 288.

97 See, for example, Krister Wahlbäck, 'Neutrality and Morality: The Swedish Experience', *American University International Law Review*, 14, 1 (1998), 103–21.

98 Arne Dahl, *Europa Blues* (Stockholm: Albert Bonniers Förlag, 2001), p. 133; my translation. The official English translation transposes 'we' into 'they'.

99 In 1997 a major nationwide Holocaust information campaign entitled 'Levande historia' (Living History) was initiated in Swedish schools, and in January 2000 the country hosted the Stockholm International Forum on the Holocaust with prominent state participants from forty-six countries. These initiatives form part of a new official policy to engage with a previously taboo past, which was launched by Prime Minister Göran Persson, who also officially admitted to the Swedish state's wrongdoings during the war in a statement to the government in 2000. *Riksdagens snabbprotokoll*, 'Protokoll 1999/2000: 52, Onsdagen den 19 januari, anförande 36, Göran Persson', *www.riksdagen.se* (accessed 15 May 2019).

100 This equivalence is made even more explicit in *Viskleken* (*Chinese Whispers*, 2011): Arto Söderstedt questions the banking world and 'thinks that what has happened the last couple of years, the financial bubble having been blown up and exploded, in a striking manner resembles the actions of a criminal. Profit maximisation without thinking about the consequences.' Arne Dahl, *Viskleken* (Stockholm: Albert Bonniers Förlag, 2011), p. 9.

101 Bob Garcia, *Jazz et polar* (Chelles: Laurent Debarre, 2007), p. 13. The cultural link between the two art forms has been exploited thematically

and allegorically not only in the Anglophone and French traditions (the focus of Garcia's analysis), but also in Scandinavian crime fiction. Other than Arne Dahl, a number of Scandinavian writers have employed jazz or blues as structuring principle or background accompaniment to their novels. In Sweden, Åke Edwardson's investigator Erik Winter, for example, listens to John Coltrane, and in Norway Gunnar Staalesen's Varg Veum is a performing jazz enthusiast.

102 Garcia, *Jazz et polar*, pp. 11–13.

103 Examples include references to Thelonious Monk's *Misterioso* (1958) in the first *Intercrime* novel from 1999 of the same name, and to Miles Davis's *Kind of Blue* (1959) in *Europa Blues*.

104 Bergman, 'Beyond National Allegory', 28.

105 Tore Mortensen og Peter Kirkegaard, 'Kind of Blue – Europa Blues: Jazzen og krimien som performative kunstarter', in Peter Stein Larsen et al. (eds), *Interaktioner: Om kunstarternes produktive* mellemværender (Aalborg: Aalborg Universitetsforlag, 2009), pp. 237–88.

106 See Stephen F. Soitos, *The Blues Detective: A Study of African American Detective Fiction* (Amherst: University of Massachusetts Press, 1996). Soitos focuses on the ways in which black American writers have subverted the detective fiction template in order to review society and reflect political concerns.

107 Kerstin Bergman, 'The Well-Adjusted Cops of the New Millennium: Neo-Romantic Tendencies in the Swedish Police Procedural', in Nestingen and Arvas (eds), *Scandinavian Crime Fiction*, pp. 34–45 (p. 35).

108 Arne Dahl, *The Blinded Man*, trans. Tiina Nunnally (London: Vintage, 2012), p. 35.

109 Translated and quoted by Bergman, 'Beyond National Allegory', 28.

110 Arne Dahl, *Viskleken* (Stockholm: Albert Bonniers Förlag, 2011), p. 502.

111 Bauman, 'Identity in the Globalising World', 129.

Chapter 3

1 Véronique Desnain, 'Gender and Genre: Women in French Crime Writing,' in Claire Gorrara (ed.), *French Crime Fiction* (Cardiff: University Press of Wales, 2009), pp. 86–106 (p. 90).

2 Nicola Barfoot, *Frauenkrimi/Polar féminin: Generic Expectations and the Reception of Recent French and German Crime Novels by Women* (Frankfurt: Peter Lang, 2007), p. 200.

3 Gill Plain, *Twentieth-Century Crime Fiction: Gender, Sexuality and the Body* (Edinburgh: Edinburgh University Press, 2001), p. 204.

4 Maureen T. Reddy, *Sisters in Crime: Feminism and the Crime Novel* (New York: Continuum, 1988), p. 174.

5 Glenwood Irons (ed.), *Feminism in Women's Detective Fiction* (Toronto: University of Toronto Press, 1995), pp. xxi–ii.

6 Deborah Hamilton, 'Barbarians at the Gate: The Case of French Women

Crime and Mystery Writers', Dossier: *Roman policier: Femme/feminisme* (Paris: Bibliothèque des Littératures Policières, n.d.).

7 Deborah Hamilton, 'The *roman noir* and the Reconstruction of National Identity in Postwar France', in Anne Mullen and Emer O'Beirne (eds), *Crime Scenes: Detective Narratives in European Culture Since 1945* (Amsterdam: Rodopi, 2000), p. 231.

8 Anne Lemonde, *Les Femmes et le roman policier: Anatomie d'un paradoxe* (Montreal: Éditions Quebec/Amérique, 1984), p. 25. All in-text translations are my own, unless otherwise stated.

9 Barfoot, *Frauenkrimi/Polar féminin*, p. 28.

10 Desnain, 'Gender and Genre', pp. 88–9.

11 Queneau, who was a friend of Marcel Duhamel, the creator of the Série noire, expressed admiration for the imprint. See *http://www.gallimard.fr/ Divers/Plus-sur-la-collection/Serie-noire* (accessed 10 May 2019). Sartre mentions the collection in *Les Mots*: 'Today still, I'm happier reading the Serie noire than Wittgenstein.' Jean-Paul Sartre, *Les Mots* (Paris: Gallimard, 1972), p. 64.

12 Deborah Eileen Hamilton, 'The French Detective Fiction Novel 1920's to 1990's: Gendering a Genre' (unpublished PhD dissertation, The Pennsylvania State University, 1994)

13 Anon. [untitled interview with Patrick Raynal], *Femme Actuelle*, 19–25 August 1996.

14 Some examples: the imprint 'Chemins noirs', launched in 1994 by the publishing house Viviane Hamy, publishes mainly female authors; the publisher Gaia (created in 1991) focuses entirely on Scandinavian authors in French translation; Baleine (created in 1995) and Florent Masson (created 1989) publish books with 'underground themes'.

15 See, for example, Hamilton, 'The French Detective Fiction Novel 1920's to 1990's: Gendering a Genre'; Barfoot, *Frauenkrimi/Polar féminin*; Desnain, 'Gender and Genre'.

16 Michel Abescat, 'Depuis le commencement, le polar s'écrit aussi au féminin', *Le Monde*, 11 July 1997.

17 Catherine Argand, Christine Ferniot and Pascale Frey, 'Les filles à l'assaut du polar', *Lire*, March (1997), 38–47 (38).

18 Argand, Ferniot and Frey, 'Les filles', 38.

19 Michel Rolland, 'De quelques femmes à la plume meurtrière', *NRP*, 2 (1990), 25–28 (25).

20 Michel Amelin, 'Détectives en talons aiguilles', *813*, 37, December (1991), 37–40; Rolland, 'De quelques femmes'; Delphine Peras, 'Polars, les femmes renouvellent le genre en beauté: Cérises noires, la relève', *France Soir*, 11 August 2002, 33.

21 Argand, Ferniot and Frey, 'Les filles'; Jacques-Pierre Amette, 'Polars: les femmes attaquent', *Le Point*, 1474, 15 December 2000, 134–6; Véronique Zbinden, 'Les nouvelles armes du polar se dégainent au féminin', *Le Nouveau Quotidien*, 30 August–5 September 1996, 12; Alix

de Saint-André, 'Polars: sale temps pour les durs à cuire! La mort des machos', *Elle*, 7 October 1996, 47–9.

22 Catherine Argand, 'Avec Maud Tabachnik, chaque mot est une balle', *Lire*, March 1997, 42.

23 It is important to stress here that Tabachnik is by no means representative of all female writers of crime fiction in France. As Claire Gorrara has pointed out in relation to female writers from the 1990s: 'Not all crime fiction written by women is feminist in intention and it would be misleading to believe that debates around gender inflect the work of every woman writer.' Claire Gorrara, *The Roman Noir in Post-War French Culture* (Oxford: Oxford University Press, 2003), p. 114.

24 Maud Tabachnik, 'Remarques sur la non-place des femmes', in 'Roman noir: Pas d'orchidées pour les T.M.', special issue, *Les Temps Modernes*, 595 (1997), 122.

25 Tabachnik, 'Remarques', 124–5.

26 Tabachnik, 'Remarques', 126.

27 Kerstin Bergman, *Swedish Crime Fiction: The Making of Nordic Noir* (Milan: Mimesis, 2014), p. 86.

28 Bergman, *Swedish Crime Fiction*, pp. 73–4.

29 Desnain, 'Gender and Genre', p. 93.

30 Desnain, 'Gender and Genre', p. 94.

31 Frank Egholm Andersen, *Den nordiske femikrimi: læbestiftslitteratur eller fornyelse af en genre* (Frederiksberg: Her og nu, 2008), p. 24.

32 Annemette Hejlsted, 'Femi-krimiens forhistorie: Om kvindelige detektiver hos tidlige krimiforfattere i Skandinavien', in Karin Lützen and Annette K. Nielsen (eds), *På kant med historien: Studier i køn, videnskab og lidenskab tilegnet Bente Rosenbeck på hendes 60-årsdag* (Copenhagen: Museum Tusculanums Forlag, 2008), pp. 229–47 (p. 232).

33 In an earlier article, Hejlsted goes so far as defining the *femikrimi* according to ten commandments of the genre in line with early twentieth-century's formulated rules for detective fiction (e.g. S. S. Van Dine, 'Twenty Rules for Writing Detective Stories', in Howard Haycraft (ed.), *The Art of the Mystery Story* (New York: Simon, 1946 [1928]), pp. 189–93). Hejlsted's first two commandments state, for example, that 'femikrimis are written by women' and that '[a] femikrimi always has a female detective as the main character', thus reducing the discussion to a set of restrictive and prescriptive formulas, excluding the possibility of critical engagement with gender issues by any work not fulfilling these criteria. Annemette Hejlsted, 'Femikrimiens ti bud', *Kvinder, Køn og Forskning*, 4 (2003), 48–51 (49–50).

34 Andrew Nestingen and Paula Arvas (eds), *Scandinavian Crime Fiction* (Cardiff: University of Wales Press, 2011), p. 5.

35 Nestingen and Arvas (eds), *Scandinavian Crime Fiction*, p. 5.

36 See, for example, Johan Wopenka, 'La littérature policière suédoise moderne: Policiers, femmes et étude sociale', *Études germaniques*, 260, 4 (2010), 739–59; Hejlsted, 'Femi-krimiens forhistorie'.

37 Bergman, *Swedish Crime Fiction*, p. 70.

38 Nestingen and Arvas (eds), *Scandinavian Crime Fiction*, p. 9.

39 Norwegian author Kim Småge's debut novel *Nattdykk* (Night Diving, 1983) has been claimed as the first *femikrimi*. See, for example, Hejlsted, 'Femikrimiens ti bud', 48; Egholm Andersen, *Den nordiske femikrimi*, p. 30. Småge's compatriots, Anne Holt and Karin Fossum, become established writers in 1993 and 1995 respectively with the publication of their first crime novels.

40 This prescription is included in the title of a guide published by *Jury* in 2000: Ulla Trenter, Kerstin Matz and Bo Lundin, *Kvinnor & deckare: en läsebok från jury, Poloniprisjuryn presenterar nya och gamla deckare av, om och för kvinnor* (Gothenburg: Jury, 2000).

41 *Søndag* has between 2006 and 2010 sent out five Liza Marklund titles with the magazine.

42 Sara Kärrholm, 'Swedish Queens of Crime: Self-Promotion and Feminine Agency', in Nestingen and Arvas (eds), *Scandinavian Crime Fiction*, pp. 131–47 (p. 133).

43 Egholm Andersen, *Den nordiske femikrimi*.

44 Sara Kärrholm, 'Mediernas betydelse för skapandet av två 'deckardrottningars' varumärken', in *NORLIT 2009: Codex and Code, Aesthetics, Language and Politics in an Age of Digital Media, Stockholm, August 6–9, 2009* (Linköping: Linköping University Electronic Press, 2010), pp. 467–84 (p. 477).

45 Christine Sarrimo, 'Liza Marklund och den feministiska litteraturfabrikken: Om sanning, lögn och medielogik i *Gömda*-debatten', *Tidsskrift for genusvetenskap*, 4 (2010), 90.

46 Sarrimo, 'Liza Marklund', 90.

47 Marie Morizot, 'Anne Holt: "Le monde réel est bien plus sanglant que mes romans"', *MetroNews*, 14 October 2010.

48 The World Economic Forum's Gender Gap Index 2018 places Iceland first, Norway second, Sweden third and Finland fourth of countries with the world's narrowest gender gap, *wef.ch/gggr18* (accessed 25 April 2019).

49 Ellen Rees, 'Straight Queers: Anne Holt's Transnational Lesbian Detective Fiction', in Nestingen and Arvas (eds), *Scandinavian Crime Fiction*, pp. 100–14 (p. 111).

50 Anne Holt, *The Final Murder*, trans. Kari Dickson (London: Sphere, 2007), p. 6. This edition is hereinafter referred to by page number in the text.

51 Lars Svendsen, *A Philosophy of Boredom*, trans. John Irons (London: Reaktion, 2005), pp. 26–7.

52 Svendsen, *Philosophy of Boredom*, p. 22.

53 Tzvetan Todorov, 'Typologie du roman policier', in *Poétique de la prose* (1971; Paris: Seuil, 1978), pp. 9–19 (p. 11).

54 Anne Holt, *Blessed Are Those Who Thirst*, trans. Anne Bruce (London: Corvus, 2012), p. 37. This edition is hereinafter referred to by page number in the text.

55 Rees, 'Straight Queers', p. 106.
56 Gorrara, *Roman noir*, pp. 115, 123.
57 Barfoot, *Frauenkrimi/Polar féminin*, p. 39.
58 Plain, *Twentieth-Century Crime Fiction*, p. 3.
59 The term used here is coined by Barbara Creed in *The Monstrous-Feminine: Film, Feminism, Psychoanalysis* (London: Routledge, 1993). Creed argues against the use of the term '"female monster" [as it] implies a simple reversal of "male monster"' and continues that 'the phrase "monstrous-feminine" emphasizes the importance of gender in the construction of her monstrosity' (p. 3). My employment of the term is based on these considerations.
60 Maud Tabachnik, *Un été pourri* (Paris: Viviane Hamy, 1994), p. 140. This edition is hereinafter referred to by page number in the text.
61 Plain, *Twentieth-Century Crime Fiction*, p. 247.
62 Plain, *Twentieth-Century Crime Fiction*, p. 246.
63 Jacques Derrida, *Marges de la philosophie* (Paris: Minuit, 1972), p. xvii.
64 Plain, *Twentieth-Century Crime Fiction*, p. 247.
65 Paul Maugendre, 'Maud Tabachnik: Étoile du temple', *L'Ours polar*, 2 (1998), *http://patangel.free.fr/ours-polar/auteurs/tabach1.php* (accessed 9 April 2019).
66 Christophe Dabitch, 'Le polar engagé d'une femme', *Le Matricule des Anges*, 20, July–August (1997), 54.
67 Tabachnik, 'Remarques', 129.

Chapter 4

1 Ruth Rosen, *The Lost Sisterhood: Prostitution in America, 1900–1918* (Baltimore: Johns Hopkins University Press, 1982), p. vii.
2 Christiane Schönfeld (ed.), *Commodities of Desire: The Prostitute in Modern German Literature* (Rochester, NY: Camden House, 2000), p. 24.
3 Shannon Bell, *Reading, Writing and Rewriting the Prostitute Body* (Bloomington: Indiana University Press, 1994), p. 2.
4 Kerstin Bergman, *Swedish Crime Fiction: The Making of Nordic Noir* (Milan: Mimesis, 2014), p. 84.
5 *Flickan och skulden* (Stockholm: Albert Bonniers Förlag, 2012), comprising interviews with rape victims, statistics and detailed accounts from court cases, investigates the status of the sexually abused victim as she is viewed by the Swedish legal system and broader society, while *En riktig våldtäktsman* (Stockholm: Albert Bonniers Förlag, 2004) analyses the crime from the perspective of the convicted rapist or sexual assailant.
6 Malena Rydell, 'Är mannen vedervärdig?', *Dagens nyheter*, 9 October 2002, *http://www.dn.se/arkiv/kultur/ar-mannen-vedervardig* (accessed 10 April 2019). The last quotation is from the statement of the August book prize jury. *Flickan och skulden* was awarded the August prize for best non-fiction book in 2002: *http://www.augustpriset.se/bidrag/*

flickan-och-skulden-en-bok-om-samhallets-syn-pa-valdtakt (accessed 10 April 2019). All in-text translations are my own, unless otherwise stated.

7 Katarina Wennstam, *Smuts* (Stockholm: Albert Bonniers Förlag, 2007), p. 406. This edition is hereinafter referred to by page number in the text.

8 An example of this can be seen in Mankell's *Mannen som log* (*The Man Who Smiled*, 1994) in which Wallander goes on package holidays to Barbados and Thailand: 'He had surrendered to his self-disgust and thrown himself into the arms of prostitutes, each one younger than the last.' Henning Mankell, *The Man Who Smiled*, trans. Laurie Thompson (London: Vintage, 2005), p. 13.

9 Andrew Nestingen, *Crime and Fantasy in Scandinavia: Fiction, Film and Social Change* (Seattle: University of Washington Press, 2008), p. 243.

10 Katarina Wennstam, *Flickan och skulden: En bok om samhällets syn på våldtäkt* (Stockholm: Albert Bonniers Förlag, 2002), p. 37.

11 Bell, *Prostitute Body*, p. 2.

12 Berit Åström, Katarina Gregorsdotter and Tanya Horeck (eds), *Rape in Stieg Larsson's Millennium Trilogy and Beyond: Contemporary Scandinavian and Anglophone Crime Fiction* (Basingstoke: Palgrave Macmillan, 2013).

13 Stieg Larsson, *The Girl with the Dragon Tattoo* (London: MacLehose Press, 2008), p. 235.

14 With reference to the Swedish feminist Maria-Pia Boëthius, Wennstam frames this statement in *Flickan och skulden*, arguing that it is the backbone of societal organisation. Wennstam, *Flickan och skulden*, p. 20.

15 Barbara Fister, 'The Millennium Trilogy and the American Serial Killer Narrative: Investigating Protagonists of Men who Write Women', in Åström, Gregorsdotter and Horeck (eds), *Rape in Stieg Larsson*, pp. 34–50 (p. 35).

16 Marla Harris, 'Rape and the Avenging Female in Stieg Larsson's Millennium Trilogy and Håkan Nesser's *Woman with a Birthmark* and *The Inspector and Silence*', in Åström, Gregorsdotter and Horeck (eds), *Rape in Stieg Larsson*, pp. 67–80 (p. 77).

17 Harris, 'Rape and the Avenging Female', p. 76.

18 This association is not established through the protagonist's first name only. His surname, Wahl – pronounced in Swedish in the same way as the Swedish word for whale ('val') – also points to the story from the Old Testament.

19 Nestingen, *Crime and Fantasy*, p. 11.

20 Risto Saarinen, 'The Surplus of Evil in Welfare Society: Contemporary Scandinavian Crime Fiction', *Dialog: A Journal of Theology*, 14, 2 (2003), 131–5 (134).

21 Don Kulick, 'Sex in the New Europe: The Criminalization of Clients and Swedish Fear of Penetration,' *Anthropological Theory*, 3, 2 (2003), 199.

22 Kulick, 'Sex in the New Europe', 211.

23 Kulick, 'Sex in the New Europe', 211. The association between prostitution and the EU has also been discussed by historian Lars Trägårdh, who in his analysis of Swedish anti-EU campaigning materials relating to the EU

referendum in 1994 comes to the conclusion that '"Europe" was equated with a "bordello"'. Lars Trägårdh, 'Sweden and the EU: Welfare State, Nationalism and the Spectre of "Europe"', in Lene Hansen and Ole Wæver (eds), *European Integration and National Identity: The Challenge of the Nordic States* (London: Routledge, 2002), pp. 130–81 (p. 165).

24 Kulick, 'Sex in the New Europe', 211.

25 Shirley Ann Jordan, *Contemporary French Women's Writing: Women's Visions, Women's Voices, Women's Lives* (Bern: Peter Lang, 2004), p. 121.

26 See, for example, Catherine Argand, 'Virginie Despentes toute crue', *Lire*, March 1997, 45; Christine Ferniot, 'Promenade "crade" au pays du cynisme et de la poudre', *Lire*, November 1998, 20.

27 Jordan, *Contemporary French Women's Writing*; Hamilton, *The French Detective Fiction Novel*; Barfoot, *Frauenkrimi/Polar féminin*.

28 Barfoot, *Frauenkrimi/Polar féminin*, p. 168.

29 Barfoot, *Frauenkrimi/Polar féminin*, p. 202.

30 Barfoot, *Frauenkrimi/Polar féminin*, p. 169.

31 Marianne Costa, 'Despentes: anarcho-féminist', *Le Magazine Info*, 8 June 2007, *http://www.lemagazine.info/?Despentes-anarcho-feministe* (accessed 12 March 2019).

32 Virginie Despentes, *Baise-moi (Rape Me)*, trans. Bruce Benderson (New York: Grove Press, 2003), p. 14. This edition is hereinafter referred to by page number in the text unless otherwise stated.

33 Virginie Despentes, *Baise-moi* (Paris: J'ai lu, 1999), p. 87. The English translation omits all songlines and chapter epigraphs.

34 Virginie Despentes, *King Kong Theory*, trans. Stéphanie Benson (New York: The Feminist Press, 2006), p. 58.

35 Despentes, *King Kong*, p. 60.

36 Costa, 'Despentes'.

37 Despentes, *King Kong*, p. 70.

38 Costa, 'Despentes'; the same idea is developed in Despentes, *King Kong*, pp. 55, 70–80.

39 Judith Butler, *Gender Trouble: Feminism and the Subversion of Identity* (New York: Routledge, 1999), p. 7.

40 Marie-Hélène Bourcier, *Queer zones. Politique des identités sexuelles et des savoirs* (Paris: Amsterdam, 2006), p. 13.

41 Bell, *Prostitute Body*, p. 2.

42 Bell, *Prostitute Body*, p. 137.

43 Ellen Rees, 'Straight Queers: Anne Holt's Transnational Lesbian Detective Fiction', in Andrew Nestingen and Paula Arvas (eds), *Scandinavian Crime Fiction* (Cardiff: University of Wales Press, 2011), pp. 100–14 (106).

Chapter 5

1 Wolfgang Behschnitt and Magnus Nilsson, '"Multicultural Literature" in a Comparative Perspective', in Wolfgang Behschnitt, Sarah de Mul and

Liesbeth Minnaard (eds), *Literature, Language, and Multiculturalism in Scandinavia and the Low Countries* (Amsterdam: Rodopi, 2013), pp. 1–15 (p. 1).

2 Ferruh Yilmaz, 'From Immigrant *Worker* to *Muslim* Immigrant: Challenges for Feminism', *European Journal of Women's Studies*, 22, 1 (2015), 37–52 (38).

3 Grete Brochmann and Anniken Hagelund, *Immigration Policy and the Scandinavian Welfare State, 1945–2010* (Basingstoke: Palgrave Macmillan, 2012).

4 Sverigedemokraterna won twenty parliamentary seats (5.7 per cent of votes) in the 2010 general election, a number increasing to forty-nine seats (12.9 per cent) in the 2014 general election and sixty-two seats (17.6 per cent) in the 2018 general election; Fremskrittspartiet in Norway formed a coalition with the Conservative Party in 2013 and is also currently (after the 2017 election) in government as the country's third largest party (15.2 per cent of votes); Dansk Folkeparti became Denmark's second largest party with 21.1 per cent of the votes in the general election in June 2015, but had their vote share reduced to 8.7 per cent in the June 2019 general election.

5 Yilmaz, 'From Immigrant *Worker*', 38.

6 Kerstin Bergman, *Swedish Crime Fiction: The Making of Nordic Noir* (Milan: Mimesis, 2014), pp. 52–3.

7 Edward W. Said, *Orientalism* (Harmondsworth: Penguin, 2003).

8 Eric Aeschimann, 'Les idéaux républicains sont devenus des armes de discrimination et de mépris', *Le Nouvel Observateur*, 4 April 2015, *http://bibliobs.nouvelobs.com/essais/20150403.OBS6427/jacques-ranciere-les-ideaux-republicains-sont-devenus-des-armes-de-discrimination-et-de-mepris.html* (accessed 2 May 2019). All in-text translations are my own, unless otherwise stated.

9 Michel Wieviorka, 'Introduction: Un débat nécessaire', in Michel Wieviorka et al. (eds), *Une société fragmentée: Le multiculturalisme en débat* (Paris: La Découverte and Syros, 1997), pp. 5–8 (p. 5).

10 See, for example, Charles Forsdick and David Murphy, *Francophone Postcolonial Studies: A Critical Introduction* (London: Arnold, 2003); Charles Forsdick and David Murphy, 'Introduction: The Postcolonial Turn in France', *Francophone Postcolonial Studies*, 5, 2 (2007), 7–13.

11 'Décret n° 2007-999 du 31 mai 2007 relatif aux attributions du ministre de l'immigration, de l'intégration de l'identité nationale et du codéveloppement', *www.legifrance.gouv.fr* (accessed 15 May 2019).

12 Laura Reeck, *Writerly Identities in Beur Fiction and Beyond* (Plymouth: Lexington, 2011), p. 3.

13 Behschnitt, de Mul and Minnaard (eds), *Literature, Language, and Multiculturalism*, p. ix.

14 Anne Ellingsen, 'Music and Ethnic Integration in Norwegian State Policies' (unpublished PhD dissertation, University of Oslo, 2007), 67.

15 Tariq Modood and Pnina Werbner (eds), *The Politics of Multiculturalism*

in the New Europe: Racism, Identity and Community (London: Zed Books, 1997), p. 76.

[16] Michel Wieviorka, 'Culture, société et démocratie', in Wieviorka et al. (eds), *Une société fragmentée*, pp. 9–60 (p. 35).

[17] Aleksandra Ålund and Carl-Ulrik Schierup, *Paradoxes of Multiculturalism: Essays on Swedish Society* (Aldershot: Avebury, 1991), p. 120; Thomas Hylland Eriksen, *Kulturterrorismen: Kritikk av tanken om kulturell renhet* (Oslo: Spartacus, 1993).

[18] Hylland Eriksen, *Kulturterrorismen*.

[19] Adrienne Johnson Gosselin (ed.), *Multicultural Detective Fiction: Murder from the 'Other' Side* (New York: Garland, 1999); Ed Christian (ed.), *The Post-Colonial Detective* (Basingstoke: Palgrave Macmillan, 2001); Maureen T. Reddy, *Traces, Codes and Clues: Reading Race in Crime Fiction* (New Brunswick, NJ: Rutgers University Press, 2003); Christine Matzke and Susanne Mühleisen (eds), *Postcolonial Postmortems: Crime Fiction from a Transcultural Perspective* (Amsterdam: Rodopi, 2006); Nels Pearson and Marc Singer (eds), *Detective Fiction in a Postcolonial and Transnational World* (Farnham: Ashgate, 2009).

[20] See, for example, Forsdick and Murphy, *Francophone Postcolonial Studies*; Forsdick and Murphy, 'Postcolonial Turn'; H. Adlai Murdoch and Anne Donadey (eds), *Postcolonial Theory and Francophone Literary Studies* (Gainesville: University Press of Florida, 2005); Alex G. Hargreaves and David Murphy, 'Introduction: New Directions in Postcolonial Studies', *Journal of Postcolonial Writing*, 44, 3 (2008), 221–5.

[21] Jean-Marc Moura, 'The Evolving Context of Postcolonial Studies in France: New Horizons or New Limits?', *Journal of Postcolonial Writing*, 44, 3 (2008), 263.

[22] Pim Higginson, *The Noir Atlantic: Chester Himes and the Birth of the Francophone African Novel* (Liverpool: Liverpool University Press, 2011), p. 1.

[23] Jean-Marc Moura, 'French-Language Writing and the Francophone Literary System', *Contemporary French and Francophone Studies*, 14, 1 (2010), 31.

[24] Pierre Halen, 'Pour une topologie institutionnelle du système littéraire francophone', in Papa Samba Diop and Hans-Jürgen Lüsebrink (eds), *Littératures et sociétés africaines: Regards comparatistes et perspectives interculturelles* (Tübingen: Gunter Narr, 2001), pp. 55–68 (p. 59).

[25] Muriel Barbery et al., 'Pour une "littérature-monde" en français', *Le Monde*, 'Livres', 16 March 2007.

[26] Christiane Albert, 'La littérature-monde en français: une nouvelle catégorie littéraire?', in Christiane Albert, Abel Kouvouama and Gisèle Prignitz (eds), *Le statut de l'écrit: Afrique, Europe, Amérique latine* (Pau: Presses Universitaires de Pau, 2008), pp. 161–70 (p. 162).

[27] Moura, 'French-Language Writing', 29.

[28] Compard, *Immigrés et romans noirs*, p. 249.

29 Compard, *Immigrés et romans noirs*, p. 243.

30 Compard, *Immigrés et romans noirs*, p. 242.

31 Rama Yade-Zimet, *Noirs de France* (Paris: Calmann-Lévy, 2007); Pap Ndiaye, *La condition noire* (Paris: Calmann-Lévy, 2008); Pascal Blanchard (ed.), *La France Noire* (Paris: La Découverte, 2012).

32 Foger Fodjo, *Les Poubelles du palais* (Paris: L'Harmattan, 2011), p. 85. This edition is hereinafter referred to by page number in the text.

33 Compare the allusions to this event with the fuller account of the Paris Massacre offered in Didier Daeninckx's novel *Meurtres pour mémoire* (Paris: Gallimard, 1984).

34 Lisa Downing, *The Cambridge Introduction to Michel Foucault* (Cambridge: Cambridge University Press, 2008), p. 31.

35 C(h)ris Reyns-Chikuma, 'Roger Fodjo: *Les Poubelles du palais*', *Alternative Francophone* 1, 5 (2012), 84–9 (84).

36 See, for example, Charles Forsdick, 'Colonialism, Postcolonialism and the Cultures of Commemoration', in Charles Forsdick and David Murphy (eds), *Postcolonial Thought in the French-speaking World* (Liverpool: Liverpool University Press, 2009), pp. 271–84 (pp. 277–80); Perry Anderson, *La Pensée tiède: Un regard critique sur la culture française* (Paris: Seuil, 2005), p. 50.

37 Homi K. Bhabha, *The Location of Culture* (Oxford: Routledge, 2005), p. 54.

38 Roger Fodjo, 'Extrait de la conférence prononcée le 3 avril 2012 à l'université de l'Alberta, Edmonton', *http://publifiction.jimdo.com/ conférences-débats* (accessed 19 May 2019).

39 Fodjo, 'Extrait de la conférence'.

40 The expression stems from Salman Rushdie's 1982 article 'The Empire Writes Back with a Vengeance', and is iterated by Bill Ashcroft, Gareth Griffiths and Helen Tiffin in their theoretical contribution to postcolonial studies, *The Empire Writes Back: Theory and Practice in Post-Colonial Literature* (Oxford: Routledge, 1989).

41 Graham Huggan, 'Perspectives on Postcolonial Europe', *Journal of Postcolonial Writing*, 44, 3 (2008), 241–9 (241).

42 Jean-Noël Blanc, *Polarville: Images de la ville dans le roman policier* (Lyon: Presses universitaire de Lyon, 1990), pp. 274–5.

43 Christina Horvath, *Le roman urbain contemporain en France* (Paris: Presses Sorbonne Nouvelle, 2008), p. 7.

44 Horvath, *Le roman urbain*, pp. 16–17.

45 Steve Puig, '"Enfermés dehors": représentations de la banlieue dans les romans de Rachid Djaïdani', in Jan Baetens and Bernardo Schiavetta (eds), 'Formes urbaines de la création contemporaine', special issue, *Formules*, 14 (2010), 179–90 (183).

46 Alex G. Hargreaves, *Voices from the North African Immigrant Community in France: Immigration and Identity in Beur Fiction* (Oxford: Berg, 1991), p. 87.

47 Michel Laronde, *Autour du roman beur: Immigration et Identité* (Paris: L'Harmattan, 1993), p. 21.

48 Kenneth Olsson, *Le discours beur comme positionnement littéraire: Romans et textes autobiographiques français (2005–2006) d'auteurs issus de l'immigration maghrébine* (Stockholm: Stockholm University, 2011), p. 15.

49 Reeck, *Writerly Identities*, p. 126.

50 Vincent Mongaillard, 'Il fait lire les cités', *Le Parisien*, 11 December 2011.

51 Rachid Santaki, *Les Anges s'habillent en caillera* (Paris: Moisson Rouge/Alvik, 2011), p. 81. This edition is hereinafter referred to by page number in the text.

52 Bernard Dinh, 'Le faubourg Saint-Denis, une communauté "ethnique" marchande?', in Cédric Audebert and Emmanuel Ma Mung (eds), *Les nouveaux territoires migratoires: Entre logiques globales et dynamiques locales* (Bilbao: Publications de l'Université de Deusto, 2007), pp. 127–40 (p. 128).

53 *La Haine*, directed by Mathieu Kassovitz (Paris: Canal+, 1995).

54 Timo Obergöker, 'L'impossibilité d'une île: L'histoire littéraire française à l'épreuve de la mondialisation', *Alternative Francophone*, 1, 7 (2014), 56–70 (62).

55 Stéphane here makes a reference to Thomas Gilou's comedy-drama *Raï* (1995), in which the main protagonist's heroin-addicted brother, Nordine, is shot dead by the police.

56 Laronde, *Autour du roman beur*, p. 212.

57 Laronde, *Autour du roman beur*, p. 213.

58 Forsdick and Murphy, 'Postcolonial Turn'.

59 Forsdick and Murphy, 'Postcolonial Turn', 7.

Chapter 6

1 Barry Forshaw, *Death in a Cold Climate: A Guide to Scandinavian Crime Fiction* (Basingstoke: Palgrave Macmillan, 2012), p. 5.

2 Paula Arvas and Andrew Nestingen, 'Other Knowing Others: Stieg Larsson's *Millennium* Trilogy and Peter Høeg's *Smilla's Sense of Snow*', in Jean Anderson, Carolina Miranda and Barbara Pezzotti (eds), *The Foreign in International Crime Fiction: Transcultural Representations* (London: Continuum, 2012), pp. 124–36 (p. 135).

3 The foreign-born population in Sweden was 17.0 per cent, in Norway 14.7 per cent and in Denmark 9.5 per cent, in comparison with 12.3 per cent in France, all in 2016 (OECD, International Migration Outlook 2018, *https://doi.org/10.1787/migr_outlook-2018-en* (accessed 16 April 2019).

4 Rasmus Bo Sørensen, 'Indvandreren er en statist i dansk litteratur', *Information*, 5 March 2010. All in-text translations are my own, unless otherwise stated.

5 See, for example, Emil Bergløv, 'Nu kommer opgøret med indvandreren i dansk litteraturhistorie', *Politiken*, 30 November 2013; Hans Hauge,

'Sættes indvandrerproblemer under debat i dansk samtidslitteratur?', in Søren Frank and Mehmet Ümit Necef (eds), *Indvandreren i dansk film og litteratur* (Hellerup: Spring, 2013), pp. 12–45.

6 Frank and Necef (eds), *Indvandreren*, p. 10.

7 Hauge, 'Sættes indvandrerproblemer under debat', p. 12.

8 Paulina Jankowska, 'Sverigeskildringar i samtida svenska romaner: debatten om fenomen och begreppen "invandrarlitteratur" och "invandrarförfattare"', *Acta Sueco-Polonica*, 16 (2010–11), 33–50 (33–4).

9 Magnus Nilsson, 'Swedish "Immigrant Literature" and the Construction of Ethnicity', *Tijdschrift voor Skandinavistiek*, 31 (2010), 199–218 (199).

10 Søren Frank, 'Is There or Is There Not a Literature of Migration in Denmark?', in Wolfgang Behschnitt, Sarah de Mul and Liesbeth Minnaard (eds), *Literature, Language, and Multiculturalism in Scandinavia and the Low Countries* (Amsterdam: Rodopi, 2013), pp. 197–223 (p. 220).

11 Adrienne Johnson Gosselin (ed.), *Multicultural Detective Fiction: Murder from the 'Other' Side* (New York: Garland, 1999), p. xii.

12 Wolfgang Behschnitt and Magnus Nilsson, '"Multicultural Literature" in a Comparative Perspective', in Wolfgang Behschnitt, Sarah de Mul and Liesbeth Minnaard (eds), *Literature, Language, and Multiculturalism in Scandinavia and the Low Countries* (Amsterdam: Rodopi, 2013), p. 1; Søren Frank, *Migration and Literature: Günter Grass, Milan Kundera, Salman Rushdie, and Jan Kjærstad* (Basingstoke: Palgrave Macmillan, 2008), p. 2.

13 Magnus Nilsson, *Den föreställda mångkulturen: Klass och etnicitet i svensk samtidsprosa* (Möklinta: Gidlunds förlag, 2010), 220.

14 Bergløv, 'Nu kommer opgøret'.

15 Maj Sjöwall and Per Wahlöö, *The Laughing Policeman*, trans. Alan Blair (London: Harper Perennial, 2007), pp. 113–17.

16 Nancy Fraser, *Justice Interruptus: Critical Reflections on the 'Postsocialist' Condition* (London: Routledge, 1997).

17 Henning Mankell, *Faceless Killers*, trans. Steven T. Murray (London: Harvill, 2000), p. 41.

18 Andrew Nestingen, *Crime and Fantasy in Scandinavia: Fiction, Film and Social Change* (Seattle: University of Washington Press, 2008).

19 Slavoj Žižek, 'Henning Mankell: the Artist of the Parallax View' (n.d.), *http://www.lacan.com/zizekmankell.htm* (accessed 25 February 2019).

20 Nestingen, *Crime and Fantasy*, p. 252.

21 Anna Estera Mrozewicz, 'Porous Borders: Crossing the Boundaries to "Eastern Europe" in Scandinavian Crime Fiction', *Akademisk kvarter*, 7 (2013), 350–65 (352).

22 Nestingen, *Crime and Fantasy*, p. 254.

23 Fraser, *Justice Interruptus*.

24 Nestingen, *Crime and Fantasy*, p. 227.

25 Kerstin Bergman, *Swedish Crime Fiction: The Making of Nordic Noir* (Milan: Mimesis, 2014), p. 67.

26 McCorristine, 'Place of Pessimism', p. 78.

27 McCorristine, 'Place of Pessimism', p. 86; my emphasis.

28 Nilsson, *Den föreställda mångkulturen*, pp. 195–210.

29 Fraser, *Justice Interruptus*, p. 23.

30 Anna Westerståhl Stenport, 'Bodies under Assault: Nation and Immigration in Henning Mankell's *Faceless Killers*', *Scandinavian Studies*, 79, 1 (2007), 1–24 (22); Magnus Nilsson, 'Literature and Diversity', *Inter: A European Cultural Studies Conference in Sweden, 11–13 June 2007* (Linköping: Linköbing University Electronic Press, 2009), pp. 443–47 (p. 446), *http:// www.ep.liu.se/ecp/025/047/ecp072547.pdf* (accessed 10 May 2019).

31 Nilsson, 'Literature and Diversity'.

32 See, for example, Paula Arvas, 'Next to the Final Frontier: Russians in Contemporary Finnish and Scandinavian Crime Fiction', in Nestingen and Arvas (eds), *Scandinavian Crime Fiction*, pp. 115–28; Mrozewicz, 'Porous Borders'.

33 Julie H. Kim (ed.), *Race and Religion in the Postcolonial British Detective Story* (Jefferson, NC: McFarland, 2005), p. 1.

34 Roy Jacobsen, *Marions slør* (Oslo: Cappelen Damm, 2008), p. 17; my emphasis. This edition is hereinafter referred to by page number in the text.

35 Graham Huggan, *The Postcolonial Exotic: Marketing the Margins* (London: Routledge, 2001), p. 9.

36 Kim Toft Hansen, *Mord og metafysik: Det absolutte, det guddommelige og det overnaturlige i krimien* (Aalborg: Aalborg Universitets Forlag, 2012), p. 244.

37 Nilsson, 'Literature and Diversity', p. 444.

38 Nilsson, *Den föreställda mångkulturen*, pp. 15–43. Nilsson borrows the term 'the ethnic lens' from the Swedish author Astrid Trotzig, 'Makten över prefixen', in Moa Matthis (ed.), *Orientalism på svenska* (Stockholm: Ordfront, 2005), pp. 104–27 (p. 126).

39 Terje Stemland, 'Ny, stor roman: En meget aktuell kriminalistisk studie av det tverrkulturelle Norge', *Aftenposten*, 20 October 2011, *https://www. aftenposten.no/kultur/i/8qdGx/ny-stor-roman* (accessed 31 October 2020).

40 Ellen Sofie Lauritzen and Marie Aubert, 'Etterlyser innvandrerromanen', *Dagbladet*, 25 July 2007, *http://www.dagbladet.no/kultur/2007/07/25/507078. html* (accessed 12 June 2019).

41 Lauritzen and Aubert, 'Etterlyser innvandrerromanen'.

42 Leif Ekle, 'Marions slør', NRK Kultur og Underholdning, 27 September 2007, *https://www.nrk.no/kultur/bokanmeldelse_-marions-slor-1.3589058* (accessed 12 June 2019).

43 Gregers Lohse, 'Interview: Fordomme er en nødvendighed', *Berlingske Tidende*, 16 October 2008, *https://www.berlingske.dk/kultur/ interview-fordomme-er-en-noedvendighed*.

44 Fraser, *Justice Interruptus*, p. 24.

45 Magnus Nilsson, 'Diversity and Homogeneity in a "Multicultural Society": A Critique of the Pervasive Picture of Collective Identities', *Conference Contributions/KS K3* (Bergen: University of Bergen, 2009), p. 5.

46 Lohse, 'Fordomme er en nødvendighed'.

47 See Mahmood Mamdani, *Good Muslim, Bad Muslim: America, the Cold War, and the Roots of Terror* (New York: Pantheon, 2004), pp. 20–4.

48 Toft Hansen, *Mord og metafysik*, p. 235.

49 Paul Smith, *Mordet på imanen* (Aarhus: Hovedland, 2008), pp. 183–96. This edition is hereinafter referred to by page number in the text.

50 Anderson, Miranda and Pezzotti (eds), *The Foreign in International Crime Fiction*, p. 2.

51 Karl XII (1628–1718; usually designated Charles XII in English) is considered a key national hero for Swedish neo-Nazi movements. In the 1930s the king was celebrated on the day of his death (30 November) by members of the Swedish Nazi party, a tradition taken up in the 1990s by the Nordic National Socialists. Gathering around Karl XII's statue in Stockholm, they are usually met with counter-demonstrations.

52 Nilsson, 'Swedish "Immigrant Literature"'.

53 Peter Hervik, 'What is the Scandinavian Nexus of "Islamophobia, Multiculturalism, and Muslim–Western Relations"?', *Intersections: East European Journal of Society and Politics*, 1, 1 (2015), 66–82 (68), *http:// intersections.tk.mta.hu/index.php/intersections* (accessed 20 June 2019).

54 Arne Larsen, '*Mordet på imanen* af Paul Smith', *Litteratursiden*, 17 March 2008, *http://www.litteratursiden.dk/boeger/mordet-pa-imanen* (accessed 5 May 2019).

55 Klaus Rothstein, 'Filosofisk krimi: Imammord', *Weekendavisen*, 14 March 2008.

56 Peter Nørskov, 'Imam-mord midt i en krisetid', *Århus Stiftstidende*, 2 March 2008.

57 Akkari acted as spokesman for Islamic Society in Denmark during the Mohammed controversy. He was accused of promoting fundamentalism and mobilising protests among Muslims by travelling to Egypt and other countries in the Middle East in January 2006 to draw attention to the cartoons.

58 Nørskov, 'Imam-mord'.

59 Nilsson, 'Literature and Diversity', p. 446.

60 Nestingen, *Crime and Fantasy*, p. 14.

61 Hervik, 'Scandinavian Nexus', 71.

62 Alex Honneth, 'Brutalization of the Social Conflict: Struggles for Recognition in the Early 21st Century', *Distinction: Scandinavian Journal of Social Theory*, 13, 1 (2012), 5–19 (5).

63 Michel Wieviorka, 'Introduction: Un débat nécessaire', in Michel Wieviorka et al. (eds), *Une société fragmentée: Le multiculturalisme en débat* (Paris: La Découverte and Syros, 1997), pp. 5–8 (p. 6).

Conclusion

1 Nancy Fraser, *Justice Interruptus: Critical Reflections on the 'Postsocialist' Condition* (London: Routledge, 1997), p. 2.

2 Gill Plain, *Twentieth-Century Crime Fiction: Gender, Sexuality and the Body* (Edinburgh: Edinburgh University Press, 2001), p. 3.

Selected bibliography

Primary sources

Dahl, Arne, *Misterioso* (Malmö: Bra Böcker, 1999).
—— *Europa Blues* (Stockholm: Albert Bonniers Förlag, 2001).
—— *Viskleken* (Stockholm: Albert Bonniers Förlag, 2011).
—— *The Blinded Man*, trans. Tiina Nunnally (London: Vintage, 2012).
—— *Europa Blues*, trans. Alice Menzies (London: Vintage, 2015).
Despentes, Virginie, *Baise-moi* (Paris: J'ai lu, 1999).
—— *Baise-moi (Rape me)*, trans. by Bruce Benderson (New York: Grove Press, 2003).
Fodjo, Roger, *Les Poubelles du palais* (Paris: L'Harmattan, 2011).
Holt, Anne, *The Final Murder*, trans. Kari Dickson (London: Sphere, 2007).
—— *Blessed Are Those Who Thirst*, trans. Anne Bruce (London: Corvus, 2012).
Jacobsen, Roy, *Marions slør* (Oslo: Cappelen Damm, 2008).
Larsson, Stieg, *The Girl with the Dragon Tattoo*, trans. Reg Keeland (London: MacLehose Press, 2008).
Manchette, Jean-Patrick, *Chroniques* (Paris: Payot, 1996).
—— *Romans noirs* (Paris: Gallimard, 2005).
—— *Journal 1966–1974* (Paris: Gallimard, 2008).
Mankell, Henning, *Mördare utan ansikte* (Stockholm: Ordfront, 1991).
—— *Pyramiden* (Stockholm: Leopard, 1999).
—— *Faceless Killers*, trans. Steven T. Murray (London: Harvill, 2000).
—— *The Pyramid*, trans. Ebba Segerberg (London: Harvill Secker, 2008).
Manotti, Dominique, *Bien connu des services de police* (Paris: Gallimard, 2010).
Santaki, Rachid, *Les Anges s'habillent en caillera* (Paris: Moisson Rouge/ Alvik, 2011).
Sjöwall, Maj, and Per Wahlöö, *Roseanna*, trans. Lois Roth (London: Harper Perennial, 2006).
—— *The Abominable Man*, trans. Thomas Teal (London: Harper Perennial, 2007).
—— *Cop Killer*, trans. Thomas Teal (London: Harper Perennial, 2007).
—— *Murder at the Savoy*, trans. Joan Tate (London: Harper Perennial, 2007).

Smith, Paul, *Mordet på imamen* (Aarhus: Hovedland, 2008).
Tabachnik, Maud, *Un été pourri* (Paris: Viviane Hamy, 1994).
Wennstam, Katarina, *Smuts* (Stockholm: Albert Bonniers Förlag, 2007).

Secondary sources

Anderson, Jean, Carolina Miranda and Barbara Pezzotti (eds), *The Foreign in International Crime Fiction: Transcultural Representations* (London: Continuum, 2012).
Andrew Nestingen and Arvas, Paula (eds), *Scandinavian Crime Fiction* (Cardiff: University of Wales Press, 2011).
Åström, Berit, Katarina Gregorsdotter and Tanya Horeck (eds), *Rape in Stieg Larsson's Millennium Trilogy and Beyond: Contemporary Scandinavian and Anglophone Crime Fiction* (Basingstoke: Palgrave Macmillan, 2013).
Barbery, Muriel et al., 'Pour une "littérature-monde" en français', *Le Monde*, 'Livres', 16 March 2007.
Barfoot, Nicola, *Frauenkrimi/polar féminin: Generic Expectations and the Reception of Recent French and German Crime Novels by Women* (Frankfurt: Peter Lang, 2007).
Bauman, Zygmunt, 'Identity in the Globalising World', *Social Anthropology*, 9, 2 (2001), 121–9.
Behschnitt, Wolfgang, Sarah de Mul and Liesbeth Minnaard (eds), *Literature, Language, and Multiculturalism in Scandinavia and the Low Countries* (Amsterdam: Rodopi, 2013).
Bell, Shannon, *Reading, Writing and Rewriting the Prostitute Body* (Bloomington: Indiana University Press, 1994).
Bergman, Kerstin, 'Beyond National Allegory: Europeanisation in Swedish Crime Writer Arne Dahl's *Viskleken*', *Clues*, 32, 2 (2014), 20–9.
––––––– *Swedish Crime Fiction: The Making of Nordic Noir* (Milan: Mimesis, 2014).
Beyer, Charlotte, '"Death of the Author": Maj Sjöwall and Per Wahlöö's Police Procedurals', in Vivien Miller and Helen Oakley (eds), *Cross-Cultural Connections in Crime Fictions* (Basingstoke: Palgrave Macmillan, 2012), pp. 141–59.
Bourcier, Marie-Hélène, *Queer zones. Politique des identités sexuelles et des savoirs* (Paris: Amsterdam, 2006).
––––––– 'Cultural Translation, Politics of Disempowerment and the Reinvention of Queer Power and Politics', *Sexualities*, 15, 1 (2011), 93–109.
Browning, Christopher S., 'Branding Nordicity: Models, Identity and the Decline of Exceptionalism', *Cooperation and Conflict*, 42, 1 (2007), 27–51.
Compard, Nadège, *Immigrés et romans noirs (1950–2000)* (Paris: L'Harmattan, 2010).

Desnain, Véronique, 'Gender and Genre: Women in French Crime Writing', in Claire Gorrara (ed.), *French Crime Fiction* (Cardiff: University Press of Wales, 2009), pp. 86–106.

Eriksen, Thomas Hylland, *Kulturterrorismen: Kritikk av tanken om kulturell renhet* (Oslo: Spartacus, 1993).

Esping-Andersen, Gøsta, *The Three Worlds of Welfare Capitalism* (Oxford: Polity/Blackwell, 1990).

Forsdick, Charles and David Murphy, *Francophone Postcolonial Studies: A Critical Introduction* (London: Arnold, 2003).

——— 'Introduction: The Postcolonial Turn in France', *Francophone Postcolonial Studies*, 5, 2 (2007), 7–13.

Forshaw, Barry, *Death in a Cold Climate: A Guide to Scandinavian Crime Fiction* (Basingstoke: Palgrave Macmillan, 2012).

Fraser, Nancy, *Justice Interruptus: Critical Reflections on the 'Postsocialist' Condition* (London: Routledge, 1997).

Gérault, Jean-François, *Jean-Patrick Manchette* (Paris: Encrage, 2000).

Gorrara, Claire, *The Roman Noir in Post-War French Culture* (Oxford: Oxford University Press, 2003).

——— 'French Crime Fiction: from *genre mineur* to *patrimoine culturel*', *French Studies*, 61, 2 (2007), 209–14.

——— (ed.), *French Crime Fiction* (Cardiff: University of Wales Press, 2009).

——— *French Crime Fiction and the Second World War: Past crimes, Present Memories* (Manchester: Manchester University Press, 2012).

Hamilton, Deborah Eileen, 'The French Detective Fiction Novel 1920's to 1990's: Gendering a Genre' (unpublished PhD dissertation, The Pennsylvania State University, 1994). ProQuest (AAT 9428110).

Hansen, Lene and Ole Wæver (eds), *European Integration and National Identity: The Challenge of the Nordic States* (London: Routledge, 2002).

Hargreaves, Alex G. and David Murphy, 'Introduction: New Directions in Postcolonial Studies', *Journal of Postcolonial Writing*, 44, 3 (2008), 221–5.

Jameson, Frederic, 'Postmodernism, or, The Cultural Logic of Late Capitalism', *New Left Review*, 146 (1984), 59–92.

Kildal, Nanna and Stein Kuhnle (eds), *Normative Foundations of the Welfare State: The Nordic Experience* (London: Routledge, 2005).

Kosonen, Pekka, 'Globalisation and the Nordic Welfare States', in Robert Sykes, Bruno Palier and Pauline M. Prior (eds), *Globalization and European Welfare States* (Basingstoke: Palgrave, 2001), pp. 153–72.

Kuisma, Mikko, 'Social Democratic Internationalism and the Welfare State after the "Golden Age"', *Cooperation and Conflict*, 42, 1 (2007), 9–26.

McCorristine, Shane, 'The Place of Pessimism in Henning Mankell's Kurt Wallander Series', in Andrew Nestingen and Paula Arvas (eds), *Scandinavian Crime Fiction* (Cardiff: University of Wales Press, 2011), pp. 77–88.

Manotti, Dominique, 'Roman noir', *Le Mouvement Social*, 219–20, 2–3 (2007), 107–9.

——— 'BAC de Marseille: l'omertà', *Libération*, 16 October 2012, *https://www.liberation.fr/societe/2012/10/16/bac-de-marseille-l-omerta_853678*.

——— 'Schreiben, um zu verstehen', *Das Argument*, 309 (2014), 475–8.

Moura, Jean-Marc, 'The Evolving Context of Postcolonial Studies in France: New Horizons or New Limits?', *Journal of Postcolonial Writing*, 44, 3 (2008), 263–74.

——— 'French-Language Writing and the Francophone Literary System', *Contemporary French and Francophone Studies*, 14, 1 (2010), 29–38.

Nestingen, Andrew, *Crime and Fantasy in Scandinavia: Fiction, Film and Social Change* (Seattle: University of Washington Press, 2008).

Nilsson, Magnus, *Den föreställda mångkulturen: Klass och etnicitet i svensk samtidsprosa* (Möklinta: Gidlunds förlag, 2010).

Pearson, Nels and Marc Singer (eds), *Detective Fiction in a Postcolonial and Transnational World* (Farnham: Ashgate, 2009).

Plain, Gill, *Twentieth-Century Crime Fiction: Gender, Sexuality and the Body* (Edinburgh: Edinburgh University Press, 2001).

Reeck, Laura, *Writerly Identities in Beur Fiction and Beyond* (Plymouth: Lexington, 2011).

Scaggs, John, *Crime Fiction* (London: Routledge, 2005).

Schor, Naomi, 'The Crisis of French Universalism', *Yale French Studies*, 100 (2001), 43–64.

Scott, Joan Wallach, 'French Universalism in the 1990s', *Differences*, 15, 2 (2004), 32–53.

Sejersted, Francis, *The Age of Social Democracy: Norway and Sweden in the Twentieth Century*, trans. Richard Daly (Princeton, NJ: Princeton University Press, 2011).

Sjöwall, Maj and Per Wahlöö, 'Kriminalromanens fornyelse', *Politiken*, 30 July 1971.

Søholm, Ejgil, *Roman om en forbrydelse: Sjöwall/Wahlöös værk og virkelighed* (Viborg: Spektrum, 1976).

Stougaard-Nielsen, Jakob, *Scandinavian Crime Fiction* (London: Bloomsbury, 2017).

Tabachnik, Maud, 'Remarques sur la non-place des femmes', in 'Roman noir: Pas d'orchidées pour les T.M.', special issue, *Les Temps Modernes*, 595 (1997), 122–9.

Tapper, Michael, *Snuten i skymningslandet: Svenska polisberättelser i roman och film 1965–2010* (Lund: Nordic Academic Press, 2011).

Todorov, Tzvetan, *Poétique de la prose* (1971; Paris: Seuil, 1978).

Toft Hansen, Kim, 'Knowing the Unknowable: Detecting Metaphysics and Religion in Crime Fiction', in Peter Baker and Deborah Shaller (eds), *Detecting Detection: International Perspectives on the Uses of a Plot* (London: Continuum, 2012), pp. 139–68.

Wennstam, Katarina, *Flickan och skulden: En bok om samhällets syn på våldtäkt* (Stockholm: Albert Bonniers Förlag, 2012). E-book.

Wieviorka, Michel et al. (eds), *Une société fragmentée: Le multiculturalisme en débat* (Paris: La Découverte and Syros, 1997).

Index